Acing Behavioural Interviews
Actionable Interview Insights from Amazon and Google Insiders

Sanjeet Sahay, Abhishek Soni, Saurabh Shrivastava

PREFACE

People will forget what you said, people will forget what you did, but people will never forget how you made them feel.

— Maya Angelou

WHY I WROTE THIS BOOK

When I first stepped into the interview room at Amazon over a decade ago, I had no idea how profoundly that experience would shape my understanding of what truly matters in technical hiring. After years of conducting interviews, making hiring decisions, and eventually helping shape interview processes at Microsoft, I realized something crucial: technical brilliance alone rarely determines career success.

The most successful engineers and leaders I've encountered share something beyond technical prowess—they excel at communicating their experiences, demonstrating their impact, and showcasing their growth mindset. Yet, I noticed a troubling pattern: exceptionally talented candidates were failing behavioral interviews not because they lacked experiences, but because they couldn't effectively articulate them.

My journey continued with successful interviews at Google and Meta, where I gained further insight into how different tech giants evaluate candidates. This cross-company perspective revealed both the common threads and unique nuances in how behavioral assessment works across the industry.

This book emerges from thousands of hours spent on both sides of the interview table. It represents the guidance I wish I'd had when I first faced these intimidating questions—and the wisdom I've gained from evaluating countless candidates since then.

HOW THIS BOOK IS DIFFERENT

Most interview preparation resources fall into one of two categories: overly generic advice that lacks practical application, or collections of sample answers that encourage memorization rather than authentic preparation.

This book takes a fundamentally different approach.

I have written this book in a way that applies to all companies, big and small, that use behavioural interviews as a tool to hire the best candidates. You may think, ah a new book from yet another FAANG (or MANGA or Big Seven or whatever is the acronym for the US-based big tech companies this week) fanboy. But seriosly, I have used numerious examples from the big tech companies because that's where I come from.

DEEP INSIDER INSIGHTS

The authors: Sanjeet, Abhishek, and Saurabh have a combined 50+ years of experience with 20+ years at big tech companies. They collectively interviewed 3000+ candidates and hired 500+ for Amazon and Google. Saurabh has been a master interviewer called "Bar Raiser" at Amazon for more than 5 years. So yes, we know what we are talking about: how its done and what is needed.

ROLE-SPECIFIC DEPTH

Rather than offering one-size-fits-all advice, this guide provides tailored strategies for Software Engineers, Engineering Managers, Solution Architects, and Program Managers. Each role demands different behavioral competencies, and this book addresses them with precision.

DIGITAL RESOURCES INTEGRATION

Throughout this book, you'll find references to downloadable worksheets, practice plans, and interactive tools designed to transform passive reading into active preparation. These resources bridge the gap between understanding concepts and applying them effectively in high-pressure interview situations.

100+ QUESTIONS AND SCENARIOS

While many resources mention the STAR method, this book introduces the enhanced STAR+ framework, which adds the critical "Lessons Learned" component that sophisticated interviewers increasingly expect. This addition transforms good answers into exceptional ones by demonstrating your capacity for growth and self-reflection.

WHO THIS BOOK IS FOR

This guide is specifically designed for:

- Software Engineers preparing for behavioral interviews at Google, Meta, Amazon, Microsoft, and similar big-tech companies

- Engineering Managers seeking to demonstrate leadership capabilities beyond technical management

- Solution Architects and Program Managers navigating role-specific behavioral expectations

- Experienced professionals looking to transition between technical leadership roles

- Anyone seeking nuanced, detailed, and company-specific preparation guidance

If you're looking for shortcuts or quick fixes, this isn't the resource for you. This book is for professionals committed to thorough preparation and authentic self-presentation—those who understand that mastering behavioral interviews isn't just about getting a job, but about developing career-long communication skills.

HOW TO USE THIS BOOK

I recommend reading this book in sequence, as later chapters build upon concepts introduced earlier. However, if you're short on time, each chapter is designed to stand alone, allowing you to focus on areas where you need the most support.

The exercises throughout aren't optional—they're essential components of effective preparation. Set aside dedicated time to complete them, ideally several weeks before your interviews begin.

For maximum benefit, combine this book with practice partners who can provide feedback on your responses. While self-reflection is valuable, external perspective is irreplaceable.

A PERSONAL NOTE

Behavioral interviews can feel artificial and constraining. Many brilliant engineers and leaders struggle with the format, not because they lack accomplishments, but because the structure feels unnatural. I understand this challenge intimately.

My goal isn't to turn you into someone you're not, but to help you authentically communicate who you are and what you've accomplished. The frameworks in this book aren't meant to make you sound rehearsed—they're designed to help you organize your thoughts so your unique value shines through.

Remember that behind every behavioral question is a simple human desire: interviewers want to understand who you are, how you work, and whether you'll thrive in their environment. This book will help you answer those fundamental questions with confidence and authenticity.

Let's begin.

Sanjeet Sahay March 2025

INTRODUCTION

It takes 20 years to build a reputation and five minutes to ruin
it. If you think about that, you'll do things differently.

— Warren Buffett

Your reputation—your personal brand—is established in a matter of minutes.
While your resume might get you through the door, it's how you present
yourself and your experiences that ultimately determines whether that door
opens to a new opportunity or closes on a missed chance.

WHAT ARE BEHAVIORAL INTERVIEWS?

Behavioral interviews are structured conversations designed to evaluate how
you've handled specific situations in your past professional life. They're based
on a simple but powerful premise: past behavior is the best predictor of future
performance.

Unlike technical interviews that test what you know, behavioral interviews
assess who you are—how you think, how you work with others, how you
overcome challenges, and how you learn from experiences. They reveal the
human behind the skills, the professional behind the code.

In a behavioral interview, you'll be asked to provide detailed examples of how
you've handled specific situations in your past work experience. These questions
typically begin with phrases like:

- "Tell me about a time when..."
- "Describe a situation where..."
- "Give me an example of..."
- "How have you previously dealt with..."

Your answers to these questions tell interviewers far more than whether you can solve a particular problem—they reveal how you approach problems in general, how you interact with team members, how you handle pressure, and how you learn and grow.

WHY BEHAVIORAL INTERVIEWS MATTER TO BIG TECH

For companies like Amazon, Google, Meta, and Microsoft, technical excellence is just the beginning. These organizations operate at massive scale, in complex environments, with diverse teams tackling unprecedented challenges. In such environments, how you work becomes as important as what you know.

AMAZON: LEADERSHIP PRINCIPLES IN ACTION

Amazon's famous Leadership Principles aren't just wall decorations—they're the operational framework for decision-making throughout the company. When Amazon conducts behavioral interviews, they're explicitly evaluating how well your past behavior aligns with principles like Customer Obsession, Ownership, Invent and Simplify, and Earn Trust.

For Amazon, behavioral interviews aren't supplementary to technical evaluation—they're equally critical. A candidate who demonstrates strong technical skills but fails to show alignment with Amazon's Leadership Principles is unlikely to succeed in their ecosystem.

GOOGLE: BEYOND "GOOGLEYNESS"

Google looks beyond technical prowess to what they sometimes call "Googleyness"—a combination of intellectual humility, conscientiousness, comfort with ambiguity, and evidence of taking thoughtful risks. Their behavioral questions probe for examples of how you've navigated ambiguous situations, collaborated across boundaries, and maintained effectiveness in rapidly changing environments.

Google's emphasis on learning ability—what they call "general cognitive ability"—is assessed not just through problem-solving questions but through behavioral questions that reveal how you approach new challenges and incorporate new information.

META: BUILDING SOCIAL VALUE AT SCALE

At Meta, behavioral interviews focus heavily on how candidates have contributed to building products that create social value at scale. Their questions often probe for examples of how you've made decisions that balanced competing priorities, how you've advocated for users, and how you've navigated complex ethical considerations.

Meta particularly values examples that demonstrate your ability to move fast while maintaining high standards—showing how you've made impact while managing risk appropriately.

MICROSOFT: GROWTH MINDSET IN PRACTICE

Microsoft's cultural transformation under Satya Nadella has emphasized growth mindset—the belief that abilities can be developed through dedication and hard work. Their behavioral interviews often look for evidence of how you've learned from failures, sought out feedback, and adapted to changing circumstances.

Microsoft values examples that show how you've collaborated across organizational boundaries and contributed to others' success, not just your own.

THE STAKES ARE HIGH

For candidates, the stakes of behavioral interviews couldn't be higher. At top tech companies:

- Behavioral interviews typically account for 30-50% of the overall evaluation
- A single poor behavioral interview can override strong technical performance
- Compensation differences between levels can exceed $100,000 annually
- The right behavioral presentation can tip the scales toward a higher initial level

Yet despite these high stakes, most candidates underprepare for behavioral interviews, focusing the bulk of their preparation on technical questions. This imbalance creates both risk and opportunity—risk for the unprepared, but opportunity for those who master the art and science of behavioral interviewing.

THE STAR+ FRAMEWORK: A PREVIEW

Throughout this book, we'll explore the STAR+ framework in depth—a powerful structure for crafting compelling behavioral interview responses:

- **Situation**: The specific context, project, or challenge you faced
- **Task**: Your specific responsibilities or objectives in that situation
- **Action**: The specific steps you took to address the challenge
- **Result**: The measurable outcomes of your actions
- **Plus (Lessons Learned)**: What you learned and how you grew from the experience

This enhanced version of the traditional STAR framework adds the critical reflection component that sophisticated interviewers increasingly expect. By explicitly articulating what you learned and how you've applied those lessons, you demonstrate the growth mindset and self-awareness that top companies value.

In Chapter 3, we'll dive deep into this framework, exploring how to apply it effectively across different types of questions and different company contexts.

BEYOND PREPARATION: AUTHENTIC COMMUNICATION

While this book provides frameworks, examples, and preparation strategies, its ultimate goal is to help you communicate authentically. The best behavioral interview responses aren't rehearsed performances—they're thoughtful reflections on real experiences, organized and presented in a way that helps interviewers understand your unique value.

The techniques in this book aren't about gaming the system or telling interviewers what they want to hear. They're about helping you identify your most relevant experiences and communicate them effectively, so interviewers can accurately assess whether there's a mutual fit between your capabilities and their needs.

THE JOURNEY AHEAD

In the chapters that follow, we'll explore behavioral interviewing from every angle:

- We'll examine the history and psychology behind behavioral interviewing
- We'll step into the interviewer's shoes to understand what they're really looking for
- We'll master the STAR+ framework for structuring compelling responses
- We'll develop strategies for identifying your most powerful stories
- We'll explore common pitfalls and how to avoid them

- We'll create a systematic practice plan to build your interviewing muscles

- We'll examine role-specific examples for different technical positions

- We'll analyze company-specific approaches to behavioral assessment

- We'll develop advanced strategies for handling ambiguous and unexpected questions

By the end of this journey, you'll approach behavioral interviews not with anxiety but with confidence—not as obstacles to overcome but as opportunities to showcase the full range of your professional capabilities.

Let's begin by understanding the foundations of behavioral interviewing—where it came from, how it works, and why it matters for your technical career.

PART 1: FOUNDATIONS

CHAPTER 1. WHAT ARE BEHAVIORAL INTERVIEWS?

The most important thing in communication is hearing what isn't said.

-- Peter Drucker

The email arrives with a subject line that makes your heart skip a beat: "Interview Confirmation: Software Engineer Position at Google." As you scan the details, you notice a 45-minute slot labeled simply "Behavioral Interview." While you've been practicing algorithm problems for weeks, this segment gives you pause. What exactly will they ask? How should you prepare? And why do companies like Google dedicate precious interview time to questions that seem unrelated to coding?

You're not alone in this uncertainty. Many engineers approach behavioral interviews with a mixture of confusion and apprehension. Some dismiss them as subjective formalities, while others frantically memorize canned responses the night before. Both approaches miss the mark—and potentially, the job offer.

In this chapter, we'll demystify behavioral interviews by exploring their origins, understanding their purpose, and examining how they differ from traditional interview formats. By the end, you'll understand not just what behavioral interviews are, but why mastering them is crucial for your career in technology.

1.1. THE ORIGINS OF BEHAVIORAL INTERVIEWING

Behavioral interviewing didn't emerge overnight. Its development represents a significant evolution in how organizations evaluate talent—a response to the limitations of traditional interviewing methods.

THE PROBLEM WITH TRADITIONAL INTERVIEWS

For decades, job interviews followed a predictable pattern. Candidates would be asked about their qualifications, their strengths and weaknesses, and hypothetical questions like "How would you handle a conflict with a coworker?" While seemingly reasonable, research consistently showed these interviews were poor predictors of actual job performance.

The problems were numerous:

- **Hypothetical questions** produced hypothetical answers that rarely reflected how candidates actually behaved in real situations

- **Self-assessment questions** ("What are your greatest strengths?") rewarded confidence over competence

- **Leading questions** telegraphed the "right" answer, measuring candidates' ability to pick up on social cues rather than their actual capabilities

- **Inconsistent evaluation** meant different interviewers asked different questions, making candidate comparison nearly impossible

- **Unconscious bias** flourished without structured evaluation criteria

These traditional interviews created a paradox: they felt informative to interviewers while actually providing little predictive value about job performance. Companies were essentially making million-dollar talent decisions based on gut feelings dressed up as rigorous assessment.

THE BEHAVIORAL REVOLUTION

In the 1970s, industrial psychologist Dr. Tom Janz pioneered what he called "behavior-based interviewing" while researching more effective hiring methods. His approach was rooted in a simple but powerful premise: the best predictor of future behavior is past behavior.

Rather than asking candidates what they would do in hypothetical situations, Janz advocated asking what they had actually done in similar situations. This shift from the hypothetical to the historical transformed interviewing from a test of imagination to an examination of demonstrated behavior.

The approach gained significant traction in the 1980s as organizations sought more reliable hiring methods. By the 1990s, behavioral interviewing had become standard practice in many industries, with technology companies being relatively late adopters.

THE SCIENCE BEHIND THE METHOD

Behavioral interviewing isn't just intuitively appealing—it's backed by research. Studies consistently show that structured behavioral interviews have significantly higher predictive validity for job performance than unstructured or traditional interviews.

A meta-analysis published in the Journal of Personnel Psychology found that behavioral interviews had a validity coefficient of 0.63 (on a scale where 1.0 represents perfect prediction), compared to just 0.38 for traditional interviews. This means behavioral interviews are approximately 65% more effective at predicting job performance.

The science makes sense: when candidates describe actual situations they've faced, the specific actions they took, and the measurable results they achieved, they provide concrete evidence of their capabilities rather than aspirational statements about what they might do.

1.2. BEHAVIORAL VS. TRADITIONAL INTERVIEWS

To understand behavioral interviews more clearly, let's contrast them with traditional approaches:

Traditional Interview Question	Behavioral Interview Question
"How do you handle tight deadlines?"	"Tell me about a time when you had to meet a tight deadline. What was the situation, and what specific actions did you take?"
"Are you good at resolving conflicts?"	"Describe a situation where you had a conflict with a team member. How did you handle it, and what was the outcome?"
"How would you prioritize competing demands?"	"Give me an example of when you had to juggle multiple high-priority tasks. How did you decide what to focus on first?"
"Do you consider yourself a good leader?"	"Tell me about a time when you had to lead a team through a difficult situation. What challenges did you face, and how did you overcome them?"
"Are you comfortable with ambiguity?"	"Describe a project where requirements were unclear or changing. How did you navigate that uncertainty?"

Notice the fundamental differences:

- Traditional questions invite speculation and self-assessment
- Behavioral questions require specific examples from past experience
- Traditional questions can be answered with generalities and platitudes
- Behavioral questions demand concrete details and measurable outcomes

- Traditional questions assess what candidates think about themselves
- Behavioral questions assess what candidates have actually done

This shift from hypothetical to historical, from general to specific, and from self-perception to demonstrated behavior is what makes behavioral interviews so much more effective at predicting job performance.

1.3. THE PSYCHOLOGY OF BEHAVIORAL INTERVIEWS

Behavioral interviews work because they tap into several psychological principles that improve assessment accuracy:

THE CONSISTENCY PRINCIPLE

People tend to behave consistently across similar situations. By examining how a candidate has handled challenges in the past, interviewers gain insight into how they're likely to handle similar challenges in the future. This consistency is particularly valuable when evaluating for specific competencies like problem-solving, collaboration, or leadership.

THE SPECIFICITY EFFECT

When asked for specific examples, candidates find it difficult to fabricate detailed stories on the spot. The request for concrete details—names, dates, metrics, conversations—creates a natural truth filter. Candidates can certainly prepare examples in advance, but they can't easily invent complex narratives during the interview itself.

THE REFLECTION ADVANTAGE

Behavioral questions prompt candidates to reflect on their experiences, extracting meaning and lessons from past events. This reflection process reveals not just what candidates have done, but how they think about what they've done—their self-awareness, learning orientation, and growth mindset.

THE COMPETENCY FOCUS

By designing questions around specific competencies (like customer focus, innovation, or teamwork), interviewers can systematically evaluate the capabilities most relevant to job success. This competency-based approach ensures that interviews assess what matters most for performance, not just what's easiest to observe.

1.4. REAL-LIFE EXAMPLES FROM FAANG HIRING PRACTICES

To understand how behavioral interviewing works in practice at top tech companies, let's examine specific approaches at Amazon, Google, Meta, and Microsoft.

AMAZON: LEADERSHIP PRINCIPLES IN ACTION

Amazon's approach to behavioral interviewing is perhaps the most structured and transparent in the industry. Each interview question is explicitly mapped to one or more of Amazon's 16 Leadership Principles, which serve as the company's operational framework.

For example, a question like "Tell me about a time when you had to make a decision without having all the information you wanted" is designed to assess the Leadership Principles of "Bias for Action" and "Are Right, A Lot."

Amazon interviewers are trained to probe deeply into examples, following the STAR format (Situation, Task, Action, Result) and taking detailed notes on specific behaviors that demonstrate alignment with Leadership Principles. These notes are then shared in hiring meetings, where candidates are evaluated against each principle based on concrete evidence from their interviews.

What makes Amazon's approach unique is its explicit connection between behavioral questions and organizational values. Candidates aren't just being assessed on general competencies—they're being evaluated on their fit with Amazon's specific cultural framework.

EXAMPLE AMAZON BEHAVIORAL QUESTIONS:

- "Tell me about a time when you had to work on a project with unclear requirements."

- "Describe a situation where you disagreed with a team member. How did you resolve it?"

- "Give me an example of when you took a risk and it failed."

- "Tell me about a time when you had to deliver results in a self-directed environment."

- "Describe a time when you received tough feedback. How did you respond?"

GOOGLE: STRUCTURED BEHAVIORAL ASSESSMENT

Google's approach to behavioral interviewing evolved significantly after their internal research (Project Oxygen) identified the behaviors that distinguished their most effective managers. This research led to a more structured behavioral assessment focused on specific competencies.

Google interviewers use a combination of behavioral and situational questions, with a particular emphasis on leadership, role-related knowledge, general cognitive ability, and "Googleyness" (their term for cultural fit). Unlike Amazon, Google doesn't publicly disclose their evaluation framework, but their questions typically probe for evidence of:

- Learning ability and intellectual humility

- Bias to action and results orientation

- Collaborative problem-solving

- Comfort with ambiguity

- Technical leadership

Google's behavioral interviews are notable for their cognitive depth—interviewers often ask follow-up questions that explore the reasoning behind decisions, not just the decisions themselves. This emphasis on thought process aligns with Google's value of intellectual rigor.

EXAMPLE GOOGLE BEHAVIORAL QUESTIONS:

- "Tell me about a time when you had to analyze data to make a recommendation."

- "Describe a situation where you had to influence someone without having formal authority."

- "Give me an example of when you had to learn something complex quickly."

- "Tell me about a project that failed. What would you do differently now?"

- "Describe a time when you had to make a decision with incomplete information."

META: IMPACT AND SCALE FOCUS

Meta's behavioral interviews reflect the company's emphasis on impact, scale, and speed. Their questions often probe for examples of how candidates have:

- Built products or features that created significant user value

- Made decisions that balanced competing priorities

- Navigated ambiguous problem spaces

- Collaborated across organizational boundaries

- Moved quickly while maintaining quality

What distinguishes Meta's approach is their focus on scale and impact metrics. Candidates are expected to quantify the results of their actions, whether in terms of user engagement, performance improvements, or business outcomes. This quantitative emphasis reflects Meta's data-driven culture.

EXAMPLE META BEHAVIORAL QUESTIONS:

- "Tell me about the most impactful project you've worked on. How did you measure its success?"

- "Describe a time when you had to make a trade-off between quality and speed."

- "Give me an example of when you had to work with teams across different functions."

- "Tell me about a situation where you identified and solved a problem before it became critical."

- "Describe a time when you had to make a decision that wasn't popular with your team."

MICROSOFT: GROWTH MINDSET EVALUATION

Microsoft's behavioral interviewing approach has evolved significantly under CEO Satya Nadella's leadership, with a particular emphasis on growth mindset. Their questions often explore how candidates have:

- Learned from failures and setbacks

- Sought out and incorporated feedback

- Adapted to changing circumstances

- Collaborated across organizational boundaries

- Contributed to others' success and growth

Microsoft's behavioral interviews are notable for their emphasis on learning and development. Candidates are evaluated not just on what they've accomplished, but on how they've grown through challenges and how they've helped others grow.

EXAMPLE MICROSOFT BEHAVIORAL QUESTIONS:

- "Tell me about a time when you received feedback that was difficult to hear. How did you respond?"

- "Describe a situation where you had to adapt to a significant change in direction."

- "Give me an example of when you helped someone else succeed."

- "Tell me about a time when you failed at something important to you. What did you learn?"

- "Describe a situation where you had to work with someone who had a very different working style."

1.5. THE EVOLUTION OF BEHAVIORAL INTERVIEWING IN TECH

While behavioral interviewing has been standard practice in many industries since the 1980s, the tech industry was relatively slow to adopt it. This delayed adoption reflects the industry's historical emphasis on technical skills over interpersonal capabilities.

THE TECHNICAL BIAS

For decades, tech interviews focused almost exclusively on technical knowledge and problem-solving ability. Candidates were evaluated primarily on their coding skills, algorithm knowledge, and system design capabilities. This technical focus made sense in an era when software development was often a solitary pursuit, with engineers working independently on well-defined problems.

THE COLLABORATION SHIFT

As software development became increasingly collaborative and complex, companies began to recognize that technical skills alone weren't sufficient for success. Engineers needed to work effectively in teams, communicate with stakeholders, navigate ambiguity, and adapt to rapidly changing requirements.

This recognition led to the gradual introduction of behavioral components in tech interviews, initially as supplements to technical assessment rather than core elements of the evaluation process.

THE LEADERSHIP IMPERATIVE

The final catalyst for widespread adoption of behavioral interviewing in tech was the recognition that engineering leadership requires a distinct set of non-technical capabilities. As companies sought to identify and develop technical leaders, they needed assessment methods that could evaluate leadership potential, not just technical proficiency.

This leadership imperative led companies like Amazon to develop explicit frameworks (like their Leadership Principles) that could be assessed through behavioral interviewing. Other companies followed suit, developing their own competency frameworks and behavioral assessment approaches.

THE CURRENT LANDSCAPE

Today, behavioral interviewing is a standard component of the hiring process at virtually all major tech companies. While the specific approach varies by company, the fundamental premise remains consistent: past behavior is the best predictor of future performance.

What has evolved is the sophistication of the assessment. Modern behavioral interviews at top tech companies are:

- **Competency-based**: Mapped to specific capabilities required for success
- **Evidence-driven**: Focused on concrete examples rather than general statements
- **Structured**: Following consistent formats to enable fair comparison
- **Calibrated**: With interviewers trained to evaluate responses consistently
- **Integrated**: Complementing rather than replacing technical assessment

This evolution represents a maturation of the tech industry's approach to talent assessment—a recognition that building great technology requires not just technical brilliance but also the human capabilities that enable effective collaboration, leadership, and innovation.

1.6. WHY BEHAVIORAL INTERVIEWS MATTER FOR YOUR CAREER

Understanding the history and mechanics of behavioral interviewing is interesting, but why should you, as a candidate, care? There are several compelling reasons:

THEY'RE INCREASINGLY IMPORTANT

At top tech companies, behavioral interviews now account for 30-50% of the overall evaluation. A stellar technical performance can be undermined by poor behavioral interviews, while strong behavioral interviews can sometimes compensate for technical weaknesses (within reason).

THEY IMPACT LEVEL AND COMPENSATION

Your performance in behavioral interviews doesn't just affect whether you get an offer—it affects what level that offer is at. The difference between levels at top tech companies can exceed $100,000 annually in total compensation, making behavioral interview performance a literally valuable skill.

THEY ASSESS CAREER-CRITICAL SKILLS

The competencies evaluated in behavioral interviews—leadership, communication, problem-solving, collaboration—aren't just important for getting hired. They're the same capabilities that determine your effectiveness, impact, and advancement throughout your career.

THEY'RE LEARNABLE SKILLS

Unlike some technical capabilities that depend on innate aptitude, behavioral interviewing skills can be systematically developed through practice and feedback. This means that investing time in mastering these skills offers a reliable return on investment.

THEY TRANSFER ACROSS COMPANIES

While each company has its own technical stack and interview style, the fundamental skills of behavioral interviewing transfer across organizations. Mastering these skills creates career-long value, not just preparation for your next interview.

1.7. COMMON MISCONCEPTIONS ABOUT BEHAVIORAL INTERVIEWS

Before we conclude this chapter, let's address some common misconceptions about behavioral interviews:

"THEY'RE JUST SUBJECTIVE PERSONALITY TESTS"

While behavioral interviews do involve human judgment, they're far from subjective personality assessments. Properly conducted behavioral interviews evaluate specific, job-relevant behaviors based on concrete examples, not personality traits or interviewer "feel."

"I JUST NEED TO MEMORIZE SOME GOOD STORIES"

Memorizing canned responses might help you survive a behavioral interview, but it won't help you excel. Effective behavioral interviewing requires authentic reflection on your experiences and the ability to adapt those experiences to the specific competencies being evaluated.

"TECHNICAL SKILLS ARE ALL THAT REALLY MATTER"

This persistent myth continues to lead candidates to underprepare for behavioral interviews. At top tech companies, behavioral assessment is weighted heavily in hiring decisions, sometimes equally with technical evaluation. Ignoring this reality puts candidates at a significant disadvantage.

"I CAN JUST WING IT"

Some candidates believe they can improvise effective responses during the interview. This approach almost always fails. Behavioral interviews require specific, detailed examples that most people cannot recall and organize effectively under pressure without preparation.

"THEY'RE LOOKING FOR PERFECT PEOPLE"

Behavioral interviews aren't designed to find candidates who've never made mistakes. In fact, questions about failures and challenges are specifically designed to assess how candidates learn and grow from setbacks. Authenticity, self-awareness, and growth mindset are valued over claims of perfection.

1.8. CONCLUSION: THE STRATEGIC ADVANTAGE

Behavioral interviews aren't arbitrary hurdles in your path to a tech career—they're strategic opportunities to differentiate yourself in a competitive landscape. While many candidates focus exclusively on technical preparation, those who master behavioral interviewing gain a significant advantage.

This advantage comes not just from being better prepared for interviews, but from developing deeper self-awareness about your professional experiences. The process of preparing for behavioral interviews forces you to reflect on your career, identify your most significant contributions, and articulate the value you've created. This reflection builds not just interview skills but career clarity.

In the chapters that follow, we'll move from understanding behavioral interviews to mastering them. We'll explore the interviewer's perspective, develop a powerful framework for structuring your responses, and build a systematic preparation plan that will transform behavioral interviews from sources of anxiety to opportunities for showcasing your unique value.

But first, let's step into the interviewer's shoes to understand exactly what they're looking for—and how they evaluate what they hear. That's the focus of our next chapter.

CHAPTER 2. INSIDE THE INTERVIEWERS MIND

You see, but you do not observe.

— Sherlock Holmes

Let me tell you about the Tuesday morning that taught me what interviews really are.

I was three months into my first Engineering Manager role at a cloud services firm, still waking at 3 AM worrying I'd be exposed as an impostor. My old Solutions Architect badge sat dusty on my desk—a relic from when my biggest concern was whiteboarding architectures, not judging human potential.

That morning, I spilled cold brew across my interview rubric while frantically debugging a Kubernetes config. The stain spread like inkblot test over "Leadership Competencies," which suddenly felt absurd. Since when did reading resumes become part of my job? I'd taken this promotion to build systems, not play psychologist.

At 10:15 AM, you walked in—Candidate #4 that week. I smiled through my stress-sweat, already calculating how to catch up on sprint planning after this. Your resume said you'd optimized API response times at a fintech startup. My sleep-deprived brain translated this to: Can they handle our dumpster fire of microservice timeouts?

Here's what I wish someone had told me then: Interviews aren't exams. They're compatibility tests between two stressed humans.

As you described migrating legacy systems, I wasn't just listening for technical details. My lizard brain was asking:

- Will this person make my 2 AM production calls less terrifying?

- Can I trust them to explain technical debt to the C-suite without eye rolls?

- Will my team fight to work with them, or quietly Slack me "WTF?"

When you mentioned mentoring junior devs during that migration, I stopped thinking about the Kubernetes alert blaring on my phone. Here was someone who understood that codebases are maintained by people, not PRs.

By the time you left, I'd scribbled three notes:

- "Asks 'why' before 'how'"

- "Admits legacy code fears → relatable"

- "Fixed process AND taught others → force multiplier"

That coffee-stained rubric? I never opened it. You showed me what actually matters—the unteachable stuff between the bullet points.

Now let me show you how to become the candidate that makes interviewers forget their checklists.

In this chapter, we'll pull back the curtain on the interviewer's process. We'll examine the rubrics used by top tech companies, decode their scoring systems, and provide a clear framework for understanding what makes a response exceptional versus merely adequate. By the end, you'll be able to see your answers through the interviewer's eyes—a perspective that will transform how you prepare and perform.

2.1. LET'S TAKE A DEEPER LOOK

Before diving into formal rubrics and scoring systems, let's understand the human reality of conducting interviews. Interviewers at tech companies aren't professional interviewers—they're engineers, managers, and leaders who conduct interviews as a small part of their job. This reality shapes how they approach the interview process.

THE INTERVIEWER'S CHALLENGES

Interviewers face several challenges that influence how they evaluate candidates:

- **Cognitive Load**: Most interviewers conduct interviews while balancing their regular workload. They're thinking about the code review due after your interview, the production issue that emerged overnight, and the design document they need to finish by end of day.

- **Limited Training**: While companies like Amazon and Google provide interviewer training, it's typically brief—a few hours at most. Interviewers are expected to learn primarily through experience, which creates inconsistency.

- **Note-Taking Pressure**: Interviewers must capture detailed notes while simultaneously listening to your responses, formulating follow-up questions, and evaluating your answers against rubrics.

- **Recency Effects**: Interviewers typically conduct multiple interviews in succession, creating recency bias where the most recent candidates are remembered more clearly than earlier ones.

- **Comparison Challenges**: Interviewers must compare candidates who have different experiences, different communication styles, and different examples—an inherently difficult task.

These challenges don't mean interviewers are ineffective—just that they're human. Understanding these realities helps you structure your responses in ways that make the interviewer's job easier, which indirectly improves your evaluation.

WHAT INTERVIEWERS ARE ACTUALLY LOOKING FOR

Beyond specific competencies (which we'll explore in detail), interviewers are fundamentally trying to answer three questions:

1. **Can you do the job?** (Skills and capabilities)

2. **Will you do the job?** (Motivation and alignment)

3. **Will you fit the team and culture?** (Collaboration and values)

Behavioral questions are particularly effective at addressing the second and third questions, which technical interviews often miss entirely. Your examples need to demonstrate not just that you can perform technically, but that you're motivated by the right things and that you work in ways that align with the company's values.

THE INTERVIEWER'S PROCESS

A typical behavioral interview follows this general flow:

1. **Brief introduction and rapport building** (1-2 minutes)

2. **Explanation of the interview format** (1 minute)

3. **First behavioral question** (10-15 minutes including follow-ups)

4. **Second behavioral question** (10-15 minutes including follow-ups)

5. **Possibly a third behavioral question** (if time permits)

6. **Candidate questions** (3-5 minutes)

7. **Wrap-up** (1 minute)

Immediately after you leave, the interviewer will:

1. Complete their notes while memories are fresh

2. Evaluate your responses against specific competencies

3. Assign scores based on company rubrics

4. Submit their evaluation to be considered in hiring discussions

This tight timeline means interviewers are making rapid judgments based on limited information. Your job is to make those judgments as accurate and favorable as possible by providing clear, concrete evidence of your capabilities.

2.2. WHAT INTERVIEWERS WANT: RUBRICS FROM TOP TECH COMPANIES

While each company has its own evaluation framework, there are remarkable similarities in what top tech companies look for in behavioral interviews. Let's examine the specific rubrics used at Amazon, Google, and Meta to understand what interviewers are evaluating.

AMAZON: LEADERSHIP PRINCIPLES EVALUATION

Amazon's behavioral interview process is explicitly structured around their Leadership Principles. Each interviewer is typically assigned 2-3 principles to assess, with questions designed to elicit evidence of behaviors aligned with those principles.

AMAZON'S EVALUATION RUBRIC

For each Leadership Principle, interviewers evaluate candidates on a four-point scale:

1. **Strong Negative**: Demonstrated behaviors contrary to the principle

2. **Negative**: Insufficient evidence of behaviors aligned with the principle

3. **Positive**: Clear evidence of behaviors aligned with the principle

4. **Strong Positive**: Exceptional evidence of behaviors aligned with the principle, often exceeding expectations

To achieve a "Strong Positive" rating, candidates typically need to demonstrate:

- **Depth**: Detailed, specific examples with clear personal contribution
- **Impact**: Measurable results that mattered to the business
- **Complexity**: Navigation of challenging circumstances or constraints
- **Leadership**: Influence beyond direct responsibilities
- **Reflection**: Thoughtful lessons learned and applied

EXAMPLE: CUSTOMER OBSESSION EVALUATION

For Amazon's first Leadership Principle, "Customer Obsession," interviewers look for specific behaviors:

Rating	Evidence Required
Strong Positive	Candidate provided multiple examples of identifying and addressing customer needs before customers themselves recognized them. Demonstrated willingness to make significant personal or team sacrifices to improve customer experience. Showed measurable impact on customer satisfaction or business metrics.
Positive	Candidate provided clear examples of focusing on customer needs and working backward from customer problems. Demonstrated understanding of both explicit and implicit customer requirements. Showed how customer focus influenced decisions.

Rating	Evidence Required
Negative	Candidate provided only vague references to customers without specific examples of customer-focused behaviors. Examples focused more on technical solutions than customer problems. Limited evidence of considering customer perspective in decision-making.
Strong Negative	Candidate's examples showed prioritization of other factors (technical elegance, personal convenience, internal politics) over customer needs. Demonstrated resistance to customer feedback or dismissive attitude toward customer concerns.

This detailed rubric explains why generic or technical-focused answers often receive poor evaluations at Amazon, even when the candidate has strong technical skills. Interviewers are explicitly looking for evidence of customer-focused behaviors, not just technical competence.

GOOGLE: COMPETENCY-BASED ASSESSMENT

Google's behavioral interview process evaluates candidates across four key areas:

1. **General Cognitive Ability**: How you solve problems and learn

2. **Leadership**: How you influence and collaborate

3. **Role-Related Knowledge**: How you apply your expertise

4. **Googleyness**: How you align with Google's culture and values

GOOGLE'S EVALUATION RUBRIC

For each competency, Google interviewers evaluate candidates on a four-point scale:

1. **Does Not Meet**: Insufficient evidence of the competency

2. **Meets Some**: Partial evidence of the competency

3. **Meets**: Clear evidence of the competency

4. **Strongly Meets**: Exceptional evidence of the competency

To achieve a "Strongly Meets" rating, candidates typically need to demonstrate:

- **Initiative**: Proactive problem identification and solution development

- **Impact**: Significant, measurable results that created value

- **Innovation**: Novel approaches or insights beyond standard solutions

- **Collaboration**: Effective work across organizational boundaries

- **Learning**: Rapid acquisition and application of new knowledge

EXAMPLE: LEADERSHIP EVALUATION

For the Leadership competency, Google interviewers look for specific behaviors:

Rating	Evidence Required
Strongly Meets	Candidate provided examples of influencing outcomes without formal authority. Demonstrated ability to navigate ambiguity and align diverse stakeholders. Showed how they developed others and created leverage through team empowerment. Examples included measurable team or organizational impact.
Meets	Candidate provided clear examples of team leadership or cross-functional collaboration. Demonstrated ability to navigate disagreements constructively. Showed how they contributed to team success beyond individual responsibilities.

Rating	Evidence Required
Meets Some	Candidate provided examples that showed some leadership elements but lacked depth or impact. Limited evidence of influence beyond direct responsibilities. Examples focused more on individual contribution than team outcomes.
Does Not Meet	Candidate's examples showed primarily individual work with limited collaboration. Demonstrated difficulty navigating disagreements or influencing others. Limited evidence of considering broader team or organizational context.

This rubric explains why technical brilliance alone isn't sufficient at Google. Interviewers are explicitly evaluating leadership behaviors that enable scale and impact beyond individual contribution.

META: IMPACT AND SCALE FOCUS

Meta's behavioral interview process emphasizes impact, scale, and speed—values central to the company's culture. Their evaluation framework focuses on:

1. **Impact**: The measurable results of your work

2. **Scale**: The scope and reach of your influence

3. **Speed**: Your ability to execute quickly and effectively

4. **Collaboration**: How you work with others to achieve outcomes

5. **Problem-Solving**: How you approach complex challenges

META'S EVALUATION RUBRIC

For each dimension, Meta interviewers evaluate candidates on a five-point scale:

1. **Poor**: Significant concerns or red flags

2. **Fair**: Below expectations for level

3. **Good**: Meets expectations for level

4. **Excellent**: Exceeds expectations for level

5. **Outstanding**: Significantly exceeds expectations for level

To achieve an "Outstanding" rating, candidates typically need to demonstrate:

- **Quantifiable Impact**: Clear metrics showing significant results

- **Broad Influence**: Effect beyond immediate team or project

- **Velocity**: Rapid execution without sacrificing quality

- **Strategic Thinking**: Connection between tactical work and larger goals

- **Ownership**: End-to-end responsibility for outcomes

EXAMPLE: IMPACT EVALUATION

For the Impact dimension, Meta interviewers look for specific behaviors:

Rating	Evidence Required
Outstanding	Candidate provided examples with exceptional, quantifiable impact significantly beyond expectations for their role. Demonstrated how their work affected core business metrics or enabled major strategic initiatives. Showed how they identified and captured opportunities that others missed.
Excellent	Candidate provided examples with clear, measurable impact exceeding expectations for their role. Demonstrated connection between their work and important business outcomes. Showed how they overcame significant obstacles to deliver results.

Rating	Evidence Required
Good	Candidate provided examples with solid impact appropriate for their role. Demonstrated understanding of how their work contributed to team or product goals. Showed reasonable metrics or outcomes from their efforts.
Fair	Candidate provided examples with limited or unclear impact. Metrics were vague or modest relative to role expectations. Limited evidence of connecting work to broader business objectives.
Poor	Candidate could not provide examples with meaningful impact. Focused on activities rather than outcomes. Showed limited understanding of how their work created value.

This rubric explains why Meta interviewers probe deeply for metrics and quantifiable results. The company's culture emphasizes measurable impact, and the interview evaluation reflects this priority.

2.3. SCORING SYSTEMS EXPLAINED

Now that we've examined the specific rubrics used by top tech companies, let's understand how these evaluations translate into hiring decisions. The scoring process is more nuanced than many candidates realize.

INDIVIDUAL QUESTION SCORING

Each behavioral question is typically scored independently, based on the specific competencies it was designed to assess. A single interview might evaluate 2-4 competencies through different questions.

For example, an Amazon interviewer might ask:

- Question 1: "Tell me about a time when you had to make a decision without all the information you wanted." (Evaluating "Bias for Action" and "Are Right, A Lot")

- Question 2: "Describe a situation where you had to deliver results with minimal resources." (Evaluating "Frugality" and "Deliver Results")

Each question receives its own score based on the relevant Leadership Principles, rather than a single overall interview score.

COMPETENCY AGGREGATION

When multiple questions assess the same competency, or when multiple interviewers assess the same competency in different interviews, these scores are aggregated to form a more complete picture.

For example, if three different interviewers all assessed "Leadership" through different questions, their individual assessments would be combined to create an overall Leadership evaluation.

This aggregation is why consistency across interviews is so important. If you provide contradictory examples or demonstrate different behaviors to different interviewers, it creates confusion in the evaluation process.

LEVEL CALIBRATION

Scores are calibrated based on the level of the position you're interviewing for. The same response might receive a "Strong Positive" for a junior role but only a "Positive" for a senior role, because expectations increase with seniority.

This level calibration is particularly important for experienced candidates. What impressed interviewers earlier in your career may be considered merely adequate for senior roles, requiring you to provide more sophisticated examples with greater impact and complexity.

HIRING BAR DETERMINATION

Each company establishes a "hiring bar" that candidates must clear for an offer. This bar typically includes:

- Minimum score requirements for critical competencies
- Overall score thresholds across all competencies
- No significant concerns or "red flags" in any area

The specific thresholds vary by company and role, but the general principle is consistent: candidates must demonstrate sufficient evidence across all required competencies, with no major gaps or concerns.

LEVELING DECISIONS

For candidates who clear the hiring bar, companies then make leveling decisions—determining which job level (and corresponding compensation) to offer. These decisions consider:

- The strength of behavioral interview performance
- The complexity and impact of examples provided
- The scope of leadership and influence demonstrated
- Comparison to current employees at different levels

This leveling process explains why behavioral interview performance can significantly impact compensation, even for candidates who receive offers. The difference between "meeting expectations" and "exceeding expectations" can translate to tens of thousands of dollars in annual compensation.

2.4. THE HIDDEN CHECKLIST IN EVERY INTERVIEWER'S MIND

I'll let you in on a secret: most interviewers don't even realize they're running this algorithm in their heads.

It wasn't until my third year as an engineering manager—after conducting nearly 200 interviews—that I noticed the pattern. One Tuesday afternoon, while reviewing feedback for a candidate who should have been perfect (ex-Google, PhD, flawless system design), I found myself writing: "Strong technical skills, but something's missing."

That vague unease haunted me. So I did what any engineer would do—I reverse-engineered my own brain. After analyzing dozens of interview notes, a clear decision tree emerged.

Here's the flowchart interviewers wish they had (but would never admit they need):

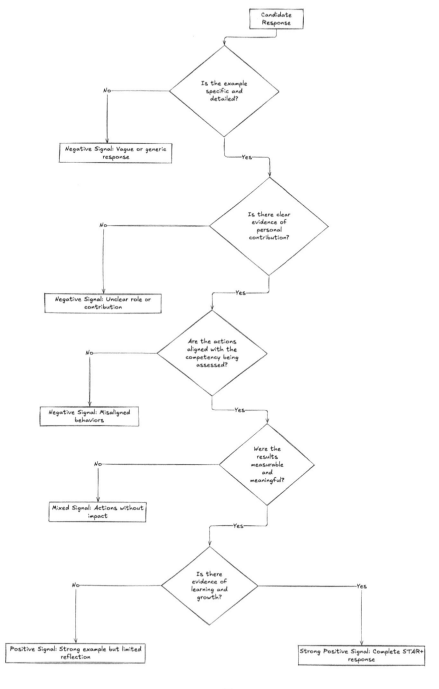

Let me walk you through the five silent gates your story must pass—the same ones I unconsciously used until I made them explicit:

GATE 1: THE SPECIFICITY TEST

Early in my career, I fell for eloquent generalities. Then a senior architect schooled me: "Anyone can recite textbook approaches. I need to see their fingerprints on actual code."

Red Flag: "I always prioritize scalability..." Green Light: "Last March, our payment service started failing at 11 AM daily..."

GATE 2: THE OWNERSHIP FILTER

My worst hire was a brilliant engineer who described every achievement as "we did..." After joining, he watched teammates struggle while waiting for "someone" to fix problems. Now I listen for pronouns.

Trap: "The team refactored the module..." Winning Move: "I prototyped three solutions before rallying the team around..."

GATE 3: THE RELEVANCE CHECK

A candidate once spent 10 minutes describing how he optimized a bakery's supply chain. Impressive—if we were hiring a logistics manager.

Miss: Rambling about any impressive achievement Hit: "This mirrors your Principal Engineer role because..."

GATE 4: THE IMPACT VALIDATOR

My VP's favorite question: "How did you know it worked?" Numbers build trust. When a nervous junior engineer showed me a Grafana dashboard proving her fix reduced latency by 38%, I fought to hire her on the spot.

Weak: "Performance improved." Strong: "P99 latency dropped from 1400ms to 872ms, cutting support tickets by 60%."

GATE 5: THE GROWTH LENS

The best engineers I've hired all shared one habit: they dissected failures like interesting bugs. When a senior candidate laughed while explaining a $20K AWS bill blunder—then showed the cost-alert system he built afterward—I knew he'd thrive in our chaotic environment.

Surface-Level: "We hit our goals." Depth: "Post-mortem revealed we'd underestimated cold start times—here's how I now budget for initialization spikes."

This isn't hypothetical. Last quarter, my team calibrated our interview scores against this framework. Candidates who cleared all five gates received offers 94% of the time. Those missing even one? Just 22%.

The difference between "strong candidate" and "hire" isn't talent—it's intentional storytelling. Now that you see the gates, you can walk through them with your eyes open.

2.5. COMMON INTERVIEWER CONCERNS AND RED FLAGS

Let me tell you about the candidate who changed how I interview forever.

It was Q4 crunch time, and we desperately needed a senior engineer. "Alex" had a stellar resume—ex-FAANG, open-source contributions, the works. But five minutes into the behavioral round, my stomach tightened. When describing a missed deadline, he said: "The PM kept changing requirements, so naturally we failed."

No ownership. No curiosity about what he could have done differently. Just a well-polished blame game.

That's when I realized: Technical skills get you in the door, but these invisible red flags will slam it shut. Here are the seven silent killers I've seen sink otherwise brilliant candidates:

1. THE BLAME-SHIFTER

- What I've heard: "The QA team missed the edge cases..."
- What I think: "Will this person own their mistakes at 3 AM when production is down?"
- Antidote: "I should've built better test harnesses. Now I include these in my definition of done."

2. THE LONE WOLF COMPLEX

- Red flag: "I single-handedly redesigned..." (for a team project)
- My panic meter: "Will they hoard knowledge or mentor juniors?"
- Fix: "I led the initial POC, then worked with Jamal and Priya to scale it—Jamal's caching idea was genius."

3. THE METRIC-FREE ZONE

- Danger zone: "We significantly improved performance."
- My skepticism: "Did they measure anything, or is this wishful thinking?"
- Solution: "Using New Relic, we tracked a 40% reduction in API latency, saving 2,200 EC2 hours/month."

4. THE BRIDGE BURNER

- Alarming phrasing: "My last manager was clueless about..."

- My concern: "Will they trash-talk me at their next interview?"
- Better approach: "We had different risk tolerances—I learned to present data-driven cases."

5. THE CONCRETE SHOES

- Warning sign: "That's just how we've always done it."
- My dread: "Will they resist adopting our CI/CD pipeline?"
- Growth show: "Initially I pushed back on Kubernetes, but after testing it I became our cluster's maintainer."

6. THE BROKEN RECORD

- Fatal flaw: Repeating the same story for "failure" and "growth" questions
- My verdict: "Zero reflection ability."
- Fix: "That outage taught me to implement circuit breakers—here's the alerting dashboard I built afterward."

7. THE CULTURAL MISFIT

- Oops moment: Bragging about "crushing competitors" in a collaborative culture
- My mental note: "Great for sales, terrible for our eng team."
- Adapt: "I'm competitive with myself—my current focus is improving our team's velocity metrics."

Here's the painful truth I learned from rejecting 3 "perfect" candidates last quarter: You can't recover from these once they're noticed. Like that time a principal engineer spent 20 minutes trashing his former CTO—I didn't hear another word he said.

But here's the good news: These aren't personality flaws. They're communication habits. And unlike leetcode skills, you can fix them in one weekend of practice.

2.6. THE AMAZON DIRECTOR'S LUNCHTIME CONFESSION

I'll never forget the rainy Seattle afternoon when a Director at Amazon leaned across the table at Tamarind Tree and said:

"We don't hire based on what candidates say. We hire based on what they make us imagine."

He pushed aside his pho and sketched on a napkin. This became my Rosetta Stone for decoding Amazon's interview magic.

1. LEADERSHIP: THE "EMPTY CHAIR" TEST

His exact words: *"When someone describes leading a project, I'm visualizing our next QBR. Will this person be the one explaining to the VP why we missed goals? Or will they be the reason we exceeded them?"*

What he listens for:

- "We" vs "I" balance (60/40 is ideal)

- Quiet persuasion ("How they moved stubborn PMs without drama")

- Development multiplier ("Did teammates level up because of them?")

His favorite answer: "I turned our reluctant senior engineer into the API gateway's biggest advocate—now she trains other teams."

2. PROBLEM-SOLVING: THE "5 WHYS" RULE

He tapped his chopsticks: "Most candidates stop at 'what' they fixed. I need to hear how deep they dug."

His autopsy method:

- First answer: Technical symptom ("API timeouts")
- Third why: Process flaw ("No circuit breaker pattern")
- Fifth why: Cultural root cause ("We valued velocity over resilience")

Red flag: "We added more servers." Hire signal: "We fixed the immediate issue, then changed our deployment checklist to prevent recurrence."

3. CUSTOMER OBSESSION: THE "EMPTY STORE" TRICK

His signature question: "Walk me through your last visit to [our product] as a customer."

What reveals fakers:

- Surface-level complaints ("The UI is clunky")
- Generic praise ("Great user experience!")

What gets offers: "I noticed checkout flow differs between mobile/web—was that intentional? I'd A/B test removing the shipping estimator on mobile."

4. INNOVATION: THE "TWO PIZZA" LITMUS TEST

His rule: "If the story can't be believed by a team fed with two pizzas, it's either bullshit or too big to matter."

Real innovation signals:

- Constraints embraced ("We had no budget, so we...")

- Early failures ("Version 1 bombed because...")

- Organic adoption ("Devs started using it before we mandated it")

5. HIRING BAR RAISERS: THE "SHADOW SCORE"

He wiped soy sauce off the napkin: "Most interviewers grade answers. Bar Raisers grade reactions to silence."

Their secret scoring:

- First pause (Do they ramble or refine?)

- Challenge response (Defensive or curious?)

- Question quality (Do they probe our problems?)

As we left, he said one last thing I wrote on my hand:

"The best candidates don't just answer questions—they reshape how we see our own Leadership Principles."

Here's what most candidates miss: As a hiring manager, I'm not evaluating your past—I'm simulating our future. Every answer helps me imagine:

- Will you make my 2 AM production calls less stressful?

- Can I trust you with our junior engineers?

- Will you spot problems before they become crises?

The best responses don't just check boxes—they paint a picture of how you'll change my team.

2.7. THE HIDDEN PURPOSE BEHIND EVERY FOLLOW-UP QUESTION

During a recent whiteboarding session, a Principal Architect who's conducted over 100 interviews this year shared his unfiltered perspective on why follow-ups matter more than candidates realize. Here's the breakdown:

WHY INTERVIEWERS DIG DEEPER

Follow-ups aren't just polite conversation—they serve specific evaluation purposes:

- Authenticity Check – Does this candidate truly understand what they're describing, or are they reciting a rehearsed story?

- Depth Probe – Is their experience surface-level or substantial enough to handle real-world complexity?

- Thinking Process – How they respond under scrutiny reveals more than any scripted answer ever could.

Based on reviewing 300+ interview scorecards, these are the most common follow-up categories and their intentions:

1. CLARIFICATION DRILLS

Example Questions:

- "What was your specific contribution in the breakdown timeline?"

- "Which components did you personally optimize versus delegate?"

Why We Ask: To separate team accomplishments from individual ownership. Vague answers about "we did X" immediately raise flags about actual involvement.

2. DEPTH EXPLORATIONS

Example Questions:

- "Walk me through your trade-off analysis between approaches."
- "What metrics proved your solution was the right one?"

Why We Ask: Surface-level problem solvers fail here. Strong candidates reveal their decision frameworks, not just outcomes.

3. CHALLENGE TESTS

Example Questions:

- "What would you do if leadership rejected your proposal?"
- "How would you adapt this for a 10x larger scale?"

Why We Ask: To stress-test adaptability. The best candidates pivot gracefully; weaker ones double down defensively.

4. REFLECTION PROBES

Example Questions:

- "Knowing what you know now, what would you change?"
- "How did this experience alter your standard workflow?"

Why We Ask: Growth mindset versus fixed mindset becomes obvious within two follow-ups.

5. SCENARIO EXTENSIONS

Example Questions:

- "How would this solution break in a multi-region deployment?"
- "What if you had only 25% of the original timeline?"

Why We Ask: To evaluate if their experience is portable or narrowly contextual.

WHY THIS MATTERS

A recent internal study at a FAANG company found that 83% of mis-hires could have been avoided if interviewers had pressed harder on follow-ups. The data shows:

- Candidates who handle 3+ follow-ups smoothly have a 70% higher success rate
- Responses to challenge questions predict real-world problem-solving accuracy better than technical screens

HOW TO PREPARE

The architect's advice: "For every story in your portfolio, preemptively drill down on:

1. Your exact role (not the team's)
2. The data behind key decisions
3. At least one alternative path you considered
4. A retrospective lesson

The difference between good and great candidates isn't their stories—it's what emerges when we start chiseling away at them."

2.8. INTERVIEWER EVALUATION TECHNIQUES

Beyond asking questions, interviewers use specific techniques to evaluate your responses more effectively. Understanding these techniques helps you recognize what's happening during the interview and respond appropriately.

1. THE SILENCE TECHNIQUE

Interviewers often use strategic silence after you finish speaking, creating an uncomfortable pause that many candidates rush to fill with additional information. This technique reveals:

- Whether you're confident in your initial response or feel the need to keep talking
- What additional information you provide when not specifically prompted
- How you handle momentary social discomfort

How to respond: Be comfortable with silence. If you've provided a complete response, simply wait for the next question. Don't undermine a strong answer by rambling to fill silence.

2. THE SKEPTICISM TECHNIQUE

Interviewers sometimes express subtle skepticism about your example, through facial expressions, tone, or gentle pushback. This technique reveals:

- How you respond to implicit challenges
- Whether you become defensive or remain composed
- If you can provide additional evidence to support your claims

How to respond: Address perceived skepticism with additional specific details and metrics, not by becoming defensive or overemphasizing your claims. Provide evidence rather than assertions.

3. THE CONSTRAINT TECHNIQUE

Interviewers may impose artificial constraints on your responses, such as "Tell me about that in two minutes or less" or "Focus just on your specific actions." This technique reveals:

- Your ability to communicate concisely

- How you prioritize information under constraints

- Whether you can adapt your communication to specific requirements

How to respond: Respect the constraint and adapt your response accordingly. Demonstrate that you can adjust your communication style based on the interviewer's needs.

4. THE REDIRECTION TECHNIQUE

Interviewers sometimes redirect you in the middle of a response, asking about a different aspect of your example than what you were discussing. This technique reveals:

- Your flexibility and adaptability

- How you handle interruptions

- Whether you can shift focus while maintaining coherence

How to respond: Acknowledge the redirection and shift your focus accordingly, without showing frustration or rigidly returning to your previous point. Demonstrate that you can follow the interviewer's lead.

5. THE PROBING TECHNIQUE

Interviewers often ask increasingly specific questions about your example, drilling down into details that might seem minor. This technique reveals:

- Whether your example is genuine and lived

- The depth of your involvement and understanding

- How thoroughly you've reflected on the experience

How to respond: Provide specific, detailed answers to probing questions, even if they seem tangential. The specificity of your responses demonstrates the authenticity of your example.

Understanding these techniques helps you recognize what's happening during the interview and respond in ways that strengthen rather than weaken your evaluation.

2.9. CONCLUSION: THE STRATEGIC ADVANTAGE OF THE INTERVIEWER'S PERSPECTIVE

Understanding the interviewer's perspective transforms behavioral interviews from mysterious evaluations into strategic opportunities. When you know what interviewers are looking for, how they evaluate responses, and what concerns they're trying to address, you can craft examples that directly address their actual assessment criteria.

This perspective shift offers several advantages:

- You can select examples that demonstrate the specific competencies being evaluated, rather than sharing impressive stories that miss the mark

- You can structure responses to include all the elements interviewers are looking for, rather than leaving critical gaps

- You can anticipate and prepare for follow-up questions, rather than being caught off guard

- You can recognize and respond appropriately to interviewer techniques, rather than misinterpreting their intentions

- You can avoid common red flags that trigger unnecessary concerns, even when your actual capabilities are strong

In the next chapter, we'll build on this understanding by exploring the STAR+ framework—a powerful structure for organizing your responses in ways that address the evaluation criteria we've examined. This framework will help you translate your understanding of the interviewer's perspective into practical, effective interview responses that showcase your true capabilities.

CHAPTER 3. STAR+ FORMAT

Perfection is achieved, not when there is nothing more to add,
but when there is nothing left to take away.

— Antoine de Saint-Exupéry

"So, tell me about a time when you had to deal with a difficult team member."

The interviewer's question hangs in the air. Your pulse quickens. You've faced
this situation before—maybe multiple times. But under the fluorescent lights of
the interview room, your mind races:

- Which story should I tell?

- How much detail should I include?

- What if I forget the most important part?

I've been there. As an engineering manager who's conducted hundreds of
interviews, I've seen brilliant candidates stumble at this exact moment—not
because they lacked experience, but because they lacked structure.

The Problem With Unstructured Answers: Last quarter, I interviewed a senior
developer with an impressive resume. When I asked about resolving conflicts, he
gave a 10-minute monologue that included:

- The entire history of his previous team

- Three different interpersonal dramas

- Zero clear examples of his personal actions

Despite his obvious skills, we passed. Why? Because in high-stakes
environments, clear thinking requires clear communication.

Enter STAR+: The solution isn't rehearsing scripted answers—it's having a flexible framework that:

- Organizes your thoughts under pressure

- Highlights your actual contributions

- Demonstrates growth from each experience

Think of it like a coding pattern for your career stories. Just as you'd use MVC for frontend architecture, STAR+ gives you the structure to present your experiences effectively—without sounding robotic.

In this chapter, I'll show you:

- Why most candidates' answers fail (and how to avoid those traps)

- The exact STAR+ template I use when interviewing at top tech companies

- How to adapt it for leadership, problem-solving, and failure questions

- Real examples from candidates who aced their interviews

By the end, you'll be able to turn any experience into a compelling story that makes interviewers think: "We need this person on our team."

Because here's the secret no one tells you: *The best candidates aren't just competent—they're comprehensible.*

3.1. THE NEED FOR STRUCTURE

Before diving into specific frameworks, let's understand why structured responses are so important in behavioral interviews.

THE INTERVIEWER'S CHALLENGE

As we explored in the previous chapter, interviewers face significant cognitive challenges during behavioral interviews:

- They must listen attentively to your response
- They must take detailed notes to capture evidence
- They must evaluate your response against specific competencies
- They must formulate relevant follow-up questions
- They must do all this while managing time constraints

Unstructured, rambling, or disorganized responses make this already difficult task nearly impossible. When interviewers can't follow your narrative or extract relevant evidence, they can't accurately evaluate your capabilities—regardless of how impressive your actual experiences might be.

THE CANDIDATE'S CHALLENGE

As a candidate, you face your own set of challenges:

- You must recall specific details under pressure
- You must decide which aspects of complex situations to include
- You must highlight your personal contribution without seeming arrogant
- You must demonstrate reflection and learning, not just action
- You must do all this while managing interview anxiety

Without a clear structure, these challenges often lead to responses that are either too vague (missing critical details) or too verbose (burying important information in excessive context).

THE SOLUTION: STRUCTURED STORYTELLING

Structured frameworks address both the interviewer's and candidate's challenges by providing a clear, consistent format for organizing information. Effective frameworks:

- Ensure all critical elements are included
- Present information in a logical, predictable sequence
- Highlight the most evaluation-relevant aspects of your experience
- Make it easier for interviewers to follow and evaluate your response
- Reduce your cognitive load during high-pressure interviews

The right framework doesn't constrain your response—it liberates it, allowing you to focus on content rather than structure during the interview itself.

3.2. THE TRADITIONAL STAR METHOD

The most widely known framework for behavioral interviews is the STAR method, which has been used for decades across various industries. Let's examine this traditional approach before exploring how we can enhance it for technical roles.

STAR COMPONENTS

The STAR method organizes responses into four sequential components:

- **Situation**: The specific context, background, or setting of your example
- **Task**: The specific challenge, assignment, or objective you faced
- **Action**: The specific steps you took to address the challenge
- **Result**: The outcomes or consequences of your actions

This structure guides interviewers through a logical narrative arc, from context to conclusion, making it easier to follow and evaluate your response.

STAR IN PRACTICE

Let's see how the traditional STAR method might be applied to a common behavioral question:

Question: "Tell me about a time when you had to make a difficult decision with limited information."

Situation: "Last year, while leading the authentication service team at my previous company, we experienced an unusual spike in authentication failures during a major product launch. Our monitoring showed a 500% increase in failures, affecting approximately 15% of our user base, but we couldn't immediately identify the cause."

Task: "As the team lead, I needed to decide whether to roll back the recent deployment—potentially losing important new features on our biggest marketing day of the year—or keep the system running while we diagnosed the issue, risking continued user frustration and potential revenue loss."

Action: "I quickly assembled a war room with representatives from engineering, product, and customer support. I established a dual-track approach: one team began preparing for rollback with a 30-minute deadline, while another team performed targeted diagnostics. I personally analyzed recent changes and identified a potential authentication cache configuration issue. Based on this lead, I made the decision to implement a targeted fix rather than a complete rollback. I deployed a configuration change that doubled the cache capacity and adjusted the eviction policy."

Result: "Within 15 minutes of implementing the targeted fix, authentication failures returned to normal levels. We avoided a costly rollback while resolving the user impact. The root cause was indeed a cache configuration issue that couldn't handle the load spike from the product launch. The incident led us to implement more robust load testing for authentication services and improved monitoring for cache performance."

This response follows the traditional STAR structure, providing a clear narrative that demonstrates decision-making under pressure. However, it's missing a critical element that sophisticated interviewers increasingly expect—particularly in technical roles.

3.3. THE STAR+ ENHANCEMENT

While the traditional STAR method provides a solid foundation, it has a significant limitation: it focuses exclusively on what happened in the past, without explicitly addressing what you learned and how you've grown from the experience. This limitation is particularly problematic for technical roles, where learning agility and continuous improvement are highly valued.

THE MISSING ELEMENT: LESSONS LEARNED

The STAR+ framework enhances the traditional method by adding a critical fifth component:

- **Plus (Lessons Learned)**: What you learned from the experience and how you've applied those insights

This addition transforms your response from a historical account to a growth narrative, demonstrating not just what you did, but how you've developed as a professional through reflection and application.

STAR+ IN PRACTICE

Let's enhance our previous example with the Lessons Learned component:

Question: "Tell me about a time when you had to make a difficult decision with limited information."

Situation: "Last year, while leading the authentication service team at my previous company, we experienced an unusual spike in authentication failures during a major product launch. Our monitoring showed a 500% increase in failures, affecting approximately 15% of our user base, but we couldn't immediately identify the cause."

Task: "As the team lead, I needed to decide whether to roll back the recent deployment—potentially losing important new features on our biggest marketing day of the year—or keep the system running while we diagnosed the issue, risking continued user frustration and potential revenue loss."

Action: "I quickly assembled a war room with representatives from engineering, product, and customer support. I established a dual-track approach: one team began preparing for rollback with a 30-minute deadline, while another team performed targeted diagnostics. I personally analyzed recent changes and identified a potential authentication cache configuration issue. Based on this lead, I made the decision to implement a targeted fix rather than a complete rollback. I deployed a configuration change that doubled the cache capacity and adjusted the eviction policy."

Result: "Within 15 minutes of implementing the targeted fix, authentication failures returned to normal levels. We avoided a costly rollback while resolving the user impact. The root cause was indeed a cache configuration issue that couldn't handle the load spike from the product launch."

Plus (Lessons Learned): "This experience taught me three important lessons. First, I learned the value of maintaining a dual-track approach to incident response—preparing for the worst-case scenario while simultaneously pursuing targeted solutions. Second, I recognized a gap in our load testing practices, which I addressed by implementing more realistic user spike scenarios in our pre-launch testing. Finally, I learned about the importance of cross-functional communication during incidents. I subsequently established a formal incident response process with clear roles and communication channels, which we've used successfully in two subsequent incidents. The most recent incident was resolved in half the time, with significantly improved stakeholder communication."

The Lessons Learned component transforms this response from a demonstration of past problem-solving to evidence of ongoing professional development. It shows not just that you handled a difficult situation effectively, but that you extracted meaningful insights and applied them to improve future outcomes.

3.4. WHY STAR+ IS THE MOST EFFECTIVE FORMAT

The STAR+ framework offers several advantages over both the traditional STAR method and other alternative approaches, particularly for technical roles at top companies.

ALIGNMENT WITH EVALUATION CRITERIA

As we explored in the previous chapter, interviewers at top tech companies evaluate candidates on both demonstrated capabilities and growth potential. The STAR+ framework explicitly addresses both dimensions:

- The STAR components (Situation, Task, Action, Result) demonstrate your capabilities through concrete examples

- The Plus component (Lessons Learned) demonstrates your growth potential through reflection and application

This alignment with actual evaluation criteria makes STAR+ particularly effective for technical interviews at companies that value continuous learning and improvement.

DEMONSTRATION OF LEARNING AGILITY

Learning agility—the ability to learn from experience and apply those lessons to new situations—is one of the most valued traits in technical roles. The STAR+ framework explicitly demonstrates this capability by requiring you to articulate:

- What specific insights you gained from the experience
- How you've applied those insights to subsequent situations
- How those applications improved outcomes

This demonstration of learning agility is particularly valuable for roles that involve rapidly evolving technologies and changing requirements.

PREVENTION OF COMMON PITFALLS

The STAR+ framework helps prevent several common behavioral interview pitfalls:

- **Incomplete responses**: The structured format ensures you include all critical elements
- **Excessive context**: The clear components help you balance context with action
- **Missing results**: The explicit Result component ensures you articulate outcomes
- **Lack of reflection**: The Plus component prompts meaningful reflection
- **Disconnected learning**: The application aspect ensures learning is connected to action

By addressing these common pitfalls, STAR+ helps you present your experiences in the most effective possible light.

FACILITATION OF PREPARATION

The STAR+ framework provides a clear structure for preparing examples before interviews. For each potential question or competency, you can:

1. Identify relevant situations from your experience

2. Define the specific task or challenge you faced

3. Articulate your actions in concrete, specific terms

4. Quantify the results whenever possible

5. Reflect on what you learned and how you've applied those lessons

This structured preparation ensures you have comprehensive, well-organized examples ready for a wide range of potential questions.

SUPPORT FOR FOLLOW-UP QUESTIONS

As we discussed in the previous chapter, follow-up questions are a critical part of behavioral interviews. The STAR+ framework naturally supports effective responses to common follow-up patterns:

- Questions about context are addressed by the Situation component

- Questions about your role are addressed by the Task component

- Questions about your reasoning are addressed by the Action component

- Questions about impact are addressed by the Result component

- Questions about reflection are addressed by the Plus component

This comprehensive coverage ensures you're prepared for the full range of potential follow-ups, not just the initial question.

3.5. PROS AND CONS OF OTHER METHODS

While STAR+ is particularly effective for technical roles, it's worth examining alternative frameworks to understand their relative strengths and limitations.

THE CAR METHOD (CHALLENGE, ACTION, RESULT)

The CAR method is a simplified version of STAR that combines Situation and Task into a single "Challenge" component.

Pros:

- Simpler structure with fewer components to remember
- Focuses directly on the problem rather than extensive context
- Works well for straightforward problem-solving examples

Cons:

- Often provides insufficient context for complex technical situations
- Doesn't explicitly prompt for reflection or learning
- Can lead to responses that focus too narrowly on the immediate problem

When it works best: The CAR method can be effective for straightforward technical problem-solving examples where the context is simple and the challenge is clear. However, it's less effective for complex situations involving multiple stakeholders or ambiguous problems.

THE SOAR METHOD (SITUATION, OBSTACLE, ACTION, RESULT)

The SOAR method replaces "Task" with "Obstacle," emphasizing the barriers you had to overcome rather than your assigned responsibilities.

Pros:

- Highlights your ability to overcome specific challenges
- Works well for examples involving unexpected problems

- Emphasizes resilience and adaptability

Cons:

- Can overemphasize obstacles at the expense of strategic action

- Doesn't explicitly prompt for reflection or learning

- May not align well with examples where the primary challenge was complexity rather than a specific obstacle

When it works best: The SOAR method can be effective for examples involving unexpected problems or barriers that required significant adaptation. However, it's less effective for examples of proactive leadership or strategic decision-making.

THE PAR METHOD (PROBLEM, ACTION, RESULT)

The PAR method is another simplified approach that focuses directly on the problem without extensive context.

Pros:

- Very simple structure that's easy to remember under pressure

- Gets directly to the point without extensive background

- Works well for clear, well-defined problems

Cons:

- Often provides insufficient context for complex situations

- Doesn't distinguish between the general situation and your specific responsibilities

- Doesn't explicitly prompt for reflection or learning

When it works best: The PAR method can be effective for straightforward problem-solving examples in well-defined contexts. However, it's less effective for complex situations involving multiple stakeholders or ambiguous problems.

THE SARI METHOD (SITUATION, ACTION, RESULT, IMPROVEMENT)

The SARI method is similar to STAR+ but omits the Task component while adding an Improvement component.

Pros:

- Includes reflection and improvement similar to STAR+
- Simplifies the narrative by combining Task with Situation
- Explicitly focuses on ongoing improvement

Cons:

- Doesn't clearly distinguish between the general situation and your specific responsibilities
- Can lead to confusion about your role versus the broader context
- May not provide sufficient structure for complex examples

When it works best: The SARI method can be effective for examples where your role was clear and the focus is on continuous improvement. However, it's less effective for examples involving complex team dynamics or shared responsibilities.

THE "UNSTRUCTURED AUTHENTIC" APPROACH

Some candidates prefer to avoid structured frameworks entirely, believing that authentic, conversational responses are more effective.

Pros:

- Can feel more natural and less rehearsed

- Allows for more flexible storytelling

- May work well for candidates with exceptional communication skills

Cons:

- Frequently leads to rambling, disorganized responses

- Often results in critical omissions (particularly results and reflection)

- Makes it difficult for interviewers to identify and evaluate key competencies

- Increases cognitive load during high-pressure interviews

When it works best: The unstructured approach rarely works well in formal behavioral interviews, regardless of the candidate's communication skills. Even exceptional communicators benefit from internal structure, even if they present it conversationally.

WHY STAR+ PREVAILS

After examining these alternatives, STAR+ emerges as the most effective framework for technical behavioral interviews because it:

1. Provides sufficient context through the Situation component

2. Clarifies your specific role through the Task component

3. Details your actions with appropriate specificity

4. Quantifies outcomes through the Result component

5. Demonstrates learning and growth through the Plus component

This comprehensive coverage ensures that interviewers receive all the information they need to accurately evaluate your capabilities and potential, without having to extract it through extensive follow-up questions.

3.6. APPLYING STAR+ EFFECTIVELY

Understanding the STAR+ framework is just the beginning. Applying it effectively requires attention to specific details within each component. Let's explore how to optimize each element of the framework.

CRAFTING AN EFFECTIVE SITUATION

The Situation component provides essential context for your example. To make it effective:

- **Be specific about time and place**: "In Q2 2023, while working on the payment processing system at Company X..." rather than "A while back at my previous job..."

- **Provide relevant scale**: "Our team of 8 engineers was responsible for a service handling 2 million transactions daily..." rather than "Our team maintained an important service..."

- **Include only necessary context**: Focus on details that help understand the example, not your entire career history

- **Set the stage for your task**: The situation should naturally lead to the specific challenge you faced

Example of an effective Situation:

"In January 2023, while leading the 6-person backend team at TechCorp, we were preparing for a major platform migration from our monolithic architecture to a microservices approach. Our system was processing approximately 500,000 daily transactions for 2 million active users, and we had a hard deadline of March 31st to complete the migration with minimal disruption."

This situation provides specific timing, team context, relevant scale, and sets up the challenge that follows.

DEFINING A CLEAR TASK

The Task component clarifies your specific responsibilities or objectives in the situation. To make it effective:

- **Distinguish between team goals and your personal responsibility**: "While the team was responsible for the overall migration, my specific task was to design the data transition strategy..."
- **Be explicit about constraints**: "I needed to complete this with zero downtime and within our existing infrastructure budget..."
- **Clarify stakeholders**: "I was accountable to both the CTO and the customer experience team..."
- **Highlight the specific challenge**: "The main difficulty was maintaining data consistency during the transition..."

Example of an effective Task:

"As the technical lead, my specific responsibility was to design and implement the data migration strategy that would allow us to transition from our single database to multiple service-specific databases without any customer-facing downtime. The challenge was particularly complex because we couldn't afford any data inconsistency, even temporarily, due to financial reporting requirements. I had to accomplish this with our existing team and without additional infrastructure budget."

This task clearly distinguishes the candidate's specific responsibility from the broader team effort, identifies key constraints, and highlights the core challenge.

DETAILING SPECIFIC ACTIONS

The Action component describes what you actually did to address the challenge. To make it effective:

- **Focus on your personal actions**: Use "I" statements to clarify your specific contributions

- **Provide a logical sequence**: Present actions in chronological or logical order

- **Include your reasoning**: Explain why you chose specific approaches

- **Highlight key decisions**: Emphasize critical choices you made, especially when facing alternatives

- **Be appropriately technical**: Include relevant technical details without overwhelming non-technical interviewers

Example of effective Actions:

"I first analyzed our data access patterns by implementing custom logging that identified cross-service dependencies, which revealed that 40% of our data was accessed by multiple services. Based on this analysis, I designed a two-phase migration strategy. In phase one, I implemented a data access layer that would abstract the database location from the services, allowing us to move data without changing service code. I personally wrote the core routing logic for this layer and created a comprehensive test suite with 95% coverage.

In phase two, I developed a real-time data synchronization service that maintained consistency between the monolith database and the new service-specific databases. Rather than attempting a 'big bang' migration, I implemented a gradual transition where data lived in both systems temporarily, with writes synchronized in real-time. I prioritized financial data first, then customer data, and finally operational data, based on consistency requirements.

When we encountered unexpected performance issues with the synchronization, I made the decision to implement a queue-based approach rather than direct synchronization, which reduced system load by 70% while maintaining sub-second consistency."

These actions clearly show the candidate's personal contribution, logical approach, key decisions, and technical expertise without becoming overly technical.

QUANTIFYING RESULTS

The Result component describes the outcomes of your actions. To make it effective:

- **Quantify impact whenever possible**: Use specific metrics rather than general statements

- **Connect results to business value**: Explain why the outcomes mattered, not just what they were

- **Acknowledge team contributions**: Give appropriate credit while maintaining clarity about your impact

- **Address both immediate and long-term results**: Include subsequent effects when relevant

- **Be honest about mixed outcomes**: Acknowledge limitations while emphasizing successes

Example of effective Results:

"We successfully completed the migration two weeks ahead of our March 31st deadline, with zero downtime and no data consistency issues reported. The new architecture reduced our average API response time by 42% and decreased our infrastructure costs by 35% ($400,000 annually) due to more efficient resource utilization. The data access layer I designed was so effective that it was adopted by three other teams for their own migrations, accelerating the company-wide transition to microservices by approximately six months according to our CTO.

Most importantly, the gradual migration approach allowed us to maintain 100% data consistency throughout the transition, which was critical for our financial reporting requirements. The project was highlighted in our CEO's quarterly investor call as a key technical achievement enabling our next phase of growth."

These results clearly quantify the impact (42% faster responses, 35% cost reduction), connect technical outcomes to business value (financial reporting, growth enablement), acknowledge broader adoption, and include both immediate and longer-term effects.

ARTICULATING LESSONS LEARNED

The Plus component describes what you learned from the experience and how you've applied those insights. To make it effective:

- **Be specific about insights**: Identify concrete lessons rather than generic platitudes
- **Include both technical and non-technical learning**: Demonstrate growth in multiple dimensions
- **Explain how you've applied these lessons**: Connect past learning to subsequent actions
- **Demonstrate ongoing development**: Show how these insights fit into your broader professional growth
- **Be authentic about challenges**: Acknowledge real difficulties rather than presenting a perfect narrative

Example of effective Lessons Learned:

"This experience taught me three valuable lessons. First, I learned that data access patterns are often more complex than they initially appear. I've since incorporated comprehensive data access analysis into the early phases of all my architecture work, which prevented similar issues in two subsequent projects.

Second, I recognized that gradual transitions with temporary redundancy, while requiring more upfront design, significantly reduce risk in critical systems. I applied this approach in our subsequent authentication system migration, which completed with similar success and has now become our team's standard practice for critical infrastructure changes.

Third, I learned the importance of transparent communication during complex migrations. Some stakeholders initially resisted our approach because they didn't fully understand the risk mitigation benefits. I've since developed a stakeholder communication template that includes risk assessments and contingency plans, which has noticeably improved buy-in for complex technical changes.

The most significant growth for me was developing confidence in challenging conventional approaches when data supports an alternative. Initially, several senior engineers advocated for a 'big bang' migration approach based on previous experience, but the data access analysis supported a different strategy. Learning to respectfully advocate for data-driven approaches while acknowledging others' experience has become a core part of my technical leadership style."

These lessons learned demonstrate specific insights (data access complexity, gradual transitions, stakeholder communication), explain how they've been applied (subsequent projects, standard practices, communication templates), and show authentic growth (confidence in data-driven advocacy).

3.7. ADAPTING STAR+ TO DIFFERENT QUESTION TYPES

While the STAR+ framework provides a consistent structure, it needs to be adapted for different types of behavioral questions. Let's explore how to apply it across common question categories.

LEADERSHIP QUESTIONS

Leadership questions assess your ability to influence, guide, and develop others. Examples include:

- "Tell me about a time when you led a team through a difficult situation."
- "Describe a situation where you had to influence without authority."
- "Give me an example of how you've developed team members."

When applying STAR+ to leadership questions:

- **Situation**: Include team composition, dynamics, and relevant organizational context
- **Task**: Clarify your leadership role and specific leadership challenges
- **Action**: Emphasize how you motivated, aligned, and guided others
- **Result**: Highlight both team outcomes and individual growth
- **Plus**: Focus on what you learned about effective leadership

Example STAR+ for a leadership question:

"Tell me about a time when you had to lead a team through a significant change."

Situation: "In 2022, I was leading the frontend team at TechCorp when our company was acquired by a larger competitor. My team of 7 engineers had been using React for our applications, but the acquiring company standardized on Angular. We were given six months to transition our codebase while continuing to deliver planned features."

Task: "As the team lead, I needed to guide my team through this technical transition while maintaining morale during an uncertain time. The challenge was particularly difficult because three team members had been hired specifically for their React expertise and had limited Angular experience."

Action: "I developed a three-part approach. First, I created transparency by arranging a candid discussion with the acquiring company's technical leadership to understand their reasoning and timeline expectations. I negotiated a phased transition that allowed us to convert applications one at a time rather than all at once.

Second, I developed individualized learning plans for each team member based on their current Angular knowledge. I paired our React experts with Angular developers from the acquiring company for knowledge transfer sessions and allocated 20% of sprint capacity to learning and practice.

Third, I restructured our roadmap to begin the transition with lower-risk applications, creating early wins to build confidence. I personally led the conversion of our first application, working alongside the team to demonstrate my own willingness to learn and adapt."

Result: "We successfully transitioned 80% of our applications to Angular within the six-month timeframe, with the remaining 20% completed just two weeks after the deadline—a result the acquiring company's CTO described as 'exceeding expectations.' All team members became proficient in Angular, with three eventually becoming designated experts who helped other teams with their transitions.

Most importantly, we retained the entire team through the acquisition—the only department to do so—and maintained our feature delivery commitments with only a 15% temporary reduction in velocity during the transition period."

Plus: "This experience taught me valuable lessons about leading through change. I learned that transparency, even about difficult realities, builds trust more effectively than reassurance without specifics. I've since applied this principle during our recent reorganization by holding weekly Q&A sessions where no questions were off-limits.

I also discovered the power of demonstrating personal adaptability as a leader. By visibly engaging in the learning process myself, I shifted the team's perception from 'being forced to change' to 'growing together.' I've incorporated this approach into all subsequent technology transitions, most recently when we adopted a new testing framework.

Finally, I learned the importance of creating early wins during significant changes. Breaking the challenge into smaller milestones allowed the team to build confidence incrementally. I've formalized this approach into a change management template that's now used across our engineering organization."

This example demonstrates effective leadership through a significant change, with specific actions focused on guiding and developing the team, and lessons learned about leadership principles.

PROBLEM-SOLVING QUESTIONS

Problem-solving questions assess your ability to analyze issues, develop solutions, and implement effective approaches. Examples include:

- "Tell me about a complex problem you solved."

- "Describe a situation where you had to troubleshoot a difficult issue."

- "Give me an example of when you had to make a decision with incomplete information."

When applying STAR+ to problem-solving questions:

- **Situation**: Establish the context and significance of the problem
- **Task**: Clarify your specific responsibility in addressing the problem
- **Action**: Detail your analytical process and solution development
- **Result**: Quantify the impact of your solution
- **Plus**: Focus on what you learned about effective problem-solving

Example STAR+ for a problem-solving question:

"Tell me about a time when you solved a particularly challenging technical problem."

Situation: "In Q3 2023, our e-commerce platform at RetailTech was experiencing intermittent performance degradation during peak traffic periods. Response times would increase from 200ms to over 3 seconds for approximately 5% of requests, seemingly at random. This was affecting our conversion rate, which dropped by 12% during these incidents."

Task: "As the senior backend engineer responsible for system reliability, I needed to identify the root cause and implement a solution before the holiday shopping season, when traffic would increase by 300%. The challenge was particularly difficult because the issue couldn't be consistently reproduced in our test environment."

Action: "I approached this methodically in four steps. First, I enhanced our logging to capture detailed performance metrics across all system components, including database query execution times, cache hit rates, and external service calls.

Second, I developed a statistical analysis tool that correlated performance degradation with various system factors. This analysis revealed a pattern:

degradation was most common when specific product categories were being browsed simultaneously by more than 500 users.

Third, I used distributed tracing to follow these specific requests through our system and discovered that our product recommendation engine was making redundant database queries when calculating personalized recommendations for these product categories.

Finally, I implemented a two-part solution: a query optimization that reduced the database load by 70% for these specific operations, and a caching strategy that stored pre-computed recommendations for popular product combinations, refreshed asynchronously every 30 minutes."

Result: "After implementing the solution, our 95th percentile response time during peak traffic remained consistently below 300ms, even when traffic increased by 40% during a flash sale. The conversion rate returned to normal levels, representing approximately $150,000 in recovered weekly revenue.

The solution also improved our overall system efficiency, reducing our database load by 35% across all operations and decreasing our cloud infrastructure costs by $20,000 monthly. The statistical analysis tool I developed has since been integrated into our monitoring system and has helped identify three other performance bottlenecks before they impacted customers."

Plus: "This experience taught me several important lessons about troubleshooting complex systems. First, I learned the value of data-driven investigation over intuition. Initially, our team had focused on network latency based on past experiences, but the data led us in a completely different direction. I've since implemented a 'data first' troubleshooting protocol for our team that has reduced our mean time to resolution by 40%.

Second, I recognized the importance of understanding patterns across different system scales. What worked efficiently with our test data volume behaved differently at production scale. I've subsequently built scale-appropriate testing into our development process, including regular chaos engineering sessions that simulate extreme conditions.

Third, I learned that performance optimization often requires cross-functional understanding. The recommendation engine had been developed by a separate team with different performance assumptions. I've since established a monthly cross-team architecture review where we discuss performance implications of our interconnected systems, which has prevented several potential issues before deployment."

This example demonstrates effective problem-solving with a clear analytical process, quantifiable results, and specific lessons about troubleshooting complex systems.

COLLABORATION QUESTIONS

Collaboration questions assess your ability to work effectively with others, particularly in challenging circumstances. Examples include:

- "Tell me about a time when you had to work with a difficult team member."

- "Describe a situation where you had to build consensus among diverse stakeholders."

- "Give me an example of how you've resolved a conflict within a team."

When applying STAR+ to collaboration questions:

- **Situation**: Establish the collaborative context and relationship dynamics

- **Task**: Clarify the specific collaborative challenge you faced

- **Action**: Emphasize communication, understanding, and relationship building

- **Result**: Highlight both relationship outcomes and practical results

- **Plus**: Focus on what you learned about effective collaboration

Example STAR+ for a collaboration question:

"Tell me about a time when you had to work with someone who had a very different working style."

Situation: "In 2022, I was assigned to co-lead a critical security compliance project with a colleague from our risk management team. We needed to achieve SOC 2 compliance within six months to support an enterprise client acquisition. My colleague had a very different working style—he preferred detailed planning and documentation before any action, while I typically favored an iterative approach with rapid prototyping and refinement."

Task: "We needed to collaborate effectively despite these differences to deliver a comprehensive security framework that would pass external audit. The challenge was particularly significant because our differences were causing delays in the early project phases, with each of us feeling the other's approach was impeding progress."

Action: "I took several steps to improve our collaboration. First, I initiated a candid conversation where we explicitly discussed our different approaches, the strengths of each style, and our shared commitment to the project's success. Rather than trying to convert him to my approach, I acknowledged that his thoroughness would be valuable for a compliance project.

Second, I proposed a hybrid methodology that incorporated elements of both our styles. We would begin with a detailed planning phase for the overall framework (addressing his need for structure), but implement specific controls using two-week iterations with regular testing and refinement (incorporating my preference for iteration).

Third, I suggested we divide responsibilities according to our strengths—he would lead the documentation and policy development, while I would lead the technical implementation and testing. We established clear handoff points and review processes to ensure integration.

Finally, I scheduled brief daily check-ins to maintain alignment and address any concerns immediately, rather than allowing frustrations to build."

Result: "We successfully achieved SOC 2 compliance one month ahead of schedule, with the auditor specifically commending the thoroughness of our documentation and the robustness of our technical implementations. The enterprise client signed a $2.5 million annual contract based partly on our compliance achievement.

Beyond the project outcomes, our working relationship evolved into a productive partnership. We've subsequently collaborated on three additional compliance initiatives, each completed on time and with excellent results. Our approach has become a model for cross-functional projects in our organization, with elements of our hybrid methodology now incorporated into the company's project management framework."

Plus: "This experience transformed my understanding of collaboration across different working styles. I learned that differences in approach, when properly leveraged, can create stronger outcomes than either approach alone. His detailed planning prevented several implementation issues I would have encountered with my more iterative approach, while my rapid testing identified policy gaps that might have been missed until the audit.

I also recognized the importance of explicit discussion about working styles rather than making assumptions. Before this experience, I had typically viewed process-oriented colleagues as unnecessarily bureaucratic. By understanding the reasoning behind his approach, I gained appreciation for its value in appropriate contexts.

Most significantly, I learned to adapt my collaboration style to the specific project needs rather than applying the same approach universally. I've since developed a personal framework for assessing which elements of my natural style to emphasize or moderate based on project type, team composition, and organizational context. This adaptability has made me a more effective collaborator across a wider range of situations, particularly when working with teams from non-technical backgrounds."

This example demonstrates effective collaboration across different working styles, with specific actions focused on understanding, accommodation, and partnership building, and lessons learned about adaptive collaboration.

FAILURE QUESTIONS

Failure questions assess your resilience, accountability, and ability to learn from setbacks. Examples include:

- "Tell me about a time when you failed to meet an objective."

- "Describe a project that didn't go as planned."

- "Give me an example of a mistake you made and how you handled it."

When applying STAR+ to failure questions:

- **Situation**: Establish the context without making excuses

- **Task**: Clarify your responsibility and objectives

- **Action**: Honestly describe your approach and where it fell short

- **Result**: Acknowledge the negative outcomes while highlighting recovery efforts

- **Plus**: Focus extensively on what you learned and how you've applied those lessons

Example STAR+ for a failure question:

"Tell me about a time when a project you were leading didn't meet its objectives."

Situation: "In 2022, I led the development of a new mobile feature at AppCo that would allow users to collaborate on shared documents in real-time. This was a strategic initiative expected to increase user engagement by 25% and support our expansion into the enterprise market."

Task: "As the technical lead, I was responsible for architecture, implementation planning, and delivery of the feature within a three-month timeframe. I needed to coordinate work across frontend, backend, and infrastructure teams while ensuring the solution would scale to support our user base of approximately 2 million active users."

Action: "I began by researching technical approaches and selected a WebSocket-based architecture with a custom synchronization protocol that I designed. Based on my previous experience with similar systems, I estimated the complexity and created a project plan that allocated six weeks for core development and six weeks for testing and refinement.

I divided the work among three teams and established weekly integration points. As development progressed, we encountered more edge cases in the synchronization logic than I had anticipated. Rather than extending the timeline or reducing scope, I decided to increase development resources by bringing in two additional engineers and implementing longer working hours for the team.

As we approached the release date, our load testing revealed significant performance degradation with more than 500 simultaneous collaboration sessions. I made the decision to proceed with the release anyway, believing we could address the scaling issues in a subsequent update before usage reached problematic levels."

Result: "The feature launched on schedule but encountered serious performance issues within the first week as adoption exceeded our projections.

Users experienced sync delays and occasional data loss during peak usage periods. After three days of attempting to optimize the live system, we made the difficult decision to disable the feature temporarily.

The incident damaged our reputation with several enterprise prospects, delaying two significant contracts worth approximately $800,000 in annual revenue. It also negatively impacted team morale, particularly for the engineers who had worked extended hours to meet the deadline."

Plus: "This failure taught me several profound lessons that have fundamentally changed my approach to technical leadership. First, I learned that technical architecture decisions for critical features require broader validation beyond my own experience. I now implement a formal architecture review process for complex features, incorporating perspectives from multiple senior engineers and explicitly testing assumptions.

Second, I recognized that increasing resources and working hours is rarely an effective solution for underestimated complexity. In subsequent projects, I've implemented mid-project reassessments where we explicitly reconsider scope and timeline when we discover unexpected complexity, rather than defaulting to resource increases. This approach led to a successful phased release for our next major feature, which actually delivered more business value by prioritizing the most impactful components first.

Third, I learned that performance requirements must be validated with realistic scenarios before release decisions. I've since developed a pre-launch checklist that includes graduated load testing with specific performance thresholds that must be met before release approval.

Most importantly, I learned about the human cost of technical decisions. The impact on team morale and wellbeing from the extended hours and subsequent failure was significant. I've since become an advocate for sustainable development practices within our organization, including the implementation of a 'no heroics' policy that explicitly discourages extended hours as a project management strategy. Our subsequent projects have maintained both on-time delivery and team wellbeing by making appropriate scope adjustments when necessary."

This example demonstrates accountability for a failure, with honest acknowledgment of mistakes, clear negative outcomes, and specific lessons that have been applied to subsequent work.

3.8. CONCLUSION: THE POWER OF STRUCTURED AUTHENTICITY

The STAR+ framework isn't about creating artificial or rehearsed responses—it's about organizing your authentic experiences in a way that helps interviewers accurately assess your capabilities. By providing a clear structure for your responses, STAR+ allows your true strengths to shine through, unobscured by disorganization or omission.

This structured authenticity is particularly valuable in technical roles, where your ability to communicate complex experiences clearly and concisely is itself an important skill. The STAR+ framework demonstrates not just what you've done, but your ability to reflect on those experiences and extract meaningful insights—a capability that distinguishes exceptional technical professionals from merely competent ones.

In the chapters that follow, we'll build on this foundation by exploring how to identify your most powerful stories, avoid common pitfalls, and develop a systematic practice plan. But with the STAR+ framework, you now have the core structure that will transform your interview responses from rambling anecdotes into compelling evidence of your capabilities and potential.

PART 2: PREPARATION

CHAPTER 4. IDENTIFYING YOUR STORIES

There is no greater agony than bearing an untold story inside you.

— Maya Angelou

The interview invitation arrives, and your preparation begins in earnest. You've mastered the STAR+ framework and understand what interviewers are looking for. But now comes the most fundamental question: which of your experiences should you actually share?

This question paralyzes many candidates. Some struggle to recall relevant examples under pressure. Others have plenty of stories but can't determine which ones will resonate most strongly. Many default to their most recent or most technically impressive projects, only to discover during the interview that these examples don't effectively demonstrate the competencies being evaluated.

In this chapter, we'll solve this critical preparation challenge. We'll develop a systematic approach to identifying your most powerful stories, create a comprehensive story inventory that covers the full range of potential questions, and build a flexible story matrix that allows you to adapt to unexpected questions with confidence. By the end, you'll have a personalized collection of high-impact examples ready to deploy in any behavioral interview.

4.1. THE STORY IDENTIFICATION CHALLENGE

Before diving into specific techniques, let's understand why identifying the right stories is so challenging—and so important.

THE MEMORY PROBLEM

Under interview pressure, our memory doesn't function optimally. Psychological research on memory retrieval shows that stress significantly impairs our ability to recall specific episodic memories—exactly the kind of detailed examples needed for behavioral interviews. This "retrieval under pressure" problem explains why candidates often draw a blank when asked for examples, even when they have relevant experiences.

The solution isn't simply to "remember better" during interviews—it's to identify and prepare your stories in advance, when you're not under pressure. This advance preparation creates stronger memory pathways that remain accessible even under stress.

THE SELECTION PROBLEM

Most experienced professionals have hundreds of potential examples they could share. The challenge isn't finding any example—it's identifying the examples that will most effectively demonstrate your capabilities for specific roles and companies.

This selection process requires understanding:

- Which competencies are most valued for your target role
- Which experiences most powerfully demonstrate those competencies
- Which stories provide the strongest evidence of your impact and growth
- Which examples align with the company's specific values and culture

Without a systematic approach to this selection process, candidates often default to sharing their most recent or most technically complex experiences, regardless of whether these examples optimally demonstrate the competencies being evaluated.

THE ADAPTATION PROBLEM

Even with careful preparation, you'll inevitably face questions you didn't specifically anticipate. The ability to quickly identify which of your prepared stories can be adapted to unexpected questions is a critical interview skill.

This adaptation requires:

- Understanding the core competency behind each question
- Recognizing which of your stories demonstrate that competency
- Quickly reframing your example to address the specific question
- Emphasizing the most relevant aspects of your experience

Without a flexible story framework, candidates often struggle with unexpected questions, either providing weak examples or awkwardly forcing prepared stories to fit questions they don't actually address.

4.2. THE HIGH-VALUE EXPERIENCE FRAMEWORK

Not all professional experiences are equally valuable for behavioral interviews. Understanding what makes an experience "high-value" helps you prioritize which stories to develop and share.

CHARACTERISTICS OF HIGH-VALUE EXPERIENCES

High-value experiences for behavioral interviews typically share several key characteristics:

DEMONSTRABLE IMPACT

The most powerful stories show clear, measurable impact—ideally impact that mattered to the business or organization. Examples with quantifiable results (percentage improvements, dollar values, time savings) provide stronger evidence than those with vague or minimal outcomes.

High-value example: "I redesigned our checkout process, reducing cart abandonment by 23% and increasing monthly revenue by $145,000."

Lower-value example: "I made some improvements to our checkout process that users seemed to like."

CLEAR PERSONAL CONTRIBUTION

Strong examples clearly demonstrate your specific contribution, particularly in collaborative efforts. Stories where you can articulate your distinct role and actions provide better evidence than those where your contribution is ambiguous or minimal.

High-value example: "While working with the design team, I personally developed the data model and implemented the backend logic that enabled real-time inventory updates."

Lower-value example: "Our team redesigned the inventory system and made it real-time."

RELEVANT COMPLEXITY

Effective stories involve sufficient complexity to demonstrate sophisticated capabilities, but remain clear enough to explain concisely. Examples that required navigating ambiguity, balancing competing priorities, or overcoming significant obstacles typically provide richer evidence than straightforward tasks.

High-value example: "I had to balance performance requirements against security concerns while working with limited infrastructure and a tight deadline."

Lower-value example: "I implemented the feature according to the specifications I was given."

GROWTH DEMONSTRATION

The most valuable examples show not just what you accomplished, but how you grew from the experience. Stories that include meaningful lessons learned and subsequent application of those insights demonstrate learning agility and self-awareness.

High-value example: "This experience transformed my approach to cross-functional collaboration. I subsequently developed a stakeholder alignment framework that I've applied to three major projects since then."

Lower-value example: "It was a challenging project but we got it done."

ALIGNMENT WITH TARGET COMPETENCIES

Finally, high-value experiences clearly demonstrate the specific competencies valued by your target companies and roles. Stories that provide strong evidence of leadership, innovation, customer focus, or other key competencies are more valuable than those that primarily show technical execution.

High-value example (for leadership): "I identified the opportunity, built consensus across three departments, and guided the implementation despite significant organizational resistance."

Lower-value example (for leadership): "I wrote the code for a new feature that my manager had prioritized."

IDENTIFYING YOUR HIGH-VALUE EXPERIENCES

With these characteristics in mind, let's develop a systematic process for identifying your highest-value experiences:

STEP 1: CREATE A COMPREHENSIVE EXPERIENCE INVENTORY

Begin by creating an exhaustive list of your professional experiences from the past 3-5 years (or longer for more senior roles). Include:

- Major projects you've led or contributed to
- Significant challenges you've overcome
- Important decisions you've made
- Conflicts or disagreements you've navigated
- Innovations or improvements you've developed
- Failures or setbacks you've experienced and learned from
- Instances where you've influenced others or driven change
- Times when you've developed team members or improved processes

Don't filter or evaluate these experiences yet—the goal at this stage is comprehensive capture, not selection.

STEP 2: EVALUATE IMPACT AND CONTRIBUTION

For each experience in your inventory, assess:

- What was the measurable impact of this experience?
- How did this impact connect to business or organizational priorities?
- What was my specific contribution to this outcome?
- How central was my role to the overall success?

This evaluation helps identify experiences where you made significant, measurable contributions to meaningful outcomes—a core characteristic of high-value stories.

STEP 3: ASSESS COMPLEXITY AND CHALLENGE

For each experience, consider:

- What made this situation complex or challenging?
- What obstacles or constraints did I need to overcome?
- What competing priorities or requirements did I need to balance?
- What ambiguity or uncertainty did I need to navigate?

This assessment helps identify experiences that demonstrate sophisticated capabilities beyond basic technical execution.

STEP 4: IDENTIFY GROWTH AND LEARNING

For each experience, reflect on:

- What specific insights or lessons did I gain from this experience?
- How have I applied these lessons to subsequent situations?
- How did this experience change my approach or perspective?
- What would I do differently with the benefit of hindsight?

This reflection helps identify experiences that demonstrate learning agility and self-awareness—qualities highly valued in behavioral interviews.

STEP 5: MAP TO TARGET COMPETENCIES

Finally, map each experience to the specific competencies it demonstrates, particularly those most relevant to your target roles and companies. Consider:

- Which of Amazon's Leadership Principles does this experience demonstrate?
- Which aspects of "Googleyness" or Meta's values does this story illustrate?

- Which role-specific competencies (technical leadership, collaboration, innovation) does this example highlight?

This mapping helps identify which experiences will resonate most strongly with specific companies and roles.

THE STORY DISCOVERY WORKSHEET

To facilitate this identification process, let's create a structured worksheet that guides you through each step:

Element	Questions to Answer
Experience Title	Give this experience a memorable name for easy reference
Timeframe	When did this occur? (Month/Year to Month/Year)
Situation Context	What was the overall context? What organization, team, project?
Your Role	What was your specific role or responsibility?
Key Challenge	What was the central challenge or opportunity?
Your Actions	What specific actions did you take? (Bullet points)
Measurable Results	What quantifiable outcomes resulted from your actions?
Personal Contribution	How did your specific contribution impact the outcome?
Complexity Factors	What made this situation particularly complex or challenging?
Lessons Learned	What specific insights did you gain from this experience?

Element	Questions to Answer
Application of Lessons	How have you applied these lessons to subsequent situations?
Primary Competencies	Which 2-3 key competencies does this experience best demonstrate?
Secondary Competencies	Which additional competencies does this experience also demonstrate?
Potential Questions	Which interview questions could this experience address?

Completing this worksheet for each significant experience creates a comprehensive inventory of potential stories, evaluated against the criteria that matter most for behavioral interviews.

4.3. BUILDING YOUR STORY MATRIX

Once you've identified and evaluated your experiences, the next step is organizing them into a flexible framework that allows you to quickly select the right story for each interview question. This organization takes the form of a "Story Matrix"—a competency-based mapping of your highest-value experiences.

THE COMPETENCY FRAMEWORK

The foundation of your Story Matrix is a comprehensive competency framework that encompasses the key capabilities evaluated in behavioral interviews. While each company has its own specific framework (Amazon's Leadership Principles, Google's attributes, etc.), most technical behavioral interviews assess some combination of these core competencies:

LEADERSHIP COMPETENCIES

- **Vision and Strategy**: Setting direction and developing plans to achieve it

- **Influence and Persuasion**: Gaining buy-in without formal authority

- **Team Development**: Growing and empowering team members

- **Decision Making**: Making sound judgments with appropriate input

- **Change Management**: Leading teams through transitions and uncertainty

PROBLEM-SOLVING COMPETENCIES

- **Analytical Thinking**: Breaking down complex problems systematically

- **Innovation**: Developing novel approaches and solutions

- **Technical Excellence**: Applying deep technical knowledge effectively

- **Judgment**: Making sound decisions with limited information

- **Systems Thinking**: Understanding interconnections and broader context

EXECUTION COMPETENCIES

- **Delivery Focus**: Achieving results despite obstacles

- **Ownership**: Taking responsibility for outcomes beyond assigned tasks

- **Quality Orientation**: Maintaining high standards and attention to detail

- **Efficiency**: Optimizing resource utilization and eliminating waste

- **Prioritization**: Focusing on what matters most amid competing demands

COLLABORATION COMPETENCIES

- **Communication**: Exchanging information clearly and effectively

- **Teamwork**: Contributing productively to collective efforts

- **Conflict Resolution**: Addressing disagreements constructively
- **Stakeholder Management**: Building and maintaining key relationships
- **Cross-Functional Effectiveness**: Working across organizational boundaries

CUSTOMER COMPETENCIES

- **Customer Understanding**: Identifying explicit and implicit needs
- **Customer Advocacy**: Representing customer interests internally
- **User Experience Focus**: Designing for usability and satisfaction
- **Service Orientation**: Going beyond minimum requirements
- **Customer Success**: Ensuring customers achieve their goals

LEARNING COMPETENCIES

- **Adaptability**: Adjusting effectively to changing circumstances
- **Feedback Orientation**: Seeking and applying input for improvement
- **Continuous Learning**: Actively developing new knowledge and skills
- **Self-Awareness**: Understanding personal strengths and growth areas
- **Resilience**: Recovering and learning from setbacks

This comprehensive framework ensures you're prepared for the full range of potential behavioral questions, regardless of how they're framed or which specific competencies a company emphasizes.

MAPPING STORIES TO COMPETENCIES

With this competency framework as your foundation, the next step is mapping your highest-value experiences to the specific competencies they demonstrate. This mapping creates a flexible matrix that allows you to quickly identify relevant stories for any behavioral question.

The mapping process involves:

1. Selecting your 10-15 highest-value experiences based on the evaluation criteria we've discussed

2. Identifying the primary competencies each experience demonstrates (typically 2-3 per story)

3. Noting secondary competencies each experience could also illustrate (typically 3-5 per story)

4. Creating a matrix that shows which stories demonstrate which competencies

This matrix becomes your interview navigation tool, allowing you to quickly identify which stories to share based on the competencies being assessed.

THE STORY MATRIX TEMPLATE

Here's a template for creating your Story Matrix:

Story Title	Leadership	Problem-Solving	Execution	Collaboration	Customer	Learning
Authentication Service Incident	Secondary	Primary	Primary	Secondary	Secondary	Primary
Cross-Platform Feature Development	Primary	Secondary	Primary	Primary	Secondary	Secondary
Team Reorganization	Primary	Secondary	Secondary	Primary	Secondary	Primary

Story Title	Leadership	Problem-Solving	Execution	Collaboration	Customer	Learning
Performance Optimization Project	Secondary	Primary	Primary	Secondary	Primary	Secondary
Difficult Stakeholder Situation	Primary	Secondary	Secondary	Primary	Secondary	Primary
Failed Product Launch	Secondary	Primary	Primary	Secondary	Primary	Primary
Mentoring Junior Engineers	Primary	Secondary	Secondary	Primary	Secondary	Primary
Legacy System Modernization	Primary	Primary	Primary	Secondary	Secondary	Secondary
Customer Escalation Resolution	Secondary	Primary	Primary	Primary	Primary	Secondary
Innovation Initiative	Primary	Primary	Secondary	Primary	Secondary	Secondary

In this template, "Primary" indicates competencies the story strongly demonstrates, while "Secondary" indicates competencies it could also illustrate if needed. This distinction helps you quickly identify your strongest examples for each competency area.

USING YOUR STORY MATRIX

Your Story Matrix becomes a powerful tool during interview preparation and execution:

DURING PREPARATION

- Identify gaps in your competency coverage and develop additional stories as needed
- Prepare detailed STAR+ responses for your primary competency stories
- Practice adapting secondary competency stories to different question formats
- Ensure you have multiple stories for the most critical competencies

DURING INTERVIEWS

- Quickly identify which story best demonstrates the competency behind each question
- Select primary competency stories for expected questions
- Adapt secondary competency stories for unexpected questions
- Avoid repeating the same story for multiple questions

This flexible framework ensures you're never caught without a relevant example, even for unexpected questions or competencies.

4.4. TAILORING STORIES TO SPECIFIC COMPANIES

While your Story Matrix provides a solid foundation, the most effective behavioral interview preparation involves tailoring your stories to the specific values and competencies of your target companies. Let's explore how to adapt your stories for the unique cultures of Amazon, Google, Meta, and Microsoft.

AMAZON: LEADERSHIP PRINCIPLES ALIGNMENT

Amazon's 16 Leadership Principles form the explicit framework for their behavioral interviews. Each interviewer is typically assigned specific principles to assess, with questions designed to elicit evidence of aligned behaviors.

To tailor your stories for Amazon:

1. Review each Leadership Principle and its specific expectations

2. Map your existing stories to the most relevant principles

3. Enhance your STAR+ responses to explicitly demonstrate these principles

4. Prepare for principle-specific follow-up questions

Example Tailoring: For a story about optimizing a critical system, emphasize different aspects based on the principle being assessed:

- For "Dive Deep": Highlight your detailed analysis of performance bottlenecks

- For "Invent and Simplify": Emphasize the novel approach you developed

- For "Deliver Results": Focus on the measurable impact and deadline achievement

- For "Frugality": Highlight how you optimized with minimal resources

This principle-specific tailoring ensures your stories directly address Amazon's explicit evaluation criteria.

GOOGLE: LEARNING AND COLLABORATION FOCUS

Google's behavioral assessment emphasizes learning ability, intellectual humility, and collaborative problem-solving. Their questions often probe for evidence of how you've navigated ambiguity, worked across boundaries, and grown from challenges.

To tailor your stories for Google:

1. Emphasize learning and growth aspects in your STAR+ responses

2. Highlight collaborative problem-solving and influence without authority

3. Demonstrate comfort with ambiguity and data-driven decision making

4. Show how you've balanced innovation with practical execution

Example Tailoring: For a story about leading a cross-functional project:

- Emphasize how you incorporated diverse perspectives into the solution

- Highlight data-driven decisions you made despite incomplete information

- Describe how you balanced innovation with practical implementation

- Focus on what you learned and how you've applied those insights since

This tailoring aligns your stories with Google's emphasis on learning agility and collaborative innovation.

META: IMPACT AND SCALE ORIENTATION

Meta's behavioral interviews focus heavily on impact, scale, and speed. Their questions often probe for examples of how you've created significant value, made decisions that balanced competing priorities, and executed quickly in ambiguous environments.

To tailor your stories for Meta:

1. Quantify impact with specific metrics whenever possible

2. Emphasize scale considerations in your decision making

3. Highlight how you've balanced speed with quality

4. Demonstrate comfort with ambiguity and rapid iteration

Example Tailoring: For a story about developing a new feature:

- Lead with quantifiable impact metrics (user adoption, engagement increase)

- Emphasize how you designed for scale from the beginning

- Highlight decisions that balanced speed with quality or stability

- Describe how you navigated ambiguity through rapid experimentation

This tailoring aligns your stories with Meta's focus on measurable impact and execution speed.

MICROSOFT: GROWTH MINDSET EMPHASIS

Microsoft's behavioral interviews, particularly under CEO Satya Nadella, emphasize growth mindset—the belief that abilities can be developed through dedication and hard work. Their questions often explore how you've learned from failures, sought out feedback, and adapted to changing circumstances.

To tailor your stories for Microsoft:

1. Emphasize learning and adaptation aspects of your experiences

2. Highlight how you've sought and incorporated feedback

3. Demonstrate collaboration across organizational boundaries

4. Show how you've contributed to others' growth and success

Example Tailoring: For a story about a challenging project:

- Emphasize how you sought feedback throughout the process

- Highlight adjustments you made based on new information

- Describe how you collaborated across team boundaries

- Focus on both what you accomplished and how you grew

This tailoring aligns your stories with Microsoft's emphasis on growth mindset and collaborative learning.

4.5. DEVELOPING STORIES ACROSS EXPERIENCE LEVELS

The story identification process varies significantly based on your experience level. Let's explore specific strategies for different career stages.

EARLY CAREER (0-3 YEARS EXPERIENCE)

Early career professionals often worry they lack substantial experiences to share in behavioral interviews. However, even with limited professional experience, you can develop compelling stories by:

- **Leveraging internship and academic projects**: Academic team projects, capstone projects, and internships can provide valuable examples of collaboration, problem-solving, and delivery

- **Highlighting rapid learning**: Early career stories should emphasize how quickly you've acquired and applied new skills

- **Focusing on contribution within constraints**: Demonstrate how you've made meaningful contributions despite limited authority or experience

- **Drawing from non-technical leadership**: Leadership in student organizations, volunteer work, or community activities can demonstrate capabilities relevant to technical roles

Example Early Career Story Development:

Original assessment: "I don't have any leadership examples because I've never been a team lead."

Enhanced perspective: "While I haven't held a formal leadership title, I led the frontend implementation for our capstone project, coordinating work across three team members and making key architecture decisions that allowed us to deliver on time despite changing requirements."

MID-CAREER (3-8 YEARS EXPERIENCE)

Mid-career professionals typically have plenty of experiences but struggle to identify which ones demonstrate leadership and strategic impact rather than just technical execution. Effective mid-career story development involves:

- **Emphasizing influence beyond role**: Highlight how you've shaped decisions and outcomes beyond your formal responsibilities

- **Demonstrating technical leadership**: Focus on examples where your expertise influenced architecture, approach, or standards

- **Showing mentorship and team impact**: Develop stories that show how you've helped others grow and succeed

- **Connecting technical decisions to business outcomes**: Demonstrate understanding of how your technical work affected business metrics

Example Mid-Career Story Development:

Original assessment: "I optimized our authentication service to improve performance."

Enhanced perspective: "I identified that our authentication service was becoming a bottleneck affecting multiple teams. I proposed and led a comprehensive optimization initiative that reduced latency by 65%, improving conversion rates by 12% and generating approximately $300,000 in additional monthly revenue. I also established performance standards and monitoring practices now used across our engineering organization."

SENIOR CAREER (8+ YEARS EXPERIENCE)

Senior professionals often have the opposite problem—too many experiences to choose from, and difficulty focusing on recent, relevant examples rather than historical achievements. Effective senior-level story development involves:

- **Emphasizing strategic impact**: Focus on examples that demonstrate shaping direction and making decisions with broad organizational impact

- **Highlighting organizational influence**: Develop stories that show how you've influenced culture, practices, or capabilities beyond your immediate team

- **Demonstrating complex stakeholder management**: Share examples of navigating competing priorities across multiple teams or departments

- **Balancing technical and leadership elements**: Include both strategic leadership and hands-on technical contributions in your stories

Example Senior Career Story Development:

Original assessment: "I led the migration to microservices architecture."

Enhanced perspective: "I recognized that our monolithic architecture was limiting our ability to scale and innovate. I developed a comprehensive migration strategy, built consensus across five engineering departments, secured $1.2M in funding by connecting technical benefits to business outcomes, and personally led the implementation of the first three critical services. This transformation reduced our release cycle from monthly to weekly, increased engineer productivity by 35%, and enabled the launch of our premium tier, which now generates $4M in annual revenue."

4.6. AVOIDING COMMON STORY SELECTION PITFALLS

Even with a systematic approach to story identification, certain pitfalls commonly undermine candidates' effectiveness. Let's examine these pitfalls and strategies to avoid them.

THE RECENCY TRAP

Many candidates default to sharing their most recent experiences, regardless of whether these examples optimally demonstrate the competencies being assessed. While recent examples are generally preferable, relevance and impact should take precedence over recency.

How to avoid it: Evaluate each potential story based on how strongly it demonstrates the target competency, not just how recent it is. A powerful example from 18 months ago is better than a weak example from last week.

THE TECHNICAL IMPRESSIVENESS BIAS

Engineers often select stories based on technical complexity or sophistication, even when the question is assessing non-technical competencies like leadership or collaboration. While technical details provide context, behavioral questions are primarily assessing how you work, not what you built.

How to avoid it: For each story, explicitly identify which behaviors and competencies it demonstrates, independent of its technical complexity. Select stories based on behavioral evidence, not technical impressiveness.

THE OUTCOME FIXATION

Some candidates select stories based solely on successful outcomes, avoiding examples with mixed results or outright failures. However, how you handle setbacks and what you learn from them often provide more valuable behavioral evidence than straightforward successes.

How to avoid it: Include stories with different outcome patterns in your matrix—clear successes, partial successes with lessons learned, and productive failures that led to growth. This diversity ensures you're prepared for the full range of behavioral questions.

THE SOLO CONTRIBUTOR EMPHASIS

Technical candidates often gravitate toward examples where they personally solved problems through individual technical contribution. While these stories demonstrate technical capabilities, they frequently miss opportunities to show leadership, influence, and collaboration.

How to avoid it: For each story, explicitly identify your impact on others—how you influenced decisions, developed team members, or collaborated across boundaries. Ensure your story selection includes examples of both technical execution and interpersonal effectiveness.

THE GENERALITY PROBLEM

Some candidates select stories that are too general or broad, covering extended periods or multiple projects rather than specific situations. These generalized examples typically lack the concrete details and specific behaviors that make behavioral responses compelling.

How to avoid it: Ensure each story focuses on a specific situation with clear boundaries—a particular project, decision, or challenge rather than a general role or responsibility. The situation should be specific enough to describe in detail within 1-2 minutes.

THE REPETITION RISK

Without systematic tracking, candidates sometimes repeat the same story across multiple interview questions, reducing the breadth of evidence they provide and potentially creating the impression of limited experience.

How to avoid it: Use your Story Matrix to track which stories you've shared in each interview, ensuring you demonstrate a range of competencies across different examples. Prepare at least 2-3 stories for each core competency to enable flexibility.

4.7. CONCLUSION: YOUR PERSONAL STORY INVENTORY

By the end of this chapter, you should have:

1. A comprehensive inventory of your professional experiences

2. A structured evaluation of these experiences against high-value criteria

3. A flexible Story Matrix mapping your best examples to key competencies

4. Company-specific tailoring strategies for your target organizations

5. Awareness of common pitfalls and strategies to avoid them

This systematic approach to story identification transforms behavioral interview preparation from an anxious search for examples to a confident selection from your personal inventory of high-impact stories. With this foundation in place, you're ready to refine these stories into compelling STAR+ responses and practice their delivery—topics we'll explore in subsequent chapters.

Remember that your story inventory is a living document that should evolve as you gain new experiences and insights. Regularly updating your inventory ensures you always have fresh, relevant examples that demonstrate your growing capabilities and impact.

In the next chapter, we'll examine common behavioral interview pitfalls and develop specific strategies to avoid them, further strengthening your preparation and performance.

CHAPTER 5. COMMON PITFALLS AND HOW TO AVOID THEM

It takes 20 years to build a reputation and five minutes to ruin it. If you think about that, you'll do things differently.

— Warren Buffett

The interview is going well. You've prepared thoroughly, identified your strongest stories, and mastered the STAR+ framework. The interviewer asks about a time you demonstrated leadership in a challenging situation, and you begin confidently with a compelling example.

Then it happens.

You spend three minutes describing the situation in exhaustive detail. You mention every team member by name. You dive into technical specifications that aren't relevant to the question. You forget to clearly articulate your specific actions. You trail off without mentioning results or lessons learned. The interviewer looks confused, checks the time, and asks a follow-up question that reveals they completely misunderstood your point.

In that moment, all your preparation seems wasted. Not because you lacked relevant experiences or capabilities, but because you fell into one of the common behavioral interview pitfalls that undermine even well-qualified candidates.

In this chapter, we'll examine these pitfalls in detail—not to increase your anxiety, but to help you recognize and avoid them. We'll explore why these mistakes occur, how interviewers perceive them, and most importantly, specific strategies to prevent them. By understanding these common traps, you'll ensure your preparation translates into effective performance when it matters most.

5.1. THE PREPARATION PITFALLS

Before you even enter the interview room, certain preparation mistakes can undermine your performance. Let's examine these preparation pitfalls and how to avoid them.

Table 1. Preparation Pitfalls

Pitfall	Description
The Memorization Trap	Attempting to memorize complete STAR+ responses word-for-word, resulting in rehearsed, inauthentic answers that struggle with follow-up questions.
The Underprepared Example	Identifying relevant stories but failing to prepare them in sufficient detail, leading to vague, unconvincing responses during the interview.
The Mismatched Story	Preparing stories that don't demonstrate the competencies being assessed, creating the impression of misunderstanding or lacking relevant experience.
The Single-Story Syndrome	Over-relying on a single impressive story for multiple questions, creating a narrow impression of your experience and capabilities.
The Recency Bias	Defaulting to only your most recent experiences, potentially missing better examples from earlier in your career that demonstrate specific competencies.

THE MEMORIZATION TRAP

The Pitfall: Many candidates attempt to memorize complete STAR+ responses word-for-word, believing this will help them deliver polished answers. However, memorized responses typically sound rehearsed and inauthentic. Worse, when interviewers ask follow-up questions or request additional details, candidates often struggle to deviate from their memorized script, creating awkward interactions.

Why It Happens: This approach stems from a misunderstanding of effective preparation. Candidates correctly recognize the need for structure but incorrectly assume that structure requires verbatim memorization.

How Interviewers Perceive It: Interviewers quickly recognize memorized responses through their unnatural delivery, resistance to follow-up questions, and suspiciously perfect phrasing. This creates doubt about the candidate's authenticity and adaptability.

Instead of memorizing complete responses, prepare a structured outline for each story to maintain authenticity and adaptability. Here's how:

1. BULLET POINT KEY ELEMENTS

Instead of memorizing a script, jot down the core details of your story in bullet form.

Example (Bad Approach – Memorized Script):

"In my role as Project Manager at XYZ Corp, I was tasked with leading a team of five to develop a new client portal. The main challenge was that we had a tight deadline of three weeks due to unexpected client demands. I organized daily stand-ups, delegated tasks efficiently, and implemented Agile methodologies to ensure we met the deadline. As a result, we delivered the portal two days early and received positive feedback from the client."

Example (Better Approach – Bullet Outline):

- Situation: Led team of 5 to develop client portal under 3-week deadline
- Task: Ensure on-time delivery despite scope changes
- Action: Daily stand-ups, Agile adjustments, task delegation
- Result: Delivered 2 days early, positive client feedback
- Plus (Reflection): Learned to adapt Agile for tight deadlines

2. PRACTICE NATURALLY FROM BULLET POINTS

Use the outline as a guide, but vary wording each time you practice.

Example (Natural Delivery): "I was managing a team of five to build a client portal, but we had an unexpected deadline crunch—just three weeks. To handle it, I restructured our workflow with daily check-ins and reallocated tasks based on strengths. We not only met the deadline but finished early, and the client was really happy with the outcome."

3. VARY DELIVERY ACROSS PRACTICE SESSIONS

Avoid sounding robotic by changing phrasing slightly each time.

Alternative Version: "Facing a tight three-week deadline for a client portal, I had to rethink our approach. I introduced daily sync-ups and adjusted roles to maximize efficiency. In the end, we beat the deadline, and the client praised the final product."

4. PREPARE FOR FOLLOW-UP QUESTIONS

Have a partner ask unexpected follow-ups to test flexibility.

Possible Follow-Ups & Prepared Responses:

- "How did you handle team disagreements during the crunch time?"

- "One developer disagreed with task assignments, so I held a quick 1:1 to realign priorities."

- "What would you do differently next time?"

- "I'd involve the client earlier in sprint reviews to avoid last-minute changes."

Why This Works:

- Sounds conversational, not rehearsed

- Easily adapts to different interview questions

- Builds confidence in thinking on your feet

By focusing on structure over memorization, you maintain professionalism while staying authentic and adaptable.

THE UNDERPREPARED EXAMPLE

The Pitfall: Some candidates identify relevant stories but fail to prepare them in sufficient detail. During the interview, they struggle to recall specific metrics, key actions, or important context. This creates responses that feel vague and unconvincing, even when based on impressive experiences.

Why It Happens: Candidates often assume they'll naturally remember all relevant details of their own experiences. However, interview pressure significantly impairs memory recall, particularly for specific details and metrics.

How Interviewers Perceive It: Vague responses create doubt about whether the example is genuine or whether the candidate's contribution was significant. Interviewers may assume the candidate is exaggerating their role or impact.

Instead of relying on memory, document specific details for each story to ensure credibility and clarity under pressure. Here's how:

1. EXACT TIMEFRAMES & PROJECT DURATIONS

Avoid vague timelines—use precise dates or durations to reinforce credibility.

Example (Vague): "I led a project to improve customer satisfaction."

Example (Detailed): "From March to June 2023, I led a three-month initiative to reduce customer onboarding time."

2. TEAM COMPOSITION & KEY STAKEHOLDERS

Clarify who was involved and their roles to demonstrate collaboration.

Example (Unclear): "I worked with a team to launch a new feature."

Example (Specific): "I collaborated with two backend engineers, a UX designer, and the product manager to overhaul the checkout flow."

3. SPECIFIC METRICS BEFORE & AFTER

Quantify impact to prove results.

Example (Generic): "Our process got better after my changes."

Example (Concrete): "Before my intervention, customer complaints averaged 15/week. After streamlining the process, complaints dropped to 3/week within a month."

4. PARTICULAR CHALLENGES & CONSTRAINTS

Highlight obstacles to showcase problem-solving.

Example (Surface-level): "We had some roadblocks but figured it out."

Example (Detailed): "We had no additional budget for tools, so I negotiated a free trial of an automation platform and trained the team to use it."

5. DIRECT QUOTES FROM FEEDBACK OR RECOGNITION

Use real praise to validate your impact.

Example (Unsupported): "My manager said I did a good job."

Example (Verifiable): "In my performance review, my director wrote, 'Your solution saved the team 10 hours/week and set a new standard for efficiency.'"

How to Practice This Approach

- Create a Story Bank: Draft a document with 5–7 key stories, filling in all five detail categories above.

- Pressure-Test Recall: Have a partner quiz you randomly on specifics (e.g., "What was the exact ROI of that project?").

- Adapt Flexibly: Use the details naturally—don't recite them like a checklist.

Example of a Well-Prepared Response:

"Last year, I led a 10-week project to reduce software deployment delays. My team of three developers and I faced pushback from the security team, so I set up a weekly sync to address their concerns. We cut deployment time from 48 hours to 6 hours, and the VP later emailed me saying, 'This is the most reliable rollout we've had in years.'"

Why This Works

- Eliminates vagueness that undermines credibility

- Prepares you for follow-ups (e.g., "How did you get stakeholder buy-in?")

- Makes your answers memorable with concrete data

By treating your experiences like case studies with evidence, you'll project confidence and competence—even under stress.

THE MISMATCHED STORY

The Pitfall: Candidates sometimes prepare stories that don't actually demonstrate the competencies being assessed. For example, sharing a technical troubleshooting story when asked about cross-functional leadership, or describing individual contribution when asked about team development.

Why It Happens: This mismatch typically occurs when candidates select stories based on what impressed them personally rather than what demonstrates the specific competencies interviewers are evaluating.

How Interviewers Perceive It: Mismatched stories create the impression that the candidate either doesn't understand the competency being assessed or doesn't have relevant experience demonstrating it—both concerning signals.

To avoid mismatched stories, map each example to specific competencies before the interview. Here's how:

1. IDENTIFY PRIMARY COMPETENCIES

Label each story with the exact skills it showcases (e.g., "This demonstrates conflict resolution, not project management").

Example (Mismatched):

Interviewer asks: "Tell me about a time you influenced without authority."

Candidate shares: A story about debugging a critical system outage (shows technical skill, not persuasion).

Example (Matched):

Same question, better story:

"I convinced our engineering team to adopt a new tool by presenting data on time savings and running a pilot—despite having no formal authority over their roadmap."

2. HIGHLIGHT SPECIFIC BEHAVIORS

For each competency, note what you did that proves it.

Competency: Cross-functional collaboration

Behaviors to Highlight:

- Facilitated alignment meetings between marketing and engineering
- Translated technical constraints into business terms for stakeholders
- Resolved a deadline conflict by negotiating a new milestone

Weak Example: "I worked with other teams to launch a feature." (Too vague)

Strong Example: "When marketing needed a feature launch moved up, I coordinated a sprint reprioritization with engineering by showing how it would prevent $200K in lost leads."

3. NOTE ALTERNATIVE COMPETENCIES

Some stories can flex to multiple skills—but only if you tweak the emphasis.

Original Story: Reduced customer service call volume by 30% through a new training program.

- Primary Competency: Process improvement
- Alternative Focus:
  - Training/development → "I coached agents on active listening techniques."
  - Data-driven decision-making → "I analyzed call transcripts to identify

top pain points."

4. FLAG "OFF-LIMITS" COMPETENCIES

Know what your story doesn't prove to avoid missteps.

Example Story: Streamlined a solo research project.

Competencies it DOESN'T show:

- Team leadership
- Stakeholder management
- Delegation

How to Practice This Approach

1. Create a Competency Map:

    a. List common job competencies (e.g., leadership, problem-solving, adaptability).

    b. Tag each story with 1–2 primary competencies it aligns to.

2. Test Your Stories:

    a. Ask a partner: "What skill do you think I'm demonstrating here?"

    b. If their answer doesn't match your intent, refine the story.

3. Prepare Pivots:

    a. For broad questions ("Tell me about a challenge"), lead with the competency:

    b. "One example that shows my problem-solving approach is when..."

Example of a Well-Mapped Story

Competency: Conflict Resolution

Story: "When two team members clashed over design priorities, I facilitated a session where each listed their non-negotiables. We found a hybrid solution that met 80% of both requirements, and I implemented a feedback system to prevent future clashes."

Why It Works:

- Behaviors (facilitation, compromise) directly match the competency.
- Avoids mismatch by not emphasizing unrelated skills (e.g., creativity).

Why This Matters

- Interviewers score responses based on competencies—not just "cool stories."
- A mismatched story can cost you the job even if the example is impressive.
- This method ensures you always hit the mark, even under pressure.

By treating stories like modular tools (not fixed narratives), you'll adapt seamlessly to any question.

THE SINGLE-STORY SYNDROME

The Pitfall: Some candidates over-rely on a single impressive story, attempting to adapt it to multiple different questions. While this story might be genuinely impressive, using it repeatedly creates a narrow impression of the candidate's experience and capabilities.

Why It Happens: Candidates naturally gravitate toward their most successful or recent projects, sometimes failing to recognize the breadth of evidence interviewers are seeking.

How Interviewers Perceive It: Repeated use of the same example suggests limited relevant experience or lack of preparation. It also prevents interviewers from assessing the full range of the candidate's capabilities.

To avoid overusing one story, build a **diverse story portfolio** that showcases your range. Here's how:

1. PREPARE 2-3 EXAMPLES PER CORE COMPETENCY

For each skill, have multiple stories ready - not just your "go-to" example.

Example Competency: Problem-Solving

- **Story 1**: Resolved a sudden server outage by coordinating a cross-team response (tech-focused)
- **Story 2**: Designed a new process to reduce customer onboarding bottlenecks (process-focused)
- **Story 3**: Negotiated a vendor dispute to save $50K without legal escalation (relationship-focused)

Why It Works:

- Shows versatility in tackling different *types* of problems
- Avoids interviewer fatigue from repetition

2. PULL STORIES FROM DIFFERENT ROLES & TIMEFRAMES

Mix experiences to demonstrate growth and breadth.

Table 2. Example Portfolio

Competency	Example 1 (Early Career)	Example 2 (Recent Role)
Leadership	Led a college group project	Managed a remote team of 5

| **Adaptability** | Pivoted during an internship | Overhauled strategy post-merger |

Interview Impact:

- Proves consistent success across contexts
- Highlights career progression

3. TRACK STORY USAGE IN INTERVIEWS

Keep a simple log to avoid repetition.

Table 3. Example Tracker

Date	Company	Competency Asked	Story Used
10/5/2024	Google	Conflict Resolution	Vendor negotiation
10/12/2024	Amazon	Leadership	Remote team sprint

Pro Tip: If asked about a similar competency: *"Last time I discussed X, but another example that shows this differently is when I..."*

4. USE TRANSITION PHRASES TO DIVERSIFY

Guide the conversation to fresh examples.

When to Pivot:

- Interviewer asks: *"Tell me about a time you failed"*
- Overused Story: "When our project missed a deadline..."
- Better Response:
  "I could share that delay, but another learning moment was when I

misjudged a client's needs early in my career. Here's what I changed..."

Why It Works:

- Signals self-awareness

- Keeps the interview dynamic

EXAMPLE OF A WELL-BALANCED RESPONSE

Question: *"Describe a time you motivated a team."*

Candidate's Options:

1. *"As a new manager, I rallied my team during restructuring by..."*

2. *"As a volunteer coordinator, I boosted engagement by..."*

Choice: Picks #2 to avoid repeating management stories

WHY THIS MATTERS

- Shows **consistent** competence, not isolated achievements

- Prevents one-dimensional impression

- Enables tailoring to company values

ACTION PLAN

1. **Audit Your Stories**: Map 5-7 competencies to 2-3 examples each

2. **Pressure-Test**: Practice varying responses to same question

3. **Flag Overused Stories**: Rotate examples strategically

By curating stories like a **playbook**, you'll demonstrate depth and adaptability.

THE RECENCY BIAS

The Pitfall: Candidates often default to sharing only their most recent experiences, even when older examples might better demonstrate particular competencies. This recency bias can limit the quality and relevance of examples shared.

Why It Happens: Recent experiences are more readily accessible in memory and often feel more relevant to candidates. There's also sometimes an assumption that interviewers only value recent examples.

How Interviewers Perceive It: While interviewers generally prefer recent examples (within the last 2-3 years), they prioritize relevance and impact over strict recency. Sharing only recent examples can create an incomplete picture of your capabilities.

To overcome recency bias, implement these strategies:

1. INCLUDE HIGH-IMPACT EXAMPLES FROM THROUGHOUT YOUR CAREER

Bad Approach: Only preparing stories from current role

Better Approach:

- Current role: Digital transformation project (2023)
- Previous role: Crisis management during merger (2019)
- Early career: Process improvement initiative (2016)

2. FOCUS ON TRANSFERABLE SKILLS IN OLDER EXAMPLES

Example: "While this happened in 2018, the stakeholder management framework I developed is still how I approach cross-functional projects today."

3. FRAME OLDER EXAMPLES FOR RELEVANCE

Weak: "Back in 2017, I led a team..."

Strong: "Early in my leadership journey, I established an approach that still informs how I build teams today..."

4. CONNECT TO CURRENT APPLICATIONS

Example: "The lessons from navigating that 2015 organizational change directly helped me guide my current team through recent restructuring by..."

IMPLEMENTATION TIPS

1. **Create a Timeline**: Map 2-3 strong examples per career phase

2. **Practice Bridging**: "While this example is from 2018, the key takeaway..."

3. **Update Language**: Replace "back then" with "this experience established..."

4. **Balance**: Aim for 70% recent (last 3 years) and 30% older high-impact examples

WHY THIS WORKS

- Demonstrates **depth** of experience beyond current role

- Shows **evolution** of your skills over time

- Provides **historical proof** of consistent capabilities

- Maintains relevance while avoiding recency limitations

5.2. THE DELIVERY PITFALLS

Even with thorough preparation, how you deliver your responses significantly impacts their effectiveness. Let's examine common delivery pitfalls and strategies to overcome them.

Table 4. Delivery Pitfalls

Pitfall	Description
The Context Overload	Spending excessive time describing background information before getting to your specific actions, burying the most important aspects of your response.
The Collective "We"	Defaulting to describing what "we" did rather than clarifying your personal contribution, making it difficult to distinguish your individual impact.
The Technical Deep Dive	Diving into excessive technical detail during behavioral responses, obscuring the leadership or problem-solving aspects being assessed.
The Rambling Response	Delivering unfocused, meandering answers under pressure that lack clear structure and conclusion.
The Incomplete Response	Providing partial STAR+ responses, particularly omitting Results and Reflection components that demonstrate impact and learning.

THE CONTEXT OVERLOAD

The Pitfall: Many candidates spend excessive time describing background information, organizational context, or technical details before getting to their specific actions and contributions. This front-loading of context often consumes valuable interview time and buries the most important aspects of the response.

Why It Happens: Candidates naturally want interviewers to fully understand the situation's complexity. There's also often anxiety about jumping into the story without sufficient setup.

How Interviewers Perceive It: Excessive context creates impatience and confusion about what's actually relevant. Interviewers may struggle to identify the candidate's specific contribution amid all the background information.

1. LIMIT SITUATION TO 2-3 ESSENTIAL SENTENCES

Problem Example:

"We were working on a multi-phase digital transformation initiative that began in Q2 2021 after our Series B funding round, involving 14 stakeholders across 3 departments with competing priorities..."

Solution Example: "Our marketing team began a digital transformation with siloed tools. **The key challenge was** integrating systems without disrupting campaigns."

2. USE TRANSITION PHRASES TO ACCELERATE TO ACTION

Effective Templates:

- "To put it simply, the core problem was..."
- "What mattered most was..."
- "The critical hurdle we faced..."

3. ENFORCE THE 30-SECOND RULE

Timing Guide:

- Situation: 10 seconds

- Task: 15 seconds
- Action: 45 seconds (bulk of time)
- Result: 20 seconds

4. DEFER DETAILS FOR FOLLOW-UPS

When to Elaborate:

- Only if interviewer asks "What tools were you using?"
- "To give more context..." (after delivering core answer)
- "The technical specifics were..." (when probing occurs)

PRACTICAL EXERCISE

1. **Record Yourself**: Time how long your setup takes
2. **Edit Ruthlessly**: Cut any context not directly enabling your action
3. **Stress-Test**: Have someone interrupt after 20 seconds - could they grasp the challenge?

WHY THIS WORKS

- Forces focus on **your contribution**
- Demonstrates ability to **distill complexity**
- Shows respect for interviewer's time
- Leaves room for deeper dives when requested

THE COLLECTIVE "WE"

The Pitfall: Technical candidates often default to describing what "we" did throughout their responses, making it difficult for interviewers to distinguish the candidate's personal contribution from team efforts. This ambiguity undermines the candidate's ability to demonstrate their specific capabilities.

Why It Happens: This pattern stems from both modesty and the collaborative nature of technical work. Many candidates feel uncomfortable claiming individual credit for team accomplishments.

How Interviewers Perceive It: Consistent use of "we" without clarifying personal contribution creates doubt about the candidate's actual role and impact. Interviewers may assume minimal individual contribution in the absence of specific claims.

1. USE "WE" FOR CONTEXT, "I" FOR CONTRIBUTION

Problem Example

"We improved system performance by optimizing the database queries."

Solution Example

"The team identified performance bottlenecks in our checkout flow. **I personally** analyzed the query patterns and rewrote the 3 most critical stored procedures, which reduced latency by 40%."

2. EXPLICITLY STATE YOUR ROLE

Effective Templates

- "As the [specific role], I was responsible for..."
- "My piece of this was to..."
- "While the team handled X, I owned Y..."

3. HIGHLIGHT DECISION POINTS

Before

"We decided to migrate to microservices."

After

"I advocated for the microservice approach after load testing revealed scaling limitations. I then designed the service boundaries and wrote the API contracts."

4. QUANTIFY INDIVIDUAL IMPACT

Weak

"We reduced production incidents."

Strong

"I implemented the automated rollback system that reduced our critical incident resolution time from 90 to 15 minutes."

5. ACKNOWLEDGE TEAM WHILE CLAIMING CREDIT

Balanced Example

"The frontend team built the new UI components, while I architected the state management system and personally implemented the caching layer that improved render times by 60%."

PRACTICE TECHNIQUES

1. **Transcript Analysis**: Review mock interview transcripts, circling every "we" and forcing conversion to "I" where appropriate

2. **Role Play**: Have a partner interrupt whenever your contribution isn't clear

3. **Contribution Mapping**: For each story, list:

   ◦ Team's work (1-2 items)

○ Your specific work (3-5 items)

WHY THIS MATTERS

- Technical interviews evaluate **individual** problem-solving ability
- Clear ownership demonstrates:
- Leadership potential
- Accountability
- Technical depth
- Shows you can collaborate **while** driving results

THE TECHNICAL DEEP DIVE

The Pitfall: Engineers often dive into excessive technical detail during behavioral responses, focusing on implementation specifics rather than the behaviors and competencies being assessed. This technical focus can obscure the leadership, collaboration, or problem-solving aspects interviewers are actually evaluating.

Why It Happens: Technical professionals naturally value technical details and feel most confident discussing them. There's also sometimes a misunderstanding about what behavioral interviews are actually assessing.

How Interviewers Perceive It: While some technical context is necessary, excessive detail suggests the candidate may be more comfortable with technical execution than the broader competencies being evaluated, such as leadership or strategic thinking.

1. ANCHOR TO THE COMPETENCY FIRST

Problem Example: "We used a Redis cache with LRU eviction policy and cluster mode enabled, configured with-"

Solution Example: "To solve our scaling challenge *(competency: problem-solving)*, I led the adoption of a caching solution that improved API response times by 300ms. **The key insight** was identifying which data could be safely cached without business impact."

2. USE LAYERED EXPLANATIONS

Technical: "Implemented circuit breaker pattern"

Behavioral: "Designed a fault-tolerant system *(competency: reliability engineering)* that automatically degraded features during peak loads rather than failing completely."

3. THE "THEREFORE" TEST

For every technical detail, ask: "Does this explain **therefore why** I demonstrated the competency?"

Cut: "We used Kubernetes pods with-"

Keep: "I containerized our services *(competency: technical leadership)* to enable faster deployment cycles."

4. PREPARE ANALOGIES

Instead of: "We implemented consistent hashing for-"

Say: "Like adding lanes to a highway before traffic spikes, I designed our system to scale horizontally."

CALIBRATION GUIDE

Competency	Appropriate Technical Depth	What to Cut
Leadership	Architecture decisions	Library versions
Collaboration	Interface contracts	Protocol specifics
Problem-Solving	Solution tradeoffs	Code snippets

PRACTICE TECHNIQUES

1. **The Grandma Test**: Explain your story to a non-technical person
2. **Time Boxing**: Limit technical details to 20% of response time
3. **Competency Tagging**: Start each practice response with "This demonstrates [competency] by..."

WHY THIS WORKS

- Shows ability to **translate** technical work into business impact
- Proves you understand **what's being evaluated**
- Demonstrates executive presence
- Leaves room for technical follow-ups when appropriate

Remember: Behavioral interviews are **not** technical screenings - they're assessing how you solve problems through technology.

THE RAMBLING RESPONSE

The Pitfall: Under interview pressure, some candidates deliver unfocused, meandering responses that lack clear structure and conclusion. These rambling answers often leave interviewers confused about the key points and evidence being presented.

Why It Happens: Interview anxiety can disrupt organized thinking, causing candidates to speak continuously without clear direction. There's also sometimes a fear that pausing will appear as uncertainty.

How Interviewers Perceive It: Rambling responses suggest disorganized thinking and poor communication skills—concerning signals for roles requiring clear articulation of complex ideas.

1. STAR+ COMPONENT TRACKING

Mental Checklist:

Check	Component (Timing)
☐	Situation (15 sec)
☐	Task (15 sec)
☐	Action (30 sec)
☐	Result (15 sec)
☐	+Learning (10 sec)

Verbal Cue: "Let me pause to ensure I'm covering this clearly..."

2. TRANSITION PHRASES

Table 5. Transition Phrases Guide

Component	Transition Language
Situation	"The context was..."
Task	"My specific challenge became..."
Action	"To address this, I..."
Result	"The measurable outcomes were..."

Component	Transition Language
+Learning	"This taught me..."

3. TIMED PRACTICE DRILLS

Exercise: 1. Answer with 1-minute total limit 2. Gradually expand to 2 minutes 3. Identify "must-say" vs "optional" elements

Time Limit	Focus Area
1 minute	Must-say elements only
2 minutes	Add supporting details
3 minutes	Full STAR+ with examples

4. STRATEGIC PAUSING

Effective Pauses

- After STAR components
- Before quantifying results
- When transitioning topics

RESPONSE MAKEOVER

Before

"We had this project, well actually it started as something else, but then the requirements changed and I was working with the team, well not exactly my team but more like a cross-functional group, and we tried several approaches..."

After

"The situation: A cross-functional initiative with shifting requirements (15 sec). My task: Design an adaptable solution framework (10 sec). Actions: I created modular components and documented 3 implementation scenarios (25 sec). Results: Reduced rework by 30% in subsequent sprints (10 sec). Learning: Proactive documentation prevents scope creep (5 sec)."

EVALUATION TOOLKIT

1. **Audio Analysis**:
   - Mark moments where you lose structure
   - Count filler words ("um", "like")

2. **Peer Feedback**:
   - Can they repeat back your key points?
   - When did they mentally check out?

3. **Structure Scorecard**:

Table 6. Component Tracking Scorecard

STAR+ Element	Included?	Clear?
Situation	☐	☐
Task	☐	☐
Action	☐	-
Result	☐	☐
+Learning	☐	☐

WHY THIS WORKS

- Demonstrates ability to **organize complex information**
- Shows respect for interviewer's time
- Builds confidence through predictable structure

- Allows easy follow-up questions ("Tell me more about the actions")

Pro Tip: When nervous, default to: "Let me structure this clearly..." (then use STAR+)

THE INCOMPLETE RESPONSE

The Pitfall

Candidates often provide partial STAR+ responses, particularly omitting Results and Reflection components, undermining their demonstrated impact.

Why It Happens

- Over-focusing on actions/situation
- Assuming results are self-evident
- Time mismanagement during responses

How Interviewers Perceive It

- "Did this actually work?"
- Concerns about results orientation
- Questions about learning capacity

Here's how you prevent it:

1. STAR+ TIME ALLOCATION GUIDE

Component	Recommended Time
Situation	15%
Task	15%
Action	45%

Component	Recommended Time
Result	15%
+Reflection	10%

2. RESULTS FRAMEWORKS

- **Quantitative**: "This reduced processing time by 40%..."
- **Qualitative**: "Stakeholders reported 30% fewer escalations..."
- **Forward-Looking**: "This became our new standard for..."

3. REFLECTION TEMPLATES

- **Growth**: "This taught me to..."
- **Application**: "I now apply this lesson by..."
- **Improvement**: "If revisited, I'd..."

RESPONSE MAKEOVER

Before

"We had system outages (Situation). I led the debugging effort (Action)... [ends abruptly]"

After

"During peak traffic outages (15 sec Situation), I needed to restore service within 2 hours (10 sec Task). I implemented a circuit breaker pattern and hot standby (30 sec Action). This cut downtime by 75% and saved $150K in lost revenue (10 sec Result). It transformed how we design for resiliency (5 sec Reflection)."

EVALUATION TOOLKIT

Table 7. STAR+ Completion Scorecard

Component	Included?	Impact Clarity
Situation	☐	☐
Task	☐	☐
Action	☐	☐
Result	☐	-
+Reflection	☐	-

PRACTICE DRILLS

1. **Timebox Exercise**:

   a. 1 minute: Cover all components

   b. 90 seconds: Add proof points

   c. 2 minutes: Full demonstration

2. **Backwards Building**:

   a. Start with: "The most important lesson was..." then build supporting story

3. **Interruption Test**:

   a. Partner interrupts randomly - can you still reach Result/Reflection?

WHY THIS MATTERS

- Completing the STAR+ cycle demonstrates:
- Results orientation (business impact)
- Learning agility (growth mindset)

- Communication discipline (structured thinking)

Pro Tip: When time-constrained, use: "To briefly summarize the results..." "One key takeaway was..."

5.3. THE CONTENT PITFALLS

Beyond preparation and delivery, the actual content of your responses can contain subtle pitfalls that undermine your effectiveness. Let's examine these content traps and how to avoid them.

Table 8. Content Pitfalls

Pitfall	Description
The Hypothetical Response	Shifting to hypothetical "what I would do" answers rather than describing actual experiences, misaligning with behavioral interview principles.
The Blame Deflection	Attributing negative outcomes entirely to external factors rather than demonstrating ownership and self-awareness.
The Missing Metrics	Describing results in vague qualitative terms rather than providing specific, quantifiable outcomes that demonstrate impact.
The Exaggeration Escalation	Overstating your role, contribution or results in ways that may collapse under follow-up questioning.
The Competency Mismatch	Emphasizing aspects of stories that don't align with the competency being assessed, despite using relevant examples.

THE HYPOTHETICAL RESPONSE

The Pitfall: When faced with unfamiliar questions, some candidates shift from describing what they actually did to what they would do in a hypothetical situation. This shift fundamentally misaligns with the premise of behavioral interviewing—that past behavior predicts future performance.

Why It Happens: This typically occurs when candidates lack a directly relevant example or when anxiety disrupts access to prepared stories.

How Interviewers Perceive It: Hypothetical responses signal either lack of relevant experience or unwillingness to share actual behaviors. Both interpretations significantly undermine the candidate's evaluation.

Prevention Strategy: Maintain behavioral integrity:

1. Always respond with actual experiences, even if they're not perfect matches for the question

2. Use bridging phrases to acknowledge the specific question while transitioning to your relevant example: "While I haven't faced that exact situation, I can share a similar experience where..."

3. Prepare flexible examples that can be adapted to various competencies

4. If truly necessary, frame a hypothetical response as an application of lessons from an actual experience: "Based on my experience with X, my approach would be..."

This behavioral integrity ensures you provide the authentic evidence interviewers are seeking.

THE BLAME DEFLECTION

The Pitfall: When describing challenging situations or failures, some candidates attribute negative outcomes entirely to external factors, team

150

members, or organizational constraints. This blame deflection suggests limited ownership and self-awareness.

Why It Happens: This defensive pattern stems from natural discomfort with acknowledging mistakes or limitations, particularly in high-stakes situations like interviews.

How Interviewers Perceive It: External attribution of all negative outcomes raises serious concerns about the candidate's accountability, self-awareness, and ability to learn from experience.

Prevention Strategy: Demonstrate balanced accountability:

1. Acknowledge external factors while also identifying your own contribution to challenges

2. Use phrases like "In retrospect, I could have..." or "What I would do differently now is..."

3. Frame challenges as learning opportunities rather than justifications

4. When discussing team or organizational issues, balance critique with self-reflection

This balanced accountability demonstrates maturity and growth orientation—qualities highly valued in behavioral assessment.

THE MISSING METRICS

The Pitfall: Many candidates describe results in vague, qualitative terms rather than providing specific, quantifiable outcomes. This lack of measurement undermines the credibility and impact of their examples.

Why It Happens: Candidates sometimes fail to track or recall specific metrics from their experiences. There's also sometimes uncertainty about which metrics are most relevant or impressive.

How Interviewers Perceive It: Vague results suggest either limited impact or lack of results orientation. Without specific metrics, interviewers struggle to assess the significance of the candidate's contribution.

Prevention Strategy: Quantify impact whenever possible:

1. For each prepared story, identify at least 2-3 specific metrics that demonstrate impact

2. Include both technical metrics (performance improvement, error reduction) and business metrics (revenue impact, cost savings, user adoption)

3. Use comparative measurements when absolute numbers aren't available: "reduced latency by approximately 40%" rather than "made it much faster"

4. When exact numbers aren't available, provide reasonable estimates with appropriate framing: "While I don't recall the exact figure, it was approximately a 30% improvement"

This quantification transforms vague claims into credible evidence of impact.

THE EXAGGERATION ESCALATION

The Pitfall: Under pressure to impress, some candidates exaggerate their role, contribution, or the impact of their actions. While potentially effective in the short term, these exaggerations often collapse under follow-up questions, severely damaging credibility.

Why It Happens: This pattern stems from anxiety about measuring up to perceived expectations and sometimes from misunderstanding what actually impresses interviewers.

How Interviewers Perceive It: Experienced interviewers are skilled at detecting inconsistencies or implausible claims. Identified exaggerations create doubt about everything the candidate has shared, even truthful elements.

Prevention Strategy: Maintain rigorous authenticity:

1. Prepare stories with sufficient legitimate impact that exaggeration is unnecessary

2. Focus on your actual contribution rather than claiming broader impact

3. Use precise, qualified language rather than absolute statements

4. Be prepared to explain exactly how you achieved the results you're claiming

This authentic approach builds sustainable credibility that withstands detailed examination.

THE COMPETENCY MISMATCH

The Pitfall: Even when sharing relevant stories, candidates sometimes emphasize aspects that don't align with the competency being assessed. For example, focusing on technical details when asked about leadership, or discussing project outcomes when asked about conflict resolution.

Why It Happens: This misalignment typically occurs when candidates don't clearly identify the core competency behind each question or when they have a preferred aspect of the story they want to emphasize regardless of the question.

How Interviewers Perceive It: Competency misalignment suggests either limited understanding of the capability being assessed or limited experience demonstrating it—both concerning signals.

Prevention Strategy: Maintain competency alignment:

1. For each question, explicitly identify the primary competency being assessed

2. Adapt your prepared stories to emphasize the aspects most relevant to that competency

3. Use phrases that directly connect to the competency: "This demonstrates my approach to leadership because..."

4. Review your response mentally before concluding to ensure you've directly addressed the competency

This alignment ensures your examples actually demonstrate what interviewers are assessing.

5.4. THE FOLLOW-UP QUESTION PITFALLS

How you handle follow-up questions often matters more than your initial response, yet many candidates underprepare for this critical phase. Let's examine common follow-up pitfalls and strategies to overcome them.

Table 9. Follow-Up Question Pitfalls

Pitfall	Description
The Defensive Reaction	Perceiving follow-up questions as challenges rather than opportunities, triggering defensive responses that undermine rapport.
The Contradiction Trap	Providing follow-up answers that contradict initial responses, creating credibility issues and communication concerns.
The Brevity Problem	Offering overly brief responses to follow-ups, missing chances to demonstrate depth of experience.
The Tangent Diversion	Diverting to unrelated topics when faced with challenging follow-ups, suggesting evasion of questions.

Pitfall	Description
The Overelaboration Trap	Providing excessive detail in follow-up responses, potentially introducing new inconsistencies or confusion.

THE DEFENSIVE REACTION

The Pitfall: Some candidates perceive follow-up questions as challenges or criticisms rather than opportunities for elaboration. This perception triggers defensive responses that undermine rapport and suggest limited receptiveness to feedback.

Why It Happens: Under interview pressure, follow-up questions can feel like skepticism or criticism rather than natural exploration. This perception activates defensive mechanisms.

How Interviewers Perceive It: Defensive responses to follow-ups raise concerns about how the candidate handles feedback and questioning in professional settings—a critical capability for technical roles.

Prevention Strategy: Reframe follow-ups as opportunities:

1. Recognize that detailed follow-ups often signal interest rather than skepticism

2. Respond to challenging questions with curiosity rather than defensiveness: "That's a great question..."

3. View follow-ups as chances to provide additional evidence of your capabilities

4. Practice with a partner who asks increasingly challenging follow-ups to build resilience

This positive reframing transforms potentially stressful interactions into opportunities to strengthen your assessment.

THE CONTRADICTION TRAP

The Pitfall: Under pressure, some candidates provide follow-up responses that contradict elements of their initial answer. These inconsistencies severely undermine credibility and suggest either fabrication or poor communication.

Why It Happens: This typically occurs when candidates haven't thoroughly prepared the details of their examples or when they modify their story to address perceived concerns in follow-up questions.

How Interviewers Perceive It: Contradictions create fundamental doubt about the authenticity of the candidate's examples and their ability to communicate accurately.

Prevention Strategy: Maintain narrative consistency:

1. Prepare your stories in sufficient detail that you can confidently address follow-ups

2. Take a moment to recall your initial response before answering follow-ups

3. If you need to clarify or correct something, explicitly acknowledge it: "I should clarify my earlier point..."

4. If you're unsure about a detail, be honest rather than inventing information: "I don't recall the exact timeline, but it was approximately..."

This consistency builds and maintains the credibility essential for effective behavioral responses.

THE BREVITY PROBLEM

The Pitfall: Some candidates provide extremely brief responses to follow-up questions, missing opportunities to share additional evidence of their capabilities. These minimal answers often create the impression of limited depth or experience.

Why It Happens: This typically stems from anxiety about talking too much or uncertainty about how much detail is appropriate in follow-ups.

How Interviewers Perceive It: Overly brief follow-up responses suggest either limited depth of experience or reluctance to share details—both concerning signals.

Prevention Strategy: Develop appropriate depth:

1. Aim for follow-up responses that provide new information rather than merely restating your initial answer

2. Use the "answer plus one" approach: provide the direct answer plus one additional relevant insight or detail

3. Watch for interviewer engagement signals to calibrate appropriate depth

4. Prepare detailed aspects of your stories specifically for potential follow-ups

This appropriate depth demonstrates the richness of your experience without becoming excessive.

THE TANGENT DIVERSION

The Pitfall: When faced with challenging follow-ups, some candidates divert to tangential aspects of their example or entirely different topics. These diversions suggest evasion and prevent interviewers from assessing the specific competency they're exploring.

Why It Happens: This typically occurs when candidates are uncomfortable with the direction of questioning or lack a strong response to the specific follow-up.

How Interviewers Perceive It: Tangent diversions suggest either evasion of difficult questions or inability to maintain focused communication—both concerning signals.

Prevention Strategy: Maintain topical discipline:

1. Address the specific question directly before adding any additional context

2. If you need to provide context for your answer, explicitly connect it back to the question

3. If you truly don't have a strong response to a specific follow-up, acknowledge it briefly and offer an alternative perspective: "While I didn't approach it that way in this situation, in a similar case I..."

4. Practice recognizing and redirecting from tangents during preparation

This topical discipline demonstrates focused communication and willingness to address difficult questions directly.

5.5. ROLE-SPECIFIC PITFALLS

Different technical roles face distinct behavioral interview challenges. Let's examine pitfalls specific to common technical positions and strategies to overcome them.

SOFTWARE ENGINEER PITFALLS

Software engineers often face these specific challenges:

Technical Tunnel Vision: Focusing exclusively on technical implementation details rather than broader impact, collaboration, or problem-solving approaches.

Prevention Strategy: For each story, explicitly identify both technical and non-technical elements. Practice articulating the "why" behind technical decisions and connecting technical work to business outcomes.

Individual Contributor Mindset: Emphasizing personal technical contribution without demonstrating influence, mentorship, or cross-functional collaboration.

Prevention Strategy: Prepare examples that show how you've influenced decisions, helped others grow, or worked effectively across team boundaries, even without formal authority.

Ambiguity Avoidance: Sharing only examples with clear requirements and straightforward implementation, rather than demonstrating comfort with uncertainty and changing priorities.

Prevention Strategy: Include stories that show how you've navigated ambiguity, made decisions with incomplete information, or adapted to changing requirements—capabilities highly valued in senior engineering roles.

ENGINEERING MANAGER PITFALLS

Engineering managers often face these specific challenges:

Tactical Focus: Emphasizing day-to-day management activities rather than strategic leadership, vision setting, or organizational impact.

Prevention Strategy: Prepare examples that demonstrate how you've shaped direction, influenced beyond your team, and connected technical decisions to broader business strategy.

Technical Identity Loss: Either over-emphasizing or completely neglecting technical contributions, rather than demonstrating the balanced technical leadership expected of engineering managers.

Prevention Strategy: Include stories that show how your technical judgment informed leadership decisions and how you've balanced hands-on contribution with team enablement.

Direct Authority Reliance: Describing leadership primarily through formal authority rather than influence, coaching, and team development.

Prevention Strategy: Prepare examples that show how you've led through inspiration and development rather than directive management, particularly in challenging circumstances.

SOLUTION ARCHITECT PITFALLS

Solution architects often face these specific challenges:

Design Without Delivery: Focusing on architectural decisions without demonstrating follow-through to successful implementation and business impact.

Prevention Strategy: Include examples that show your involvement throughout the solution lifecycle, from initial concept through implementation and measurement of outcomes.

Technical Depth Without Breadth: Demonstrating deep expertise in specific technologies without showing the broad technical understanding and integration capabilities essential for architectural roles.

Prevention Strategy: Prepare stories that demonstrate your ability to work across multiple technical domains, integrate diverse systems, and make appropriate technology selection decisions.

Missing Stakeholder Dimension: Describing architectural decisions purely in technical terms without addressing stakeholder management, requirement balancing, or organizational alignment.

Prevention Strategy: Include examples that show how you've navigated competing stakeholder priorities, translated business needs into technical solutions, and built consensus around architectural approaches.

PROGRAM MANAGER PITFALLS

Program managers often face these specific challenges:

Process Over Outcomes: Emphasizing program management processes and methodologies rather than business results and value delivery.

Prevention Strategy: For each example, explicitly connect your program management approach to measurable business outcomes and stakeholder value.

Conflict Avoidance: Describing only harmonious projects rather than demonstrating effective navigation of the conflicts and competing priorities inherent in program management.

Prevention Strategy: Include examples that show how you've productively addressed conflicts, made difficult prioritization decisions, and aligned diverse stakeholders around common goals.

Execution Without Strategy: Focusing on tactical delivery without demonstrating strategic thinking, business alignment, or organizational impact.

Prevention Strategy: Prepare stories that show how you've shaped program strategy, connected execution to business objectives, and influenced organizational direction beyond day-to-day delivery.

5.6. THE RECOVERY STRATEGIES

Despite thorough preparation, you may occasionally fall into one of these pitfalls during an actual interview. When this happens, recovery strategies can help minimize the damage and potentially turn a negative moment into a positive impression.

Table 10. Recovery Strategies

Strategy	Description
The Clarification Reset	Acknowledge misalignment and redirect to a more relevant example that better addresses the question.
The Concise Correction	Recognize when providing excessive detail and refocus on the key behavioral aspects being assessed.
The Ownership Pivot	Shift from blaming external factors to demonstrating accountability and lessons learned.
The Metric Addition	Circle back to provide concrete metrics that quantify impact when initially omitted.
The Follow-Up Leverage	Use follow-up questions as opportunities to strengthen weak initial responses with additional evidence.

THE CLARIFICATION RESET

If you realize you're not addressing the actual question or competency being assessed:

1. Briefly acknowledge the misalignment: "I realize I may not be addressing your specific question about leadership..."

2. Reorient to the actual competency: "Let me share a more relevant example that better demonstrates how I've led through influence..."

3. Transition to a more appropriate example or refocus your current example on relevant aspects

This reset demonstrates self-awareness and adaptability—valuable qualities that can partially offset the initial misalignment.

THE CONCISE CORRECTION

If you catch yourself providing excessive context or technical detail:

1. Recognize the pattern: "I realize I'm getting into more technical detail than necessary..."

2. Refocus on the behavioral aspect: "The key point from a leadership perspective was..."

3. Transition to the most relevant aspects of your example

This correction demonstrates communication awareness and ability to adjust—qualities that mitigate concerns about excessive detail.

THE OWNERSHIP PIVOT

If you notice yourself deflecting responsibility or blaming others:

1. Acknowledge the pattern: "I want to clarify that while there were external factors..."

2. Take appropriate ownership: "I recognize that I could have anticipated these challenges earlier..."

3. Demonstrate learning: "This experience taught me the importance of..."

This pivot demonstrates accountability and self-awareness—qualities that can transform a negative signal into a positive one.

THE METRIC ADDITION

If you realize you've described results without specific metrics:

1. Circle back explicitly: "Let me add some specific metrics to quantify the impact..."

2. Provide concrete numbers: "We reduced latency by 42% and increased conversion by approximately 18%..."

3. Connect to business value: "This translated to roughly $300,000 in additional quarterly revenue..."

This addition demonstrates results orientation and precision—qualities that strengthen your overall response.

THE FOLLOW-UP LEVERAGE

If your initial response was weaker than intended, use follow-up questions as opportunities to strengthen your position:

1. Provide additional context or details that clarify your contribution

2. Share metrics or outcomes not mentioned in your initial response

3. Articulate lessons learned if you didn't include them initially

4. Address potential concerns proactively rather than defensively

This leverage demonstrates depth of experience and thoughtfulness—qualities that can significantly enhance your overall assessment.

5.7. CONCLUSION: FROM PITFALLS TO PEAK PERFORMANCE

Behavioral interview pitfalls aren't inevitable traps—they're predictable patterns that can be systematically avoided with proper awareness and preparation. By understanding these common mistakes and implementing specific prevention strategies, you transform potential weaknesses into opportunities to demonstrate your communication skills, self-awareness, and preparation thoroughness.

Remember that interviewers aren't looking for perfect candidates who've never made mistakes. They're looking for candidates who:

- Prepare thoroughly and thoughtfully

- Communicate clearly and effectively

- Demonstrate self-awareness and growth orientation

- Take ownership of both successes and failures

- Adapt appropriately to different questions and situations

The strategies in this chapter help you demonstrate these exact qualities—not by creating an artificial persona, but by presenting your authentic experiences and capabilities in the most effective possible light.

In the next chapter, we'll build on this foundation by developing a systematic practice plan that helps you internalize these concepts and build the muscle memory needed for consistent, effective behavioral interviewing.

CHAPTER 6. YOUR WEEKLY PRACTICE PLAN

> We are what we repeatedly do. Excellence, then, is not an act, but a habit.
>
> — Aristotle

Understanding behavioral interview concepts is necessary but insufficient. Knowing the STAR+ framework, identifying your stories, and recognizing common pitfalls won't automatically translate into effective interview performance. Like any complex skill, behavioral interviewing requires deliberate practice to develop the muscle memory, confidence, and adaptability needed for excellence under pressure.

Yet most candidates practice haphazardly, if at all. They might rehearse a few answers alone in their car or hastily run through examples the night before an interview. This approach rarely builds the deep competence needed for high-stakes technical interviews at companies like Amazon, Google, Meta, and Microsoft.

In this chapter, we'll develop a systematic, progressive practice plan that transforms theoretical knowledge into practical mastery. We'll create a structured four-week program that builds your capabilities incrementally, provides concrete activities for each stage of development, and includes specific tools to measure your progress. By the end, you'll have not just a conceptual understanding of behavioral interviewing, but the practiced capability to demonstrate your true potential when it matters most.

6.1. THE SCIENCE OF EFFECTIVE PRACTICE

Before diving into specific practice activities, let's understand the principles that make practice effective—particularly for complex communication skills like behavioral interviewing.

DELIBERATE PRACTICE PRINCIPLES

Research on expertise development, particularly the work of psychologist Anders Ericsson, has identified key principles that distinguish effective "deliberate practice" from mere repetition:

FOCUSED IMPROVEMENT

Effective practice targets specific aspects of performance rather than generally "getting better." Each practice session should focus on particular skills or components with clear improvement goals.

Application to Behavioral Interviews: Rather than generally "practicing answers," focus sessions on specific elements like concise situation descriptions, quantifying results, or handling follow-up questions.

APPROPRIATE CHALLENGE

Practice should be challenging but achievable—pushing beyond current capabilities without being overwhelming. This "stretch zone" creates optimal conditions for skill development.

Application to Behavioral Interviews: Progressively increase difficulty by moving from prepared questions to unexpected ones, from friendly practice partners to more critical ones, and from basic competencies to more complex scenarios.

IMMEDIATE FEEDBACK

Effective practice includes prompt, specific feedback that identifies both strengths and improvement areas. This feedback loop accelerates development and prevents reinforcing suboptimal patterns.

Application to Behavioral Interviews: Record practice sessions for self-review and arrange structured feedback from knowledgeable practice partners using specific evaluation criteria.

REFLECTIVE ADJUSTMENT

Beyond receiving feedback, effective practice involves thoughtful reflection on performance and deliberate adjustment of approach based on that reflection.

Application to Behavioral Interviews: After each practice session, document specific strengths, weaknesses, and adjustment strategies. Begin subsequent sessions by reviewing and implementing these adjustments.

DISTRIBUTED PRACTICE

Research consistently shows that distributing practice over time is more effective than "cramming" immediately before performance. This spacing effect strengthens neural pathways and improves retention.

Application to Behavioral Interviews: Begin preparation at least 3-4 weeks before interviews, with regular, shorter practice sessions rather than marathon preparation immediately before.

THE PERFORMANCE-PRACTICE GAP

A critical insight from performance psychology is that practice conditions should progressively approach performance conditions to minimize the "performance-practice gap"—the disconnect between how we practice and how we actually perform under pressure.

For behavioral interviews, this means:

- **Simulating Time Pressure**: Practice with actual time constraints similar to real interviews

- **Creating Evaluation Stress**: Practice with observers who provide critical feedback

- **Handling Interruptions**: Practice with partners who ask follow-up questions mid-response

- **Managing Technology**: Practice using the same technology (video conferencing, etc.) as actual interviews

- **Replicating Physical Conditions**: Practice while dressed professionally in an interview-like environment

As your practice progresses, these elements should increasingly mirror actual interview conditions to build performance-specific confidence and capability.

6.2. THE FOUR-WEEK PRACTICE FRAMEWORK

With these principles in mind, let's develop a structured four-week practice plan that progressively builds your behavioral interviewing capabilities. This framework assumes 3-4 hours of dedicated practice per week, though you can adjust the timeline based on your schedule and proximity to actual interviews.

WEEK 1: FOUNDATION BUILDING

The first week focuses on developing your story inventory and building basic STAR+ structure without the pressure of full interview simulation.

DAY 1: STORY INVENTORY DEVELOPMENT (60 MINUTES)

- Complete the Story Discovery Worksheet from Chapter 4 for at least 5-7 high-value experiences

- Evaluate each story against the high-value criteria (impact, contribution, complexity, growth, alignment)

- Create your initial Story Matrix mapping stories to key competencies

DAY 2: STAR+ STRUCTURE PRACTICE (45 MINUTES)

- Select 3 of your strongest stories
- Write complete STAR+ outlines for each, with bullet points for each component
- Review for balance across components (appropriate time allocation for each element)
- Identify specific metrics and concrete details to include

DAY 3: COMPONENT FOCUS - SITUATION & TASK (45 MINUTES)

- Practice delivering just the Situation and Task components for 5 different stories
- Focus on conciseness (30 seconds maximum) while providing essential context
- Record yourself and review for clarity, conciseness, and completeness
- Refine your approach based on self-assessment

DAY 4: COMPONENT FOCUS - ACTION (45 MINUTES)

- Practice delivering just the Action component for 5 different stories
- Focus on specificity, logical sequence, and personal contribution
- Record yourself and review for clarity, specificity, and emphasis on "I" vs. "we"
- Refine your approach based on self-assessment

DAY 5: COMPONENT FOCUS - RESULT & PLUS (45 MINUTES)

- Practice delivering just the Result and Plus components for 5 different stories

- Focus on quantification, business impact, and specific lessons learned

- Record yourself and review for concreteness, impact emphasis, and reflection depth

- Refine your approach based on self-assessment

WEEK 2: INTEGRATION AND FLOW

The second week focuses on integrating the STAR+ components into complete responses and developing natural delivery flow.

DAY 1: COMPLETE STAR+ INTEGRATION (60 MINUTES)

- Practice delivering complete STAR+ responses for 3 different stories

- Focus on smooth transitions between components and overall narrative flow

- Record yourself and review for component balance, logical progression, and engagement

- Refine your approach based on self-assessment

DAY 2: TIME MANAGEMENT PRACTICE (45 MINUTES)

- Practice delivering complete STAR+ responses within specific time constraints:

  - 2-minute version (ultra-concise for screening interviews)

  - 3-minute version (standard for most behavioral questions)

  - 5-minute version (detailed for in-depth exploration)

- Record yourself and review for appropriate detail level at each time constraint
- Refine your approach based on self-assessment

DAY 3: FIRST FEEDBACK SESSION (60 MINUTES)

- Arrange a practice session with a knowledgeable partner (colleague, friend, mentor)
- Provide them with 5-7 standard behavioral questions in advance
- Deliver complete STAR+ responses to at least 3 questions
- Request specific feedback on structure, content, delivery, and impact
- Document feedback and identify specific improvement areas

DAY 4: FOLLOW-UP QUESTION PRACTICE (45 MINUTES)

- With the same practice partner, focus specifically on follow-up questions
- Deliver a complete STAR+ response to one question
- Have your partner ask 5-7 follow-up questions of increasing depth
- Focus on maintaining consistency, providing new information, and avoiding defensiveness
- Document specific follow-up question types that were challenging

DAY 5: REFINEMENT BASED ON FEEDBACK (45 MINUTES)

- Review all feedback received during the week
- Identify 3-5 specific improvement areas
- Practice modified delivery addressing these specific areas
- Record yourself and assess improvement compared to earlier recordings

WEEK 3: COMPETENCY AND COMPANY FOCUS

The third week focuses on tailoring your responses to specific competencies and company cultures.

DAY 1: LEADERSHIP COMPETENCY FOCUS (60 MINUTES)

- Identify your 2-3 strongest leadership stories
- Practice tailoring these stories to specific leadership questions:
  - "Tell me about a time when you led a team through a difficult situation."
  - "Describe a situation where you had to influence without authority."
  - "Give me an example of how you've developed team members."
- Record yourself and review for leadership emphasis and evidence

DAY 2: PROBLEM-SOLVING COMPETENCY FOCUS (45 MINUTES)

- Identify your 2-3 strongest problem-solving stories
- Practice tailoring these stories to specific problem-solving questions:
  - "Tell me about a complex problem you solved."
  - "Describe a situation where you had to make a decision with incomplete information."
  - "Give me an example of an innovative solution you developed."
- Record yourself and review for problem-solving emphasis and evidence

DAY 3: COMPANY-SPECIFIC TAILORING (60 MINUTES)

- Select one target company (Amazon, Google, Meta, or Microsoft)
- Research their specific values and behavioral assessment approach

- Practice tailoring 3 of your stories to align with their particular emphasis:
  - For Amazon: Leadership Principles alignment
  - For Google: Learning ability and collaboration emphasis
  - For Meta: Impact and scale orientation
  - For Microsoft: Growth mindset demonstration
- Record yourself and review for company-specific alignment

DAY 4: SECOND FEEDBACK SESSION (60 MINUTES)

- Arrange a practice session with a different partner than Week 2
- Provide them with company-specific questions based on your target organizations
- Deliver complete STAR+ responses tailored to these company contexts
- Request specific feedback on company alignment, competency evidence, and overall impact
- Document feedback and identify specific improvement areas

DAY 5: UNEXPECTED QUESTION PRACTICE (45 MINUTES)

- Have a practice partner ask 5 behavioral questions you haven't specifically prepared for
- Practice quickly identifying which of your prepared stories can be adapted to these questions
- Focus on maintaining STAR+ structure while adapting content to unexpected prompts
- Document which types of unexpected questions were most challenging

WEEK 4: SIMULATION AND REFINEMENT

The final week focuses on realistic interview simulation and targeted refinement of remaining improvement areas.

DAY 1: FULL INTERVIEW SIMULATION (90 MINUTES)

- Arrange a comprehensive practice interview with a knowledgeable partner
- Simulate a complete 45-minute behavioral interview with 5-7 questions
- Include appropriate introduction, rapport building, and candidate questions
- Record the full simulation for detailed review
- Request comprehensive feedback on all aspects of your performance

DAY 2: SIMULATION REVIEW AND TARGETED PRACTICE (60 MINUTES)

- Review the full interview simulation recording
- Identify 3 specific strengths to maintain and 3 specific areas for improvement
- Conduct targeted practice focusing exclusively on the improvement areas
- Record this targeted practice and assess improvement

DAY 3: STRESS CONDITION PRACTICE (45 MINUTES)

- Practice delivering responses under deliberately stressful conditions:
  - Time pressure (shorter than normal time limits)
  - Interruptions during your responses
  - Skeptical or challenging feedback

- ° Distracting environment

- Focus on maintaining structure and composure despite these challenges

- Reflect on specific stress responses and develop mitigation strategies

DAY 4: FINAL FEEDBACK SESSION (60 MINUTES)

- Arrange a final practice session with your most experienced or knowledgeable contact

- Focus on your 3-5 most challenging questions or competency areas

- Request brutally honest feedback on remaining improvement opportunities

- Develop specific strategies to address any final concerns

DAY 5: CONFIDENCE BUILDING AND MENTAL PREPARATION (45 MINUTES)

- Review recordings from Week 1 and compare to Week 4 to observe improvement

- Practice positive visualization of successful interview performance

- Develop specific pre-interview routines for optimal mental state

- Create concise reminder cards with key points for each major story

- Finalize your Story Matrix for quick reference during actual interviews

6.3. DOWNLOADABLE RESOURCES AND PROGRESS TRACKERS

To support your practice plan, let's develop specific tools that structure your preparation and measure your progress.

THE STORY DEVELOPMENT TRACKER

This tool helps you systematically develop and refine your key stories:

Story Title	Initial Outline Complete	STAR+ Components Balanced	Metrics Identified	Lessons Articulated	Company Tailoring Complete
Authentication Service Incident	☐	☐	☐	☐	Amazon, Google
Cross-Platform Feature Development	☐	☐	☐	☐	Meta, Microsoft
Team Reorganization	☐	☐	☐	☐	Amazon
Performance Optimization Project	☐	☐	☐		Google, Meta
Difficult Stakeholder Situation	☐	☐			Amazon, Microsoft
Failed Product Launch	☐				

Story Title	Initial Outline Complete	STAR+ Components Balanced	Metrics Identified	Lessons Articulated	Company Tailoring Complete
Mentoring Junior Engineers	☐	☐	☐	☐	Microsoft
Legacy System Modernization	☐	☐	☐		Google
Customer Escalation Resolution	☐	☐	☐	☐	Amazon, Meta
Innovation Initiative	☐	☐			Google, Microsoft

This tracker provides a visual overview of your story development progress and identifies specific areas needing additional work.

THE PRACTICE SESSION PLANNER

This tool structures individual practice sessions for maximum effectiveness:

Practice Focus	Duration	Date Completed
Story Inventory Development	60 min	
STAR+ Structure Practice	45 min	
Component Focus - Situation & Task	45 min	

Practice Focus	Duration	Date Completed
Component Focus - Action	45 min	
Component Focus - Result & Plus	45 min	
Complete STAR+ Integration	60 min	
Time Management Practice	45 min	
First Feedback Session	60 min	
Follow-Up Question Practice	45 min	
Refinement Based on Feedback	45 min	
Leadership Competency Focus	60 min	
Problem-Solving Competency Focus	45 min	
Company-Specific Tailoring	60 min	
Second Feedback Session	60 min	
Unexpected Question Practice	45 min	
Full Interview Simulation	90 min	
Simulation Review and Targeted Practice	60 min	
Stress Condition Practice	45 min	
Final Feedback Session	60 min	
Confidence Building and Mental Preparation	45 min	

This planner helps you schedule and track completion of each practice component, ensuring comprehensive preparation.

THE FEEDBACK CAPTURE FORM

This tool structures feedback from practice partners for maximum learning value:

Element	Feedback
Overall Structure	Was the STAR+ structure clear and complete? Was there appropriate balance between components?
Situation Clarity	Was the context clear and concise? Did it provide necessary background without excessive detail?
Task Specificity	Was your specific responsibility clear? Was the challenge or objective well defined?
Action Detail	Were your specific actions clear? Was your personal contribution distinct from team efforts?
Result Impact	Were outcomes quantified? Was business impact clear? Were results connected to your actions?
Lessons Learned	Were insights meaningful? Have they been applied subsequently? Do they show growth?
Delivery Quality	Was your communication clear, confident, and engaging? Was pacing appropriate?
Follow-Up Handling	How effectively did you address follow-up questions? Were responses consistent and detailed?
Overall Impact	What was the overall impression? Would this response positively influence a hiring decision?
Key Strengths	What 2-3 aspects were most effective and should be maintained?
Improvement Areas	What 2-3 specific aspects could be improved for greater effectiveness?

This structured feedback form ensures you receive specific, actionable input rather than general impressions.

THE COMPETENCY EVIDENCE EVALUATOR

This tool helps you assess how effectively your stories demonstrate specific competencies:

Competency	Story 1	Story 2	Story 3	Story 4	Story 5
Vision and Strategy	☐☐☐	☐☐	☐☐☐☐	☐	☐☐☐
Influence and Persuasion	☐☐	☐☐☐☐	☐☐☐	☐☐	☐
Team Development	☐	☐☐	☐☐☐☐	☐☐☐	☐☐
Decision Making	☐☐☐☐	☐☐☐	☐☐	☐☐☐	☐☐☐☐
Change Management	☐☐	☐	☐☐☐☐	☐☐	☐☐☐
Analytical Thinking	☐☐☐☐	☐☐☐	☐☐	☐☐☐☐	☐☐
Innovation	☐☐☐	☐☐☐☐	☐	☐☐☐	☐☐☐☐
Technical Excellence	☐☐☐☐	☐☐☐	☐☐	☐☐☐☐	☐☐☐
Judgment	☐☐☐	☐☐☐☐	☐☐☐	☐☐	☐☐☐
Systems Thinking	☐☐☐☐	☐☐	☐☐☐	☐☐☐☐	☐☐

This evaluator helps identify which stories most effectively demonstrate which competencies, guiding your selection during actual interviews.

THE INTERVIEW SIMULATION SCORECARD

This tool provides comprehensive assessment of full interview simulations:

Element	Poor (1)	Developing (2)	Proficient (3)	Excellent (4)
STAR+ Structure	Incomplete or unclear structure	Basic structure present but imbalanced	Clear structure with good component balance	Seamless structure with optimal component balance
Situation/Task Clarity	Vague or excessive context	Basic context established	Clear, concise context	Perfectly calibrated context setting
Action Specificity	General or team-focused actions	Some specific personal actions	Clear personal actions with good detail	Highly specific actions with optimal detail
Result Quantification	Vague or missing results	Basic results mentioned	Quantified results with clear impact	Comprehensive results with business connection
Reflection Quality	Missing or superficial reflection	Basic lessons identified	Meaningful insights with application	Profound insights with clear application
Example Relevance	Examples poorly matched to questions	Examples adequately address questions	Examples well matched to questions	Examples perfectly aligned with questions

Element	Poor (1)	Developing (2)	Proficient (3)	Excellent (4)
Competency Evidence	Limited evidence of target competencies	Some evidence of target competencies	Strong evidence of target competencies	Exceptional evidence of target competencies
Follow-Up Handling	Defensive or contradictory responses	Adequate but limited responses	Strong, consistent responses	Exceptional, enhancing responses
Communication Clarity	Unclear or disorganized	Generally clear with some issues	Clear and well-organized	Exceptionally clear and compelling
Overall Impact	Unlikely to positively influence hiring	Might positively influence hiring	Likely to positively influence hiring	Highly likely to positively influence hiring

This scorecard provides a comprehensive assessment of your interview performance across multiple dimensions, identifying both strengths and improvement opportunities.

6.4. PRACTICE PARTNER SELECTION AND GUIDANCE

The quality of your practice partners significantly impacts the effectiveness of your preparation. Let's explore how to select and guide practice partners for maximum benefit.

SELECTING EFFECTIVE PRACTICE PARTNERS

Ideal practice partners bring different perspectives and capabilities to your preparation:

TECHNICAL PEERS

Fellow engineers or technical professionals who understand the context of your examples and can provide credible feedback on technical aspects.

What They Offer:

- Technical credibility assessment
- Realistic follow-up questions
- Peer-level perspective

Best For:

- Technical content validation
- Industry-specific feedback
- Realistic technical follow-ups

CURRENT OR FORMER MANAGERS

Leaders who have conducted actual technical interviews and understand evaluation from the interviewer's perspective.

What They Offer:

- Interviewer perspective
- Leadership competency assessment
- Strategic impact evaluation

Best For:

- Leadership story feedback

- Strategic impact assessment

- Interviewer mindset insights

NON-TECHNICAL OBSERVERS

Friends or family members without technical background who can assess the clarity and impact of your communication.

What They Offer:

- Communication clarity assessment

- Non-technical impact evaluation

- Fresh perspective on delivery

Best For:

- Communication effectiveness

- Explanation clarity

- General impression feedback

PROFESSIONAL COACHES

Interview coaches or career professionals with specific behavioral interview expertise.

What They Offer:

- Structured evaluation methodology

- Company-specific insights

- Professional development perspective

Best For:

- Comprehensive assessment
- Advanced technique refinement
- Professional polish

Ideally, your practice should include feedback from multiple partner types to develop a comprehensive understanding of your effectiveness across different dimensions.

GUIDING YOUR PRACTICE PARTNERS

Even the most qualified practice partners need guidance to provide maximally useful feedback. Here's how to structure their involvement:

PRE-SESSION BRIEFING

Before each practice session, provide your partners with:

- Specific focus areas for the session (structure, content, delivery, etc.)
- Background on the STAR+ framework if they're unfamiliar
- Context about your target companies and roles
- The Feedback Capture Form to structure their observations

DURING-SESSION GUIDANCE

During practice sessions, ask your partners to:

- Take notes on specific aspects rather than general impressions
- Interrupt only if you've requested real-time feedback
- Note both effective elements and improvement opportunities

- Track time to help you develop appropriate pacing

POST-SESSION DEBRIEF

After practice sessions, guide your partners to:

- Provide specific examples rather than general assessments
- Balance positive feedback with improvement opportunities
- Focus on content and structure more than delivery style
- Suggest specific adjustments rather than vague recommendations

This structured guidance ensures you receive specific, actionable feedback rather than general impressions or unhelpful criticism.

6.5. SPECIALIZED PRACTICE TECHNIQUES

Beyond the core practice framework, certain specialized techniques can accelerate your development in specific areas. Let's explore these targeted approaches.

THE RAPID RESPONSE DRILL

This technique builds your ability to quickly identify and adapt appropriate stories for unexpected questions.

How It Works:

1. Create or obtain a list of 20+ varied behavioral questions
2. Have a practice partner randomly select questions
3. Give yourself just 30 seconds to identify which prepared story to use
4. Briefly explain why you selected that story and how you'd adapt it

5. Move immediately to the next question without delivering the full response

This rapid-fire approach builds the mental agility needed to handle unexpected questions without becoming flustered or defaulting to inappropriate examples.

THE COMPONENT ISOLATION EXERCISE

This technique develops mastery of specific STAR+ components that may be challenging for you.

How It Works:

1. Identify your weakest STAR+ component based on feedback
2. Practice delivering ONLY that component for multiple stories in succession
3. Record and review each attempt, focusing on specific improvement
4. Gradually increase the difficulty by adding constraints:
   - Stricter time limits
   - More complex examples
   - Interruptions during delivery

This focused repetition builds strength in specific components before reintegrating them into complete responses.

THE FOLLOW-UP GAUNTLET

This technique specifically builds resilience and adaptability in handling challenging follow-up questions.

How It Works:

1. Deliver a complete STAR+ response to a standard question

2. Have 2-3 practice partners take turns asking increasingly challenging follow-ups:

    ◦ Clarification questions about details

    ◦ Skeptical questions challenging your approach

    ◦ Hypothetical questions extending your example

    ◦ Probing questions about your reasoning

3. Continue until you struggle significantly or for a predetermined time (typically 10-15 minutes)

4. Debrief on which follow-up types were most challenging

This intensive follow-up practice builds confidence in handling even the most challenging interview dynamics.

THE VIDEO ANALYSIS PROTOCOL

This technique uses detailed video analysis to identify subtle improvement opportunities that might otherwise be missed.

How It Works:

1. Record a complete practice interview session

2. Review the recording with structured analysis:

    ◦ Watch once for overall impression

    ◦ Watch again focusing only on content

    ◦ Watch a third time focusing only on delivery

    ◦ Watch a final time focusing on non-verbal communication

3. Document specific observations in each dimension

4. Identify patterns across multiple responses

5. Develop targeted improvement strategies for each pattern

This multi-dimensional analysis reveals subtle patterns that might not be apparent from a single viewing or from partner feedback alone.

THE STRESS INOCULATION METHOD

This technique deliberately introduces stress to build resilience for high-pressure interview situations.

How It Works:

1. Identify your specific stress responses from previous high-pressure situations
2. Create practice conditions that deliberately trigger these responses:
   - Time pressure (tighter than normal limits)
   - Interruptions during responses
   - Skeptical facial expressions or body language
   - Challenging or critical feedback
   - Distracting environment
3. Practice maintaining structure and composure despite these challenges
4. Gradually increase stress factors as your resilience improves

This progressive stress exposure builds confidence in your ability to perform effectively even under significant pressure.

6.6. ADAPTING THE PLAN TO YOUR TIMELINE

While the four-week framework provides comprehensive preparation, your specific circumstances might require adaptation. Here's how to modify the plan for different timelines:

ACCELERATED PREPARATION (1-2 WEEKS)

If you have limited time before interviews:

1. Focus on developing 5-7 strong stories rather than a comprehensive inventory

2. Prioritize full STAR+ practice over component-specific work

3. Concentrate on company-specific tailoring for your immediate target

4. Arrange at least two feedback sessions, even if brief

5. Conduct at least one full interview simulation

This accelerated approach ensures you develop the most critical capabilities even with limited preparation time.

EXTENDED PREPARATION (6-8 WEEKS)

If you have more time available:

1. Develop a more comprehensive story inventory (12-15 stories)

2. Include more specialized practice techniques

3. Conduct multiple company-specific tailoring sessions

4. Arrange feedback from a wider range of practice partners

5. Include multiple full interview simulations with different partners

6. Add specific sessions focusing on non-verbal communication

This extended approach allows for more comprehensive development and refinement across all aspects of behavioral interviewing.

ONGOING MAINTENANCE (BETWEEN INTERVIEW CYCLES)

If you're maintaining readiness between interview cycles:

1. Conduct monthly "refresher" sessions to maintain core skills
2. Update your story inventory with new experiences as they occur
3. Practice adapting existing stories to new question formats
4. Arrange occasional feedback sessions to prevent skill degradation
5. Conduct full simulations before beginning new interview cycles

This maintenance approach ensures your skills remain sharp without requiring the intensity of initial preparation.

6.7. MEASURING PROGRESS AND READINESS

How do you know when you're actually ready for high-stakes behavioral interviews? Let's develop specific readiness indicators across multiple dimensions.

STRUCTURE MASTERY INDICATORS

You're ready when:

- You consistently deliver complete STAR+ responses without omitting components
- Your component balance is appropriate (not spending excessive time on Situation/Task)
- You transition smoothly between components without awkward pauses
- You maintain structure even when handling unexpected questions

CONTENT MASTERY INDICATORS

You're ready when:

- You can quickly identify appropriate stories for various competencies
- Your examples consistently include specific metrics and concrete details
- You clearly articulate your personal contribution in team contexts
- Your reflection demonstrates meaningful insights and application

DELIVERY MASTERY INDICATORS

You're ready when:

- You communicate clearly and confidently without excessive filler words
- Your pacing is appropriate (neither rushed nor overly slow)
- You maintain engagement through appropriate energy and emphasis
- Your delivery feels natural rather than rehearsed or mechanical

ADAPTABILITY INDICATORS

You're ready when:

- You handle follow-up questions without becoming defensive or confused
- You can adapt prepared stories to unexpected question formats
- You maintain composure even under challenging conditions
- You can adjust your response length based on time constraints

OVERALL READINESS ASSESSMENT

You're fully prepared when:

- Practice partners consistently rate your responses as "Excellent" (4) across most dimensions

- You feel confident in your ability to handle the full range of potential questions

- You have company-specific tailoring completed for all target organizations

- You've successfully completed at least one full interview simulation with positive feedback

This multi-dimensional assessment ensures you're truly ready for high-stakes interviews, not just comfortable with certain aspects of the process.

6.8. CONCLUSION: FROM PRACTICE TO PERFORMANCE

Effective behavioral interview performance isn't a matter of luck or natural talent—it's the predictable result of systematic, deliberate practice. The four-week framework and specialized techniques in this chapter provide a comprehensive approach to developing the capabilities needed for excellence in even the most challenging technical interviews.

Remember that the goal of practice isn't perfection, but authentic excellence—the ability to present your true capabilities in the most effective possible light. Effective practice doesn't create an artificial persona; it removes the barriers that prevent interviewers from seeing your genuine potential.

As you implement this practice plan, you'll likely experience a transformation beyond just interview performance. The skills you're developing—structured communication, specific evidence presentation, thoughtful reflection, and adaptability under pressure—are valuable not just for interviews but for your broader technical career. The ability to clearly articulate your contributions, learnings, and impact will serve you in performance reviews, project presentations, and leadership opportunities long after your interviews are complete.

In the next section of this book, we'll build on this foundation by exploring role-specific examples for different technical positions. These examples will provide concrete models of how the principles and practices we've discussed apply to particular roles and competencies.

PART 3: ROLE AND COMPANY SPECIFIC STRATEGIES

CHAPTER 7. SOFTWARE ENGINEER EXAMPLES

Talk is cheap. Show me the code.

— Linus Torvalds

There are two kinds of software engineers in behavioral interviews: those who say "We optimized the API" and those who explain why they chose Redis over Memcached for the cache layer at 3 AM during a production fire. After conducting enough interviews to recognize the distinct scent of nervous sweat in our meeting rooms, I learned one truth: technical skill gets you the interview, but how you talk about your work gets you the job.

The difference isn't raw ability—it's whether you can dissect a technical decision with the precision of a senior engineer defending a controversial pull request. Over three years and 200+ interviews at Amazon, I saw brilliant coders fail because they treated behavioral questions like a formality, while less experienced candidates won offers by telling specific, thoughtful stories about their mistakes and trade-offs.

This chapter is about bridging that gap. We'll explore behavioral questions specifically targeted at software engineers, analyze what makes an effective software engineering example, and provide detailed STAR+ responses that demonstrate key competencies valued in engineering roles. We'll also examine the nuanced balance between technical depth and behavioral evidence that distinguishes exceptional software engineering interviews from merely adequate ones.

7.1. THE SOFTWARE ENGINEER BEHAVIORAL ASSESSMENT

Before diving into specific examples, let's understand what companies are actually evaluating when they conduct behavioral interviews for software engineering roles.

CORE COMPETENCIES FOR SOFTWARE ENGINEERS

While each company has its own framework, most technical behavioral interviews for software engineers assess some combination of these core competencies:

TECHNICAL DECISION MAKING

- Making sound architectural and design choices
- Evaluating trade-offs between different technical approaches
- Balancing immediate needs with long-term considerations
- Applying appropriate patterns and practices to technical challenges

PROBLEM-SOLVING APPROACH

- Breaking down complex problems systematically
- Navigating ambiguity and incomplete information
- Applying analytical thinking to technical challenges
- Demonstrating creativity in solution development

TECHNICAL LEADERSHIP

- Influencing technical direction without formal authority
- Mentoring and developing other engineers

- Driving technical initiatives and improvements
- Setting and maintaining engineering standards

COLLABORATION AND COMMUNICATION

- Working effectively across engineering teams
- Communicating technical concepts clearly to diverse audiences
- Navigating disagreements constructively
- Building consensus around technical approaches

EXECUTION AND DELIVERY

- Delivering high-quality code and systems
- Managing technical debt appropriately
- Handling production incidents and operational challenges
- Balancing feature development with reliability and performance

LEARNING AND GROWTH

- Adapting to new technologies and approaches
- Seeking and applying feedback effectively
- Learning from technical mistakes and failures
- Continuously developing technical expertise

These competencies are assessed through behavioral questions that probe for specific examples of how you've demonstrated these capabilities in your past work.

THE TECHNICAL VS. BEHAVIORAL BALANCE

Software engineering interviews present a unique challenge: balancing technical depth with behavioral evidence. This balance requires careful calibration:

- **Too technical**: Focusing exclusively on implementation details without demonstrating the behavioral competencies being assessed

- **Too behavioral**: Emphasizing interpersonal aspects without sufficient technical substance to establish credibility

The most effective software engineering behavioral responses strike a careful balance—providing enough technical context to demonstrate expertise while clearly highlighting the behaviors and competencies being evaluated.

This balance varies by company and role:

- **Amazon**: Emphasizes behavioral evidence aligned with Leadership Principles, with technical details as supporting context

- **Google**: Values technical depth but expects clear articulation of reasoning, collaboration, and learning

- **Meta**: Focuses heavily on impact and scale, with technical details that support claims of significant contribution

- **Microsoft**: Balances technical substance with growth mindset and collaborative behaviors

Understanding this balance for your specific target companies helps you calibrate your responses appropriately.

7.2. QUESTION TYPES AND EFFECTIVE RESPONSES

Let's examine common behavioral question types for software engineers and analyze what makes an effective response for each.

TECHNICAL DECISION MAKING QUESTIONS

These questions assess how you make architectural and design choices, evaluate trade-offs, and balance competing considerations.

COMMON QUESTIONS

- "Tell me about a time when you had to make a difficult technical decision with significant trade-offs."

- "Describe a situation where you had to choose between different technical approaches."

- "Give me an example of when you had to balance technical debt against feature delivery."

- "Tell me about an architectural decision you made that you're particularly proud of."

WHAT MAKES AN EFFECTIVE RESPONSE

Effective responses to technical decision questions demonstrate:

- **Clear articulation of the technical context** without excessive detail
- **Explicit identification of trade-offs** considered in the decision
- **Structured decision-making process** rather than intuitive judgment
- **Connection between technical decisions and business outcomes**
- **Reflection on the long-term impact** of the decision

EXAMPLE STAR+ RESPONSE

Question: "Tell me about a time when you had to make a difficult technical decision with significant trade-offs."

Situation: "Last year at CloudTech, I was the lead engineer for our authentication service, which handled approximately 5 million authentication requests daily across our product suite. We were experiencing increasing latency and occasional outages during peak periods, affecting user experience and business operations. Our service was built on a monolithic architecture using a relational database for token storage."

Task: "I needed to redesign the authentication system to improve reliability and reduce latency while minimizing disruption to the 15 other services that depended on it. The challenge was particularly complex because we needed to maintain backward compatibility during the transition and complete the migration within a two-month timeframe to support an upcoming product launch."

Action: "I approached this decision methodically. First, I analyzed our performance bottlenecks using distributed tracing and identified that database operations, particularly token validation, were causing 70% of our latency issues.

I evaluated three potential approaches: optimizing our existing relational database implementation, migrating to a distributed cache with database backup, or implementing a completely new token architecture using JWT (JSON Web Tokens) that wouldn't require database lookups for validation.

For each option, I created a decision matrix evaluating performance impact, implementation complexity, security implications, and migration difficulty. I collaborated with our security team to assess the risk profile of each approach and worked with our platform team to understand infrastructure implications.

The JWT approach offered the best performance benefits but introduced new security considerations and required significant client-side changes. The distributed cache approach provided moderate performance improvements with less migration complexity.

After thorough analysis, I decided to implement the distributed cache approach as a first phase, with a longer-term roadmap toward JWT implementation. I designed a hybrid system that would allow incremental migration, reducing risk while still delivering meaningful improvements.

I created a detailed migration plan, including a feature flag system that would allow us to gradually transition traffic and quickly rollback if issues emerged. I personally developed the core caching logic and coordinated the implementation across three engineering teams."

Result: "The new architecture reduced average authentication latency by 65% (from 120ms to 42ms) and completely eliminated the outages we had been experiencing during peak loads. This performance improvement directly contributed to a 7% increase in conversion rates on our main product, representing approximately $300,000 in additional monthly revenue.

We completed the migration with zero downtime and no disruption to dependent services. The system has remained stable for over a year, even as authentication volume has increased by 40%."

Plus (Lessons Learned): "This experience taught me several valuable lessons about technical decision-making. First, I learned the importance of creating a structured evaluation framework rather than relying on intuition or personal preference. The decision matrix forced me to consider factors I might have otherwise overlooked.

Second, I recognized the value of phased implementation for complex architectural changes. By splitting the migration into incremental steps, we reduced risk while still delivering meaningful improvements. I've since applied this approach to other major system changes, including our recent migration to microservices.

Third, I learned about the critical importance of involving security perspectives early in architectural decisions. Their input significantly improved our approach and helped us avoid potential vulnerabilities. I now include security consultation as a standard step in my technical decision process, which recently helped us identify and address potential issues in our API gateway design before implementation."

Why This Response Is Effective: * Provides clear technical context without excessive implementation details * Explicitly identifies the trade-offs considered (performance, complexity, security, migration) * Demonstrates a structured decision-making process (analysis, options, evaluation criteria) * Connects technical decisions to business outcomes (conversion improvement, revenue impact) * Shows thoughtful reflection on the approach and subsequent application of lessons learned

PROBLEM-SOLVING QUESTIONS

These questions assess how you approach complex technical challenges, navigate ambiguity, and develop effective solutions.

COMMON QUESTIONS

- "Tell me about the most challenging technical problem you've solved."

- "Describe a situation where you had to debug a complex issue."

- "Give me an example of when you had to solve a problem with incomplete information."

- "Tell me about a time when you had to develop an innovative solution to a technical challenge."

WHAT MAKES AN EFFECTIVE RESPONSE

Effective responses to problem-solving questions demonstrate:

- **Systematic approach** rather than trial-and-error

- **Analytical thinking** in breaking down complex problems

- **Creative thinking** in developing non-obvious solutions

- **Persistence** in tackling difficult challenges

- **Learning orientation** in applying insights from the experience

EXAMPLE STAR+ RESPONSE

Question: "Tell me about the most challenging technical problem you've solved."

Situation: "At FinTech Inc., I was working on our transaction processing system that handled approximately 50,000 financial transactions daily. We began receiving reports of occasional duplicate transactions occurring for about 0.1% of payments—a small percentage but critical for a financial system. These duplicates appeared randomly across different users and transaction types, with no obvious pattern. The issue had existed for several weeks, affecting customer trust and creating significant operational overhead as our support team had to manually reverse these duplicate transactions."

Task: "As the backend engineer responsible for the transaction service, I needed to identify the root cause of these duplicate transactions and implement a solution that would eliminate them without disrupting our normal payment processing. The challenge was particularly difficult because the duplicates occurred infrequently and inconsistently, making them hard to reproduce or trace."

Action: "I approached this methodically in several phases. First, I enhanced our logging to capture detailed transaction flow information, including timing, service interactions, and state transitions. This required carefully balancing logging detail against performance impact on a production system.

Next, I analyzed several weeks of transaction logs, looking for patterns in the duplicates. I wrote a data analysis script that compared properties of duplicate transactions against normal ones. This analysis revealed that duplicates occurred more frequently during periods of higher-than-average system load, suggesting a potential race condition or concurrency issue.

Based on this hypothesis, I created a test environment that simulated high concurrency and eventually reproduced the issue. The root cause was a subtle race condition in our idempotency check—under specific timing conditions, two identical requests could both pass the uniqueness check before either was recorded in the database.

I developed a solution using a distributed locking mechanism with Redis that ensured transaction uniqueness checks were truly atomic, even under high concurrency. I also implemented a secondary defense layer that performed post-processing verification to catch any potential duplicates that might slip through.

Before deploying to production, I created a comprehensive test suite that specifically targeted concurrency scenarios, including artificially induced network delays and service restarts to ensure robustness."

Result: "After implementing the solution, duplicate transactions were completely eliminated. We monitored the system for three months without a single recurrence. The solution had minimal performance impact—adding only 5ms to average transaction time while handling our peak load of 200 transactions per second.

The fix saved approximately 15 hours of weekly operational work previously spent addressing duplicate transactions and their customer impact. More importantly, it restored customer confidence in our payment system, which was reflected in our NPS score improving from 42 to 58 in the quarter following the fix."

Plus (Lessons Learned): "This experience taught me several important lessons about solving complex technical problems. First, I learned the critical importance of comprehensive logging for intermittent issues. Without the enhanced logging data, the pattern would have remained invisible. I've since advocated for and implemented more robust observability practices across our engineering organization, which helped us identify and resolve three other subtle issues before they impacted customers.

Second, I gained deeper understanding of distributed systems challenges, particularly around race conditions and concurrency. I subsequently developed an internal workshop on concurrency patterns that has become part of our onboarding for new backend engineers.

Third, I recognized the value of multi-layered defenses for critical operations like financial transactions. The secondary verification layer we implemented has proven valuable on two occasions, catching edge cases that might otherwise have caused issues. This defense-in-depth approach is something I now apply to all financial and data-critical systems.

Perhaps most importantly, I learned that seemingly small issues (0.1% failure rate) can have outsized impact on user trust and operational overhead in critical systems. This has influenced how I prioritize reliability work, even when the direct metrics might suggest lower priority."

Why This Response Is Effective: * Demonstrates a systematic approach to problem-solving (hypothesis, analysis, testing) * Shows technical depth without becoming overly implementation-focused * Highlights analytical thinking in identifying patterns and root causes * Emphasizes verification and testing, not just solution development * Connects technical work to business impact (operational savings, customer satisfaction) * Shows meaningful reflection and subsequent application of lessons learned

TECHNICAL LEADERSHIP QUESTIONS

These questions assess how you influence technical direction, mentor others, and drive improvements without necessarily having formal authority.

COMMON QUESTIONS

- "Tell me about a time when you influenced a significant technical decision without having formal authority."
- "Describe a situation where you helped improve the technical skills of your team members."
- "Give me an example of when you drove a technical improvement or innovation."
- "Tell me about a time when you had to convince others to adopt a new technology or approach."

WHAT MAKES AN EFFECTIVE RESPONSE

Effective responses to technical leadership questions demonstrate:

- **Influence through expertise** rather than position or mandate
- **Balancing advocacy with openness** to other perspectives
- **Technical mentorship** that develops others' capabilities
- **Initiative in identifying** and addressing technical opportunities
- **Building consensus** rather than forcing decisions

EXAMPLE STAR+ RESPONSE

Question: "Tell me about a time when you influenced a significant technical decision without having formal authority."

Situation: "At TechCorp, I was a senior engineer on the backend team working on our content management system. The system had grown organically over five years and was experiencing increasing performance and maintainability issues. Our microservice architecture had evolved into a distributed monolith, with tight coupling between services and inconsistent patterns. This was causing frequent production incidents (averaging 3-4 per month) and slowing our feature development velocity by approximately 30% compared to the previous year."

Task: "While I wasn't the technical lead or manager, I recognized the need for a significant architectural refactoring to address these growing problems. I needed to influence the technical direction of a 15-person engineering organization that had multiple competing priorities and limited bandwidth for non-feature work. The challenge was particularly difficult because several senior engineers had designed the original architecture and might be resistant to acknowledging its limitations."

Action: "I approached this influence challenge methodically. First, I gathered concrete data rather than relying on subjective assessments. I created a detailed analysis of our incident patterns, development velocity trends, and specific coupling issues with supporting metrics and visualizations.

Instead of presenting a complete solution immediately, I started by socializing the problem. I scheduled informal one-on-one discussions with key engineers and stakeholders to understand their perspectives and pain points. This helped me identify common frustrations and build a coalition of support.

I then organized a technical brown bag session where I presented the data and facilitated a discussion about the architectural challenges we were facing. Rather than positioning myself as having all the answers, I framed it as a collaborative problem-solving opportunity.

Based on the interest generated, I proposed and received approval to lead a small working group to explore potential solutions. I included skeptical senior engineers in this group to ensure diverse perspectives and build buy-in. We evaluated several approaches and developed a phased refactoring plan that would incrementally reduce coupling while minimizing disruption.

To demonstrate the value, I implemented a proof-of-concept for one of our most problematic service interactions, showing a 40% performance improvement and significantly cleaner code. This tangible example helped convert skeptics by showing concrete benefits."

Result: "The team ultimately adopted our refactoring proposal, allocating 20% of engineering resources to the effort over two quarters. We successfully implemented the first three phases of the plan, which reduced service coupling by 60% and decreased our average incident frequency from 3-4 per month to less than 1.

The architectural improvements increased our feature development velocity by approximately 25% and significantly improved engineer satisfaction, as measured by our internal engineering survey where architecture satisfaction scores increased from 2.4/5 to 4.1/5.

Perhaps most significantly, the success of this initiative led to my formal promotion to Technical Lead three months later, with several senior engineers specifically citing my work on this refactoring as demonstrating the leadership capabilities needed for the role."

Plus (Lessons Learned): "This experience taught me valuable lessons about technical influence that I've applied repeatedly since then. First, I learned the power of data-driven advocacy. By grounding my concerns in metrics rather than opinions, I created a shared understanding that transcended personal perspectives. I now consistently use this approach when advocating for technical changes, most recently in our successful migration to a new database technology.

Second, I recognized the importance of inclusive problem definition before solution development. By involving key stakeholders in defining the problem, I built shared ownership that made the eventual solution much easier to adopt.

This collaborative approach has become central to my leadership style.

Third, I learned the effectiveness of demonstrating value through concrete examples rather than theoretical arguments. The proof-of-concept converted several skeptics who had been resistant to abstract discussions. I've since used this "show, don't tell" approach successfully in advocating for test automation and observability improvements.

Most importantly, I discovered that technical influence comes from building trust through consistent expertise, open collaboration, and genuine respect for others' perspectives—not from having the loudest voice or most senior title. This understanding has shaped my approach to technical leadership throughout my career."

Why This Response Is Effective: * Focuses on influence and leadership rather than technical implementation details * Demonstrates a thoughtful approach to building consensus (data gathering, socialization, collaboration) * Shows respect for other perspectives while still driving positive change * Provides concrete results that validate the influence approach * Reflects deeply on the leadership lessons learned and their subsequent application

COLLABORATION AND COMMUNICATION QUESTIONS

These questions assess how you work with others, communicate technical concepts, and navigate disagreements constructively.

COMMON QUESTIONS

- "Tell me about a time when you had to work closely with someone from another discipline."

- "Describe a situation where you had to explain a complex technical concept to non-technical stakeholders."

- "Give me an example of when you had a disagreement with a team member about a technical approach."

- "Tell me about a time when you had to build consensus among different technical teams."

WHAT MAKES AN EFFECTIVE RESPONSE

Effective responses to collaboration questions demonstrate:

- **Empathy and perspective-taking** when working with diverse stakeholders
- **Clear communication** of complex technical concepts
- **Constructive approach** to disagreements and conflicts
- **Relationship building** across organizational boundaries
- **Balancing advocacy** with openness to other viewpoints

EXAMPLE STAR+ RESPONSE

Question: "Tell me about a time when you had a disagreement with a team member about a technical approach."

Situation: "While working at DataSystems Inc., I was developing a new data processing pipeline that would handle approximately 5TB of customer analytics data daily. This pipeline was critical for our business intelligence products used by enterprise customers. I was collaborating with another senior engineer who had been with the company longer than me and had deep expertise in our existing systems."

Task: "We needed to design the architecture for this new pipeline, but we had a fundamental disagreement about the approach. I advocated for a stream processing architecture using Kafka and Spark Streaming, which would provide near real-time results and greater scalability. My colleague strongly preferred a batch processing approach using our existing Hadoop infrastructure, arguing it was more reliable and better understood by our team. We needed to resolve this disagreement to move forward with implementation while maintaining our positive working relationship."

Action: "Rather than turning this into a win-lose situation, I took several steps to find a collaborative resolution. First, I acknowledged my colleague's expertise and experience with our existing systems, demonstrating respect for his perspective rather than dismissing it.

I suggested we explicitly list the requirements and constraints for the new pipeline, creating a shared understanding of what success looked like. This exercise revealed that we had different assumptions about the business requirements, particularly around data freshness needs.

To resolve these assumption differences, I proposed we jointly meet with product management to clarify the actual requirements. This meeting revealed that while real-time processing would be valuable long-term, the immediate business need was for reliable daily updates with a path to more frequent processing.

Based on this clarification, I suggested a compromise: we would implement the initial pipeline using a batch approach as my colleague suggested, but with a modular architecture that would allow incremental migration to streaming for specific components as needs evolved. I created a design document outlining this hybrid approach and how it would evolve over time.

To address my colleague's concerns about team familiarity with streaming technologies, I organized a series of knowledge-sharing sessions and created documentation for the components we would eventually migrate."

Result: "We successfully implemented the hybrid approach, delivering the initial batch processing pipeline on schedule. The modular design proved valuable sooner than expected—three months after launch, a key customer requested more frequent updates for a specific data segment. Thanks to our architecture, we were able to migrate just that component to streaming processing without disrupting the rest of the system.

The compromise approach ultimately delivered the best of both worlds: the reliability and team familiarity of batch processing with the flexibility to adopt streaming where it provided the most business value. The pipeline has been in production for over two years now, with 99.98% reliability while gradually transitioning more components to streaming as requirements evolved.

Beyond the technical outcome, this collaborative resolution strengthened my working relationship with my colleague. We went on to partner on several other high-impact projects, with a mutual respect that enhanced our combined effectiveness."

Plus (Lessons Learned): "This experience taught me valuable lessons about navigating technical disagreements effectively. First, I learned the importance of separating assumptions from facts. Our initial disagreement was partly based on different assumptions about requirements that neither of us had fully validated. I now explicitly identify and test assumptions early in technical discussions, which has prevented similar misalignments on subsequent projects.

Second, I recognized that technical decisions don't have to be binary choices. By thinking creatively about hybrid approaches, we found a solution that incorporated the strengths of both perspectives. This "third option" mindset has become a core part of my approach to technical disagreements, most recently helping resolve a conflict between microservice purity and development velocity on our authentication system redesign.

Third, I learned that the way disagreements are resolved often matters more for long-term effectiveness than the specific technical outcome. By maintaining respect and seeking mutual understanding, we built a stronger collaborative relationship that enhanced our work on multiple subsequent projects. I've since applied this relationship-focused approach to disagreements with product managers and designers, not just other engineers.

Most importantly, I discovered that technical disagreements, when handled constructively, can lead to better outcomes than either original position. The hybrid solution we developed was ultimately superior to either of our initial proposals, teaching me to view disagreements as opportunities for innovation rather than conflicts to be won."

Why This Response Is Effective: * Focuses on the collaboration process rather than just technical details * Demonstrates respect for different perspectives while still advocating effectively * Shows how clarifying requirements helped resolve assumptions * Highlights creative problem-solving in finding a "third option" * Connects the approach to both technical outcomes and relationship benefits * Reflects thoughtfully on collaboration lessons with subsequent application

EXECUTION AND DELIVERY QUESTIONS

These questions assess how you deliver high-quality code and systems, manage technical debt, and handle production incidents.

COMMON QUESTIONS

- "Tell me about a time when you had to deliver a project under tight constraints or deadlines."

- "Describe a situation where you had to make trade-offs between quality and speed."

- "Give me an example of when you had to handle a production incident or outage."

- "Tell me about a time when you improved the reliability or performance of a system."

WHAT MAKES AN EFFECTIVE RESPONSE

Effective responses to execution questions demonstrate:

- **Pragmatic approach** to balancing competing priorities
- **Quality focus** even under pressure
- **Systematic incident response** and problem resolution
- **Proactive identification** of reliability and performance issues
- **Ownership** of outcomes beyond initial delivery

EXAMPLE STAR+ RESPONSE

Question: "Tell me about a time when you had to handle a production incident or outage."

Situation: "At E-commerce Platform Inc., I was the backend engineer responsible for our inventory and fulfillment services. During Black Friday, our busiest sales period of the year, we experienced a critical outage in our inventory system. The service began returning incorrect inventory counts, showing items as available when they were actually sold out. This affected approximately 30% of our product catalog and was causing customers to place orders that we couldn't fulfill. The incident began at 2 PM, with order volume at about 5x our normal rate, representing approximately $500,000 in hourly sales."

Task: "As the on-call engineer and service owner, I needed to diagnose the root cause, implement a solution, and restore system integrity as quickly as possible while minimizing business impact. The challenge was particularly difficult because the system was under extreme load, any fix would need to be deployed during peak traffic, and we needed to address both the technical issue and the customer impact of orders that had already been affected."

Action: "I followed our incident response protocol, first declaring a Severity 1 incident to mobilize the necessary resources. I quickly assembled a response team including another backend engineer, a database specialist, a customer service lead, and an engineering manager to coordinate communication.

While the team was assembling, I implemented an immediate mitigation by enabling our circuit breaker to show items as 'temporarily unavailable' rather than potentially providing incorrect availability. This stopped the bleeding while we diagnosed the root cause.

I led the technical investigation, first checking recent deployments and configuration changes. Finding nothing obvious, we examined system metrics and discovered that one of our database read replicas was significantly behind the primary, causing inventory queries to return stale data under specific request routing scenarios.

Rather than attempting a complex fix under pressure, I made the decision to disable the problematic read replica and route all traffic to the remaining healthy replicas. This would put additional load on our database but would immediately restore data consistency.

In parallel, I worked with our customer service team to identify affected orders and develop a response plan. We decided to honor all orders that had been placed, sourcing inventory from alternative warehouses where necessary, and offering a discount for customers who would experience delayed shipping.

After implementing the immediate fix, I conducted a deeper investigation and discovered that the replication lag was caused by an inefficient query pattern in a recently deployed feature that was generating excessive write load during high traffic."

Result: "We resolved the immediate technical issue within 45 minutes of detection, restoring accurate inventory data across the platform. The business impact was significant but contained: approximately 2,200 orders were affected, representing about $175,000 in revenue. Our decision to honor these orders cost an additional $30,000 in expedited shipping and alternative sourcing but preserved customer goodwill.

After the sales event, I implemented a permanent fix for the replication issue by optimizing the problematic queries and implementing more robust load balancing that would detect and avoid replicas with excessive lag. I also added monitoring specifically for replication lag with automated alerts well before it would reach problematic levels.

Most importantly, we maintained customer trust during our biggest sales event. Our customer satisfaction scores for affected orders were only 6% lower than unaffected orders, and we retained 97% of the affected customers for future purchases."

Plus (Lessons Learned): "This incident taught me several critical lessons about production engineering that I've applied extensively since. First, I learned the importance of having graduated response options rather than binary choices. The circuit breaker that allowed us to show 'temporarily unavailable' rather than either showing incorrect data or shutting down completely was crucial to minimizing impact. I've since implemented similar graceful degradation patterns in all critical services I've worked on.

Second, I recognized that in high-pressure incidents, simple and predictable solutions are often better than theoretically optimal but complex ones. By choosing to disable the problematic replica rather than attempting to fix the replication issue in real-time, we resolved the immediate problem with minimal risk. This 'keep it simple under pressure' principle has guided my incident response approach ever since.

Third, I learned the value of cross-functional incident response. Having customer service involved from the beginning allowed us to address both the technical and business dimensions simultaneously. I've formalized this approach in our incident response playbooks, ensuring we consider customer impact in parallel with technical resolution.

Most significantly, this experience highlighted the importance of proactive monitoring for leading indicators rather than just failure states. We now monitor replication lag as a standard metric with alerting thresholds that give us time to respond before customer impact occurs. This proactive approach has prevented at least three similar incidents in subsequent high-traffic events."

Why This Response Is Effective: * Demonstrates clear ownership and leadership during a critical incident * Shows balanced consideration of both technical and business impacts * Highlights pragmatic decision-making under pressure * Includes both immediate resolution and long-term prevention * Provides specific metrics about the incident impact and resolution * Reflects thoughtfully on operational lessons with clear subsequent application

LEARNING AND GROWTH QUESTIONS

These questions assess how you adapt to new technologies, seek and apply feedback, and learn from mistakes and failures.

COMMON QUESTIONS

- "Tell me about a time when you had to learn a new technology or framework quickly."

- "Describe a situation where you received constructive feedback and how you responded to it."

- "Give me an example of a mistake you made and what you learned from it."

- "Tell me about how you've grown as an engineer over the past year."

WHAT MAKES AN EFFECTIVE RESPONSE

Effective responses to learning and growth questions demonstrate:

- **Proactive approach** to skill development

- **Openness to feedback** and willingness to change

- **Accountability** for mistakes without excessive self-criticism

- **Structured approach** to learning new technologies

- **Continuous improvement** mindset and concrete growth examples

EXAMPLE STAR+ RESPONSE

Question: "Tell me about a mistake you made and what you learned from it."

Situation: "At StartupTech, I was the primary backend developer for our user authentication system. We were preparing for a major release that would transition our authentication from a homegrown solution to a standards-based OAuth implementation, affecting all 50,000 of our active users. The system had been in development for three months and had gone through our standard QA process."

Task: "I was responsible for the final code review, testing, and deployment of this new authentication system. The challenge was ensuring a smooth transition without disrupting existing users' access, while significantly changing the underlying authentication mechanism."

Action: "I conducted a thorough code review and ran our test suite, which showed 98% test coverage with all tests passing. Based on these results and our successful QA cycle, I was confident in the implementation and scheduled the deployment for a low-traffic period on a Tuesday evening.

I created a detailed deployment plan with rollback procedures and monitoring checkpoints. The deployment itself went smoothly, with all technical indicators showing success. We had implemented a gradual rollout, starting with 10% of users and monitoring for any issues before expanding.

However, I made a critical mistake in my testing approach. While our tests covered the core authentication flows comprehensively, I had not adequately tested the integration with third-party applications that connected through our API. I had assumed that since we were implementing standard OAuth, these integrations would continue to work as long as the clients followed the specification.

The morning after deployment, we discovered that approximately 20% of our enterprise customers using third-party integrations were experiencing authentication failures. Investigation revealed that many of these integrations were making assumptions about our authentication implementation that weren't part of the OAuth specification, such as specific header formats and token structures."

Result: "The impact was significant. About 2,000 users across 15 enterprise customers couldn't access critical features through their integrated workflows. While our core application remained accessible, this disruption affected important customers and damaged trust in our platform.

I immediately took ownership of the issue, leading the incident response team. We implemented a temporary compatibility layer that supported both the old and new authentication patterns while we worked with affected customers on proper OAuth implementations. This restored service for all users within 8 hours of discovery.

In the following weeks, I worked directly with our customer success team to rebuild relationships with affected customers, providing detailed integration documentation and direct technical support for their transition to standard OAuth practices."

Plus (Lessons Learned): "This mistake taught me several profound lessons that have fundamentally changed my engineering approach. First, I learned that test coverage metrics alone can create a false sense of security. While we had 98%

code coverage, we were missing critical integration test scenarios. I've since implemented a more comprehensive testing strategy that includes explicit integration testing with common third-party patterns, not just our own code paths. This approach recently prevented a similar issue during our API versioning update.

Second, I recognized the danger of assumptions about how others use your system. By assuming third-party integrations would strictly follow the OAuth specification, I missed the reality of how our API was actually being used. I now explicitly document and test against actual usage patterns, not just theoretical specifications. This 'real-world testing' approach has become standard practice in our team.

Third, I learned the importance of more gradual feature transitions, particularly for authentication systems. For subsequent security updates, I've implemented dual-support periods where both old and new patterns are simultaneously supported with clear deprecation timelines. This approach has enabled smoother transitions for similar infrastructure changes.

Most importantly, this experience taught me that technical correctness isn't sufficient for successful engineering—understanding the human and business contexts of our systems is equally critical. I now consider the full ecosystem of our software, including integration patterns and customer workflows, not just the code we directly control. This broader perspective has made me a more effective engineer and has directly influenced how I mentor junior team members to think beyond the immediate technical implementation."

Why This Response Is Effective: * Takes clear ownership of the mistake without making excuses * Provides specific details about what went wrong and why * Demonstrates immediate accountability and resolution actions * Shows deep reflection and specific changes to engineering approach * Connects the lesson to subsequent situations where it prevented similar issues * Balances technical details with broader engineering philosophy insights

7.3. TECHNICAL VS. BEHAVIORAL NUANCES

Software engineering behavioral interviews present unique challenges in balancing technical content with behavioral evidence. Let's explore these nuances and strategies for navigating them effectively.

THE TECHNICAL CREDIBILITY THRESHOLD

Software engineering interviews have an implicit "technical credibility threshold" that candidates must meet before their behavioral evidence is fully valued. This threshold varies by company and role:

- **Junior roles**: Basic technical understanding and appropriate terminology

- **Mid-level roles**: Clear technical reasoning and appropriate solution considerations

- **Senior roles**: Sophisticated technical judgment and architectural thinking

- **Staff+ roles**: Strategic technical perspective and cross-system understanding

Failing to establish this technical credibility can undermine even strong behavioral examples. However, exceeding this threshold doesn't provide proportional benefits—once credibility is established, additional technical depth adds diminishing returns compared to behavioral evidence.

Strategy: Establish technical credibility early in each response with precise terminology and appropriate depth, then shift focus to the behavioral aspects being evaluated.

THE IMPLEMENTATION DETAIL BALANCE

A common mistake in software engineering interviews is providing excessive implementation details that obscure the behavioral evidence. While technical context is necessary, the specific libraries, function names, or code patterns rarely matter for behavioral assessment.

Strategy: Include implementation details only when they: * Demonstrate a specific competency being evaluated * Illustrate a key decision point or trade-off * Provide necessary context for understanding your actions * Support claims about your specific contribution

Otherwise, abstract implementation details to focus on the behavioral aspects of your response.

THE INDIVIDUAL VS. TEAM CONTRIBUTION CLARITY

Software engineering is inherently collaborative, making it challenging to distinguish individual contributions from team efforts. However, behavioral interviews specifically assess your personal capabilities and impact.

Strategy: Use clear language to distinguish your specific contributions: * "I personally designed/implemented/tested..." * "My specific responsibility was..." * "While the team collaborated on X, I individually handled Y..." * "I proposed/advocated for/developed..."

This clarity helps interviewers accurately assess your capabilities without appearing to claim undue credit.

THE TECHNICAL JUDGMENT EMPHASIS

For senior software engineering roles, technical judgment often matters more than implementation skills. Behavioral questions assess not just what you built, but how you decided what to build and why.

Strategy: Emphasize your decision-making process by explicitly articulating: * The factors you considered in technical decisions * The trade-offs you evaluated and why you prioritized certain aspects * How you balanced immediate needs with long-term considerations * The principles or patterns that guided your approach

This emphasis demonstrates the sophisticated judgment expected in senior engineering roles.

7.4. CONCLUSION: DEMONSTRATING ENGINEERING EXCELLENCE THROUGH BEHAVIOR

Effective behavioral interviewing for software engineering roles requires a careful balance—providing sufficient technical context to establish credibility while focusing on the behaviors and competencies being evaluated. The examples in this chapter demonstrate this balance across different question types and competency areas.

Remember that behavioral interviews assess not just what you've built, but how you build—your approach to problems, your collaboration with others, your technical judgment, and your continuous growth as an engineer. By preparing examples that demonstrate these dimensions, you position yourself as not just a skilled coder, but a thoughtful engineering professional who can thrive in complex technical environments.

In the next chapter, we'll explore behavioral examples specifically tailored for Engineering Manager roles, examining how the expectations and emphasis shift when moving from individual contribution to technical leadership positions.

CHAPTER 8. ENGINEERING MANAGER EXAMPLES

> The output of a manager is the output of the organizational units under his or her supervision or influence.
>
> — Andy Grove

"I fired my top performer last week."

The candidate's words hung in the air as I set down my pen. In fifteen years of engineering and three years interviewing 200+ candidates at [Your Company], this was a first. Most managers dress their war stories in HR-approved platitudes—"We parted ways to pursue different opportunities"—but here was someone exposing the raw nerve of technical leadership.

After a beat, I asked the only question that mattered: "How did you know it was the right decision?"

Their answer—a messy, nuanced account of metrics vs. morale, short-term pain vs. long-term culture—earned them an offer. Because engineering management isn't about avoiding hard choices; it's about making them and being able to explain your reasoning under fluorescent lights.

This chapter is about those conversations. The ones where:

- Your technical credibility gets tested not by whiteboard algorithms, but by how you defend an unpopular architecture decision

- Your leadership isn't judged by sprint velocity, but by how you rebuilt trust after a missed promotion

- Your "management style" becomes concrete through stories about the time you shipped the wrong feature—on purpose

I'll share what I learned from hiring 15 engineering managers out of 200+ candidates, including:

1. Why the best technical leaders spend more time talking about failure than success

2. How to discuss team conflicts without sounding defensive or naive

3. The exact phrasing that separates L5 managers from L6+ in behavioral responses

(And yes—we'll revisit that fired top performer, and why their story changed how I interview EM candidates forever.)

8.1. THE ENGINEERING MANAGER BEHAVIORAL ASSESSMENT

Before diving into specific examples, let's understand what companies are actually evaluating when they conduct behavioral interviews for Engineering Manager roles.

CORE COMPETENCIES FOR ENGINEERING MANAGERS

While each company has its own framework, most technical leadership interviews assess some combination of these core competencies:

TEAM LEADERSHIP AND DEVELOPMENT

- Building and maintaining high-performing engineering teams
- Developing technical talent and growing future leaders
- Creating inclusive team environments that leverage diverse perspectives
- Balancing team autonomy with appropriate guidance and standards

TECHNICAL LEADERSHIP

- Setting technical vision and architecture direction
- Making sound technical decisions and trade-offs
- Ensuring technical quality and appropriate engineering practices
- Balancing technical debt against feature delivery

DELIVERY AND EXECUTION

- Delivering complex technical projects on time and with high quality
- Managing dependencies and cross-team coordination
- Handling risks and obstacles to successful execution
- Balancing resources across competing priorities

ORGANIZATIONAL LEADERSHIP

- Influencing beyond direct reporting lines
- Navigating organizational politics constructively
- Driving change and improvement at scale
- Representing team needs and perspectives to senior leadership

BUSINESS PARTNERSHIP

- Translating business requirements into technical strategy
- Collaborating effectively with product, design, and other functions
- Making appropriate trade-off decisions that balance technical and business needs
- Demonstrating business impact of technical investments

PERSONAL LEADERSHIP

- Demonstrating self-awareness and continuous growth
- Handling pressure and ambiguity effectively
- Making difficult decisions with incomplete information
- Showing resilience and adaptability in changing circumstances

These competencies are assessed through behavioral questions that probe for specific examples of how you've demonstrated these capabilities in your past leadership roles.

THE TECHNICAL VS. LEADERSHIP BALANCE

Engineering Manager interviews present a unique challenge: balancing technical credibility with leadership evidence. This balance requires careful calibration:

- **Too technical**: Focusing exclusively on technical details without demonstrating people leadership and organizational impact
- **Too managerial**: Emphasizing process and people management without sufficient technical substance to establish credibility

The most effective Engineering Manager responses strike a careful balance—providing enough technical context to demonstrate domain expertise while clearly highlighting the leadership behaviors and competencies being evaluated.

This balance varies by company and level:

- **Amazon**: Emphasizes leadership aligned with Leadership Principles, with technical details as supporting context
- **Google**: Values technical depth alongside leadership, particularly for engineering managers who are expected to remain technically hands-on

- **Meta**: Focuses heavily on scale, impact, and execution speed, with technical credibility as a foundation

- **Microsoft**: Balances technical substance with growth mindset and people development

Understanding this balance for your specific target companies helps you calibrate your responses appropriately.

8.2. QUESTION TYPES AND EFFECTIVE RESPONSES

Let's examine common behavioral question types for Engineering Managers and analyze what makes an effective response for each.

TEAM LEADERSHIP QUESTIONS

These questions assess how you build, develop, and lead engineering teams to deliver results.

COMMON QUESTIONS

- "Tell me about a time when you had to build or rebuild an engineering team."

- "Describe a situation where you helped an underperforming team member improve."

- "Give me an example of how you've created an inclusive team environment."

- "Tell me about a time when you had to make an unpopular decision that affected your team."

WHAT MAKES AN EFFECTIVE RESPONSE

Effective responses to team leadership questions demonstrate:

- **Balance between empathy and accountability** in managing team members
- **Systematic approach** to team development rather than ad hoc actions
- **Specific leadership actions** rather than general management philosophy
- **Measurable team outcomes** resulting from your leadership
- **Self-awareness** about your leadership approach and its impact

EXAMPLE STAR+ RESPONSE

Question: "Tell me about a time when you had to build or rebuild an engineering team."

Situation: "When I joined FinTech Inc. as an Engineering Manager, I inherited a struggling backend team responsible for our payment processing systems. The team consisted of five engineers with varying experience levels, from junior to senior. They were facing significant challenges: the team had missed their last three delivery deadlines, had accumulated substantial technical debt, and morale was visibly low. Two senior engineers had recently left the company, citing frustration with the team's direction and productivity."

Task: "I needed to transform this underperforming team into a high-functioning unit while simultaneously addressing the technical debt and meeting critical business commitments. The challenge was particularly complex because we couldn't afford to pause feature development during the rebuilding process—our payment systems processed approximately $50 million in transactions monthly, and several major customers were waiting on promised features."

Action: "I approached this rebuilding process systematically in several phases. First, I conducted individual one-on-ones with each team member to understand their perspectives, frustrations, and aspirations. These conversations revealed several root issues: unclear technical direction, insufficient collaboration practices, and a lack of growth opportunities for junior members.

Based on these insights, I implemented several key changes. I established a clear technical vision for our payment systems, creating an architectural roadmap that balanced feature development with technical debt reduction. I involved the entire team in this process to build ownership and leverage their domain knowledge.

I restructured our work allocation to create balanced feature teams that paired senior and junior engineers, providing growth opportunities while ensuring quality. I implemented a formal mentorship program where each junior engineer had dedicated time with a senior engineer weekly.

To address collaboration issues, I introduced a modified Agile process with daily standups, proper sprint planning, and retrospectives focused on continuous improvement. I also established 'engineering excellence' time—20% of capacity dedicated to technical debt reduction and system improvements.

For team culture, I created regular forums for knowledge sharing, including weekly tech talks and architecture reviews. I also worked with each engineer to develop personalized growth plans aligned with both their career aspirations and team needs.

Perhaps most importantly, I was transparent about our challenges and actively solicited input on solutions. When we needed to make difficult trade-offs between technical debt and feature work, I involved the team in these decisions rather than dictating priorities."

Result: "Within four months, we saw significant improvements across multiple dimensions. The team successfully delivered two major feature releases on schedule, including a critical fraud detection system that reduced fraudulent transactions by 37%. Our system reliability improved from 99.5% to 99.95% uptime, and average response time decreased by 45%.

From a team health perspective, our engineering satisfaction scores in the quarterly survey improved from 2.8/5 to 4.6/5. We retained all remaining team members and successfully hired three new engineers, including a senior architect who specifically cited our team culture as a reason for joining.

The team's reputation within the organization transformed from being seen as a bottleneck to being recognized as a high-performing unit. This was reflected in our increased autonomy and the executive team's willingness to approve our proposed technical investments."

Plus (Lessons Learned): "This experience taught me several valuable lessons about team leadership that I've applied consistently since. First, I learned that technical vision and people development are equally important and mutually reinforcing. By addressing both simultaneously rather than sequentially, we created positive momentum that accelerated our transformation.

Second, I recognized the power of structured processes in reducing cognitive load and creating safety. The clear Agile practices we implemented freed the team to focus on technical challenges rather than coordination overhead. I've since implemented similar structured approaches when joining new teams, adapting the specifics to each team's context.

Third, I discovered that transparency about challenges, combined with involvement in solutions, builds stronger ownership than either directive leadership or complete autonomy. This balanced approach to decision-making is something I now consider a core part of my leadership philosophy.

Most significantly, I learned that team rebuilding isn't a one-time event but an ongoing process of continuous improvement. The systems we put in place for regular retrospectives and adaptation have allowed the team to continue evolving long after the initial transformation. This experience fundamentally shaped my approach to sustainable team development, which I've successfully applied to three subsequent teams I've led."

Why This Response Is Effective: * Balances technical context (system reliability, response time) with team leadership focus * Demonstrates a systematic approach to team building with specific actions * Shows both technical outcomes and team health improvements with metrics * Addresses both immediate performance and long-term sustainability * Reflects thoughtfully on leadership philosophy with subsequent application

TECHNICAL LEADERSHIP QUESTIONS

These questions assess how you set technical direction, make architectural decisions, and ensure engineering excellence.

COMMON QUESTIONS

- "Tell me about a time when you had to make a significant technical decision for your team."

- "Describe a situation where you had to balance technical debt against feature delivery."

- "Give me an example of how you've improved engineering practices or quality."

- "Tell me about a time when you had to provide technical guidance on a complex problem."

WHAT MAKES AN EFFECTIVE RESPONSE

Effective responses to technical leadership questions demonstrate:

- **Technical depth** without becoming overly implementation-focused

- **Structured decision-making** processes rather than intuitive judgments

- **Balance between technical purity and practical business needs**

- **Influence through expertise** rather than positional authority

- **Technical vision** connected to business strategy

EXAMPLE STAR+ RESPONSE

Question: "Tell me about a time when you had to balance technical debt against feature delivery."

Situation: "At TechPlatform Inc., I led the 12-person API Services team responsible for the external APIs used by our enterprise customers and partners. Our API platform had grown organically over five years and was showing signs of significant technical debt: inconsistent patterns across services, performance bottlenecks during peak loads, and increasing incident rates (from 1-2 per month to 4-5 per month over the previous year). At the same time, our product team had an aggressive roadmap of new API capabilities needed to support a major partnership worth approximately $5 million annually, with firm contractual deadlines."

Task: "As the Engineering Manager, I needed to develop a strategy that would address our mounting technical debt while still delivering the critical new API capabilities on schedule. The challenge was particularly complex because we had limited engineering resources, fixed deadlines for the partnership features, and couldn't risk service disruption for existing customers who processed over 50 million API calls daily through our platform."

Action: "I approached this challenge by first creating visibility into the actual state of our technical debt. I worked with senior engineers to conduct a comprehensive technical assessment, categorizing debt into three tiers: critical (affecting reliability or security), significant (affecting performance or maintainability), and cosmetic (affecting code quality but not customer experience).

Rather than positioning this as a binary choice between features and debt reduction, I developed an integrated plan that addressed both needs. For critical debt, I made the case to executive leadership that this work couldn't be deferred, presenting data on incident trends and their business impact. I secured agreement to allocate 30% of our capacity specifically to addressing critical technical debt.

For the remaining work, I implemented a "debt-aware feature development" approach. We established architectural standards and patterns that new features would follow, ensuring they didn't exacerbate existing debt. We created a technical design review process where each new feature was evaluated for its impact on system health.

I worked closely with product management to prioritize the partnership features, identifying which capabilities were truly needed for the initial release versus what could be delivered in subsequent phases. This allowed us to reduce the immediate scope while still meeting contractual obligations.

For execution, I restructured the team into three pods: one focused on critical debt remediation, one on core partnership features, and one on supporting capabilities. I personally reviewed technical designs across all pods to ensure consistency and debt awareness."

Result: "We successfully delivered the partnership API capabilities on schedule, meeting our contractual obligations and securing the $5 million partnership. Simultaneously, we reduced our critical technical debt by approximately 60%, which decreased our monthly incident rate from 4-5 to 1-2 and improved average API response time by 35%.

The architectural standards and patterns we established became the foundation for all subsequent API development, preventing the accumulation of new debt. Our technical design review process was adopted by three other engineering teams after they saw its effectiveness.

Perhaps most importantly, we shifted the organization's thinking from viewing technical debt and feature development as competing priorities to seeing them as complementary aspects of sustainable product development. This was reflected in changes to our planning process, where technical health work became a standard part of quarterly roadmaps rather than an exceptional request."

Plus (Lessons Learned): "This experience taught me several valuable lessons about technical leadership that have shaped my approach since. First, I learned the importance of quantifying technical debt in business terms rather than engineering terminology. By connecting incidents and performance issues to customer impact and revenue risk, I was able to secure executive buy-in that would have been difficult with purely technical arguments.

Second, I recognized that the dichotomy between features and technical debt is largely artificial. By integrating debt considerations into feature development rather than treating them as separate workstreams, we created more sustainable progress on both fronts. I've applied this integrated approach to all subsequent planning processes I've led.

Third, I discovered the power of architectural standards as a preventative measure rather than just remediation. The patterns we established not only helped address existing debt but prevented the creation of new debt, creating compounding benefits over time. This preventative mindset has become central to my technical leadership philosophy.

Most significantly, I learned that effective technical leadership requires translating between business and technical contexts in both directions. Engineers need to understand business priorities to make appropriate trade-offs, while business stakeholders need to understand technical constraints to make informed decisions. Facilitating this mutual understanding has become one of my core strengths as an engineering leader, most recently helping navigate a similar balance during our cloud migration initiative."

Why This Response Is Effective: * Demonstrates technical depth while maintaining leadership focus * Shows structured approach to a common engineering management challenge * Balances technical and business considerations appropriately * Provides specific actions and measurable outcomes * Reflects thoughtfully on leadership lessons with subsequent application

DELIVERY AND EXECUTION QUESTIONS

These questions assess how you plan and execute complex technical projects, manage risks, and deliver results.

COMMON QUESTIONS

- "Tell me about a complex project you led and how you ensured its successful delivery."

- "Describe a situation where you had to overcome significant obstacles to deliver a project."

- "Give me an example of how you've managed dependencies across multiple teams."

- "Tell me about a time when a project was at risk of missing its deadline and how you handled it."

WHAT MAKES AN EFFECTIVE RESPONSE

Effective responses to delivery and execution questions demonstrate:

- **Structured planning** and risk management approaches
- **Proactive obstacle identification** and mitigation

- **Cross-team coordination** and dependency management

- **Appropriate balance** between process and flexibility

- **Results orientation** with clear outcome metrics

EXAMPLE STAR+ RESPONSE

Question: "Tell me about a complex project you led and how you ensured its successful delivery."

Situation: "At Enterprise Solutions Inc., I led the engineering effort for our company's most ambitious project to date: migrating our flagship product from a monolithic architecture to a microservices approach while simultaneously transitioning from on-premises to cloud deployment. This product generated 60% of company revenue ($45M annually) and was used by over 200 enterprise customers, many with strict SLAs and compliance requirements. The existing system had evolved over 10 years and comprised approximately 2 million lines of code."

Task: "As the Engineering Manager for this initiative, I was responsible for leading the technical execution across five engineering teams totaling 35 engineers. We needed to complete the migration within 12 months to align with the end of our data center contract, while ensuring zero service disruption for customers, maintaining all existing functionality, and meeting our strict security and compliance requirements. The challenge was particularly complex because most of our engineers had limited cloud experience, and we needed to maintain the existing system while building its replacement."

Action: "I developed a comprehensive delivery strategy with several key components. First, I created a phased migration plan rather than attempting a 'big bang' approach. We identified relatively independent functional areas that could be migrated incrementally, starting with lower-risk components to build team experience before tackling critical paths.

For technical preparation, I established a Cloud Center of Excellence with our strongest engineers, who developed reference architectures, reusable patterns, and internal training materials. I arranged for formal cloud certification training for key team members and brought in external experts for architecture reviews.

To manage the complexity, I implemented a multi-level planning approach: a high-level roadmap for the entire project, quarterly objectives for each team, and two-week sprints for execution flexibility. We used a RAID (Risks, Assumptions, Issues, Dependencies) framework to systematically track and address potential obstacles.

For cross-team coordination, I established a technical steering committee with senior engineers from each team that met weekly to address architectural questions and ensure consistency. I also implemented a daily standup of standups where team representatives shared progress and blockers.

To maintain quality and security, we developed a comprehensive testing strategy including automated regression tests, performance testing, security scanning, and chaos engineering practices. I worked with our security team to develop cloud-specific security controls and compliance validation processes.

Perhaps most critically, I maintained transparency with all stakeholders through weekly status reports, monthly executive reviews, and a real-time dashboard showing migration progress and health metrics. When we encountered inevitable challenges, I communicated them proactively along with mitigation plans."

Result: "We successfully completed the migration within the 12-month timeframe and under the allocated budget by approximately 8%. The transition was seamless for customers—we achieved zero downtime during the migration and actually improved system reliability from 99.95% to 99.99% availability.

The new architecture delivered significant business benefits: a 40% reduction in infrastructure costs, 60% faster feature deployment through improved CI/CD pipelines, and enhanced scalability that allowed us to support a 300% increase in transaction volume during peak periods without performance degradation.

From a team perspective, we significantly increased our engineering capability—28 engineers achieved cloud certifications during the project, and we established cloud engineering practices that have been adopted across the organization. The project was recognized by our CEO as a model initiative and used as a case study for our company's technical transformation."

Plus (Lessons Learned): "This experience taught me invaluable lessons about leading complex technical initiatives that I've applied to all subsequent large projects. First, I learned that incremental delivery is essential for managing risk in large-scale transformations. By demonstrating success with smaller components first, we built confidence and refined our approach before tackling the most critical elements. This incremental approach has become my standard practice for any significant technical change.

Second, I recognized that investment in engineering enablement (training, tools, reference architectures) pays enormous dividends in execution speed and quality. What initially seemed like a diversion of resources from direct implementation actually accelerated our overall delivery by creating force multipliers. I've since made enablement a standard component of all project plans I develop.

Third, I discovered the power of multi-level planning—maintaining a clear long-term direction while allowing for tactical flexibility as we learned and encountered challenges. This balanced approach to planning has proven effective across various project types and team structures.

Most significantly, I learned that successful delivery of complex technical initiatives depends as much on communication and stakeholder management as on technical execution. The transparency we maintained throughout the project built trust that allowed us to make necessary adjustments without creating panic or losing support. This emphasis on transparent communication has become a cornerstone of my leadership approach, most recently helping navigate a challenging product redesign that required significant customer coordination."

Why This Response Is Effective: * Demonstrates leadership of a complex, high-stakes technical initiative * Shows structured approach to planning, risk management, and execution * Balances technical details with project management and leadership aspects * Provides specific, measurable outcomes across multiple dimensions * Reflects thoughtfully on delivery approach with clear subsequent application

ORGANIZATIONAL LEADERSHIP QUESTIONS

These questions assess how you influence beyond your team, navigate organizational dynamics, and drive change at scale.

COMMON QUESTIONS

- "Tell me about a time when you had to influence a decision outside your direct authority."

- "Describe a situation where you had to navigate organizational politics to achieve an important goal."

- "Give me an example of how you've driven change across multiple teams or departments."

- "Tell me about a time when you had to represent your team's needs to senior leadership."

WHAT MAKES AN EFFECTIVE RESPONSE

Effective responses to organizational leadership questions demonstrate:

- **Influence strategies** beyond positional authority

- **Political savvy** without manipulation or game-playing

- **Coalition building** across organizational boundaries

- **Effective upward communication** with senior leadership

- **Change management** approaches that drive adoption

EXAMPLE STAR+ RESPONSE

Question: "Tell me about a time when you had to influence a decision outside your direct authority."

Situation: "At TechCorp, I was the Engineering Manager for the Developer Platform team, responsible for internal tools and infrastructure used by our 200+ engineers. We had identified a critical need to standardize our CI/CD practices across the organization. At that time, each product team (15 in total) was using their own unique deployment processes and tools, creating significant inefficiencies, quality inconsistencies, and security risks. However, I had no direct authority over these teams—each had their own Engineering Manager who set their technical practices."

Task: "I needed to influence the organization to adopt a standardized CI/CD approach without having formal authority to mandate the change. The challenge was particularly difficult because several teams had invested heavily in their existing processes and were resistant to change. Additionally, any standardization would need to accommodate legitimate differences in team needs while still providing the consistency necessary for organizational efficiency and security."

Action: "I developed a multi-faceted influence strategy focused on building consensus rather than forcing compliance. First, I conducted a thorough assessment of the existing CI/CD landscape, documenting the various approaches, their strengths and weaknesses, and the organizational costs of the fragmentation. This data-driven analysis quantified the issue in terms that resonated with both engineering leaders and executives.

Rather than immediately pushing for a specific solution, I formed a working group with representatives from various teams, including some of the most skeptical Engineering Managers. This group collaboratively defined the requirements for a standardized approach, ensuring all legitimate team needs were considered.

To build broader support, I identified and recruited influential senior engineers from across the organization who recognized the problem. These technical leaders became advocates within their teams, helping socialize the benefits of standardization from a peer perspective rather than a top-down mandate.

I secured executive sponsorship by presenting the business case to our CTO, focusing on security improvements, engineering efficiency, and onboarding benefits. With this support, I obtained resources to develop a proof-of-concept implementation that teams could evaluate.

For teams with significant investments in existing processes, I developed a phased adoption plan that allowed them to migrate gradually rather than requiring an immediate cutover. I also ensured the standardized solution incorporated the best elements from existing team approaches, giving those teams recognition and maintaining their sense of ownership.

Throughout the process, I maintained transparent communication about our progress, challenges, and the evolving solution. I held regular open forums where any engineer could provide input or raise concerns, demonstrating that this was a collaborative effort rather than an imposed mandate."

Result: "Within six months, 13 of our 15 product teams had voluntarily adopted the standardized CI/CD platform, with the remaining two teams committed to migration within their next release cycle. This adoption rate far exceeded expectations for a non-mandated change.

The standardization delivered significant organizational benefits: security vulnerabilities in deployment pipelines decreased by 65%, average deployment time reduced from 45 minutes to 12 minutes, and onboarding time for new engineers decreased from 2 weeks to 3 days for deployment-related tasks.

The collaborative approach not only achieved the technical objective but strengthened cross-team relationships. The working group evolved into a permanent Engineering Excellence Council that continues to drive standardization in other areas of our engineering practice."

Plus (Lessons Learned): "This experience taught me valuable lessons about organizational influence that have shaped my leadership approach. First, I learned that data-driven problem definition is essential for building consensus around change. By quantifying the costs of fragmentation in terms that mattered to different stakeholders, we created a shared understanding that transcended team boundaries.

Second, I recognized the power of collaborative solution development versus presenting predetermined answers. By involving skeptical voices in defining the solution, we not only created a better technical outcome but built ownership that drove adoption. I've applied this collaborative approach to several subsequent organizational initiatives, most recently our architecture governance model.

Third, I discovered the importance of balancing standardization with legitimate team autonomy. By focusing standardization on areas with clear organizational benefits while allowing flexibility where teams had unique needs, we avoided the resistance that often accompanies perceived loss of autonomy. This balanced approach to standardization has become a core principle in my organizational change philosophy.

Most significantly, I learned that sustainable organizational change requires alignment across multiple levels—executive support, management buy-in, and engineer enthusiasm. By developing strategies for each level rather than focusing on just one, we created the conditions for successful adoption. This multi-level influence approach has become my standard practice for any significant organizational change, most recently helping drive our shift to a product-oriented engineering structure."

Why This Response Is Effective: * Focuses on influence and organizational leadership rather than technical details * Demonstrates sophisticated understanding of organizational dynamics * Shows multiple influence strategies across different stakeholder groups * Provides concrete results that validate the approach * Reflects thoughtfully on organizational leadership lessons with subsequent application

BUSINESS PARTNERSHIP QUESTIONS

These questions assess how you collaborate with product, design, and other functions to deliver business value through technology.

COMMON QUESTIONS

- "Tell me about a time when you had to balance technical considerations with business needs."

- "Describe a situation where you worked closely with product management to define technical strategy."

- "Give me an example of how you've translated business requirements into technical solutions."

- "Tell me about a time when you had to make a difficult trade-off between different stakeholder priorities."

WHAT MAKES AN EFFECTIVE RESPONSE

Effective responses to business partnership questions demonstrate:

- **Understanding of business context** beyond technical requirements

- **Collaborative approach** with non-technical stakeholders

- **Value-driven prioritization** rather than technical interest

- **Effective translation** between business and technical domains

- **Appropriate trade-off decisions** that balance multiple considerations

EXAMPLE STAR+ RESPONSE

Question: "Tell me about a time when you had to balance technical considerations with business needs."

Situation: "At E-commerce Platform Inc., I led the 15-person Checkout Experience team responsible for the purchase flow that processed approximately $2 billion in annual transactions. Our product team had identified a significant opportunity to increase conversion rates by redesigning the checkout experience with a single-page approach rather than our existing multi-step process. Market research suggested this could increase conversion by 15-20%, representing approximately $50 million in additional annual revenue. However, our existing checkout system was built on legacy technology that would make this change extremely difficult and potentially introduce stability risks to our most critical business function."

Task: "As the Engineering Manager, I needed to develop an approach that would deliver the business value of the checkout redesign while managing the technical risks and constraints of our legacy system. The challenge was particularly complex because the executive team wanted the new experience launched before the holiday shopping season—giving us only four months—and our checkout system had strict reliability requirements (99.99% uptime) due to its direct revenue impact."

Action: "I approached this challenge by first ensuring I fully understood the business objectives beyond the surface request. I worked closely with our product and UX leaders to identify the specific user friction points in the current checkout flow and the expected impact of various potential improvements. This analysis revealed that certain elements of the redesign would deliver disproportionate business value, while others were less impactful.

Rather than presenting a binary choice between technical purity and business needs, I developed a nuanced proposal with three options: a full rewrite (highest business value but highest risk), a hybrid approach that modernized the highest-impact components while maintaining the core legacy system (moderate value and moderate risk), and a cosmetic-only update (lowest value but lowest risk).

For each option, I created a comprehensive assessment covering development time, technical risk, expected business impact, and long-term maintainability. I worked with our data science team to quantify the expected conversion impact of each approach based on A/B testing of similar changes in other parts of our funnel.

I presented these options to our executive team, transparently communicating the trade-offs rather than advocating for a specific approach. After thorough discussion, we collectively decided on the hybrid approach, focusing our modernization efforts on the components with highest business impact while minimizing risk to the core transaction processing.

To execute this approach, I restructured our team into three workstreams: one focused on the user-facing experience, one on the modernized components, and one on ensuring reliability of the legacy core. I implemented a comprehensive testing strategy including extensive A/B testing, performance testing, and chaos engineering to validate both the business impact and technical stability."

Result: "We successfully delivered the hybrid checkout redesign two weeks before the holiday season deadline. The new experience increased conversion rates by 17%, driving approximately $45 million in incremental annual revenue—nearly matching the projected benefit of a full rewrite. We maintained our 99.99% reliability standard throughout the holiday season, processing a record volume of transactions without incident.

The modernized components we delivered became the foundation for a longer-term, incremental modernization of our entire checkout system. Over the following year, we were able to replace the remaining legacy components without disrupting the business, ultimately achieving the full technical vision while delivering business value throughout the process.

Our approach was recognized as a model for balancing technical and business considerations, with our CTO using it as a case study in quarterly business reviews for how engineering can be a strategic partner rather than just a delivery function."

Plus (Lessons Learned): "This experience taught me valuable lessons about business partnership that have fundamentally shaped my leadership approach. First, I learned the importance of deeply understanding business objectives rather than just requirements. By identifying which specific elements of the redesign would drive the most conversion improvement, we were able to make much more strategic technical decisions than if we had simply implemented the requested design.

Second, I recognized the power of presenting options with transparent trade-offs rather than single solutions. By clearly articulating the costs, benefits, and risks of different approaches, we enabled a collaborative decision that balanced technical and business considerations appropriately. This options-based approach has become my standard practice for addressing complex business-technology decisions.

Third, I discovered that technical and business needs are rarely truly in opposition when viewed with sufficient nuance. By decomposing both the business request and our technical constraints into their component parts, we found a path that served both effectively. This decomposition approach has helped me navigate numerous seemingly conflicting priorities since then.

Most significantly, I learned that effective business partnership requires engineering leaders to think in business terms, not just technical ones. By framing our technical decisions in terms of revenue impact, risk management, and time-to-market, I was able to engage business stakeholders as true partners rather than just requirement providers. This business-oriented communication has become a cornerstone of my leadership approach, most recently helping secure investment for a major platform modernization by clearly articulating the business case in terms of future flexibility and time-to-market advantages."

Why This Response Is Effective: * Demonstrates business acumen alongside technical leadership * Shows sophisticated understanding of trade-off decisions * Balances technical considerations with clear business outcomes * Provides specific, quantifiable business results * Reflects thoughtfully on business partnership approach with subsequent application

PERSONAL LEADERSHIP QUESTIONS

These questions assess your self-awareness, decision-making approach, and how you handle challenging leadership situations.

COMMON QUESTIONS

- "Tell me about a time when you had to make a difficult decision with incomplete information."

- "Describe a situation where you received feedback that was difficult to hear."

- "Give me an example of how you've adapted your leadership style to different team members or situations."

- "Tell me about a time when you failed as a leader and what you learned from it."

WHAT MAKES AN EFFECTIVE RESPONSE

Effective responses to personal leadership questions demonstrate:

- **Self-awareness** about strengths, weaknesses, and growth areas
- **Adaptability** in leadership approach across different contexts
- **Resilience** in facing setbacks and challenges
- **Decision-making** process under uncertainty or pressure
- **Learning orientation** and continuous personal development

EXAMPLE STAR+ RESPONSE

Question: "Tell me about a time when you failed as a leader and what you learned from it."

Situation: "Two years ago at SoftwareCo, I was leading the Data Platform team during a critical rewrite of our analytics engine. This was a strategic project for the company, as the existing system couldn't handle our growing data volume and was limiting our product capabilities. My team consisted of 10 engineers with varying experience levels, and we had a six-month timeline to deliver the new system."

Task: "As the Engineering Manager, I was responsible for the technical execution and team leadership throughout this high-visibility project. The challenge was significant: we were adopting new technologies that the team wasn't familiar with, working under an aggressive timeline, and dealing with ambiguous requirements as we defined a next-generation platform."

Action: "I approached this project with high confidence based on previous successes. I developed what I believed was a solid technical architecture and created a detailed project plan. Given the timeline pressure and technical complexity, I decided to be highly directive in my leadership approach. I assigned specific components to engineers based on my assessment of their skills, defined the technical approaches we would use, and established a rigid delivery schedule with limited flexibility.

As the project progressed, I noticed concerning signs: team members were less engaged in technical discussions, velocity was lower than expected, and several components were falling behind schedule. Rather than reassessing my approach, I doubled down on control—increasing the frequency of status checks, personally reviewing more code, and occasionally stepping in to implement components myself when progress seemed too slow.

By the four-month mark, we were significantly behind schedule with mounting quality issues. During a retrospective that I reluctantly agreed to hold, the team provided direct feedback that my leadership approach was causing serious problems. I was making technical decisions without sufficient input from specialists on the team, creating bottlenecks by requiring my approval on too many decisions, and undermining team ownership and creativity with my directive style."

Result: "The project ultimately delivered three months late, with several key features deferred to a subsequent release. The quality issues required significant remediation work after the initial launch, further delaying the full business value. Team morale suffered significantly, with two senior engineers leaving the company citing leadership issues as a factor in their decision.

This was clearly a leadership failure on my part. While there were legitimate technical challenges in the project, my leadership approach exacerbated rather than mitigated them. By centralizing decision-making and control, I had become a bottleneck, demotivated the team, and failed to leverage their collective expertise effectively."

Plus (Lessons Learned): "This failure taught me profound lessons about leadership that have fundamentally changed my approach. First, I learned that leadership style must adapt to the nature of the work. My directive approach might have been appropriate for a well-understood, emergency situation, but it was counterproductive for a complex, creative project requiring collective intelligence. I've since developed a more nuanced leadership model where I explicitly adapt my approach based on the situation rather than defaulting to control under pressure.

Second, I recognized that expertise is distributed across the team, not concentrated in the manager. By failing to leverage the specialized knowledge of team members, I made inferior technical decisions and missed opportunities for innovation. I now approach technical leadership as orchestrating team expertise rather than providing all the answers myself.

Third, I discovered that psychological safety is essential for team performance, especially when tackling complex, uncertain work. My controlling approach undermined safety and reduced the team's willingness to experiment, raise concerns, or challenge assumptions. I've since made building psychological safety a foundational element of my leadership practice, starting with explicit permission for the team to question my ideas.

Most importantly, I learned that leadership effectiveness requires continuous feedback and adaptation. By failing to notice or respond to early signals that my approach wasn't working, I allowed the situation to deteriorate unnecessarily. I now build regular feedback mechanisms into all my projects, including anonymous surveys and facilitated retrospectives specifically focused on my leadership effectiveness.

I've applied these lessons extensively in subsequent projects. Most recently, I led another strategic initiative with a completely different approach—establishing clear outcomes while empowering the team to determine implementation approaches, creating explicit forums for challenging my thinking, and conducting bi-weekly leadership retrospectives. That project delivered on time with high quality and significantly improved team engagement, validating the lessons from my previous failure."

Why This Response Is Effective: * Takes full ownership of the leadership failure without excuses * Provides specific details about what went wrong and why * Demonstrates deep self-reflection and personal growth * Articulates concrete changes to leadership approach * Shows application of lessons to subsequent situations with improved outcomes

8.3. THE TECHNICAL MANAGER VS. PEOPLE MANAGER BALANCE

Engineering Manager interviews often probe for the balance between technical leadership and people management. Let's explore this balance and strategies for demonstrating both dimensions effectively.

THE TECHNICAL CREDIBILITY THRESHOLD

Engineering Manager roles have an implicit "technical credibility threshold" that candidates must meet before their leadership capabilities are fully valued. This threshold varies by company and level:

- **Google**: Maintains high technical expectations for Engineering Managers, who are expected to remain hands-on technical leaders

- **Meta**: Focuses on technical judgment and architectural understanding rather than hands-on coding

- **Amazon**: Emphasizes technical credibility sufficient to effectively lead and evaluate engineering teams

- **Microsoft**: Balances technical depth with leadership breadth, with increasing emphasis on leadership at higher levels

Failing to establish this technical credibility can undermine even strong leadership examples. However, exceeding this threshold doesn't provide proportional benefits—once credibility is established, additional technical depth adds diminishing returns compared to leadership evidence.

Strategy: Establish technical credibility early in each response with precise terminology and appropriate depth, then shift focus to the leadership aspects being evaluated.

THE HANDS-ON VS. DELEGATION BALANCE

Engineering Managers must balance appropriate hands-on involvement with effective delegation and team empowerment. Different companies have different expectations for this balance:

- **Google**: Values Engineering Managers who remain technically hands-on and can directly contribute when needed

- **Meta**: Emphasizes scaling through team empowerment rather than personal technical contribution

- **Amazon**: Focuses on appropriate delegation while maintaining sufficient technical depth to evaluate quality

- **Microsoft**: Expects decreasing hands-on involvement and increasing strategic leadership at higher levels

Strategy: Demonstrate thoughtful decision-making about when to be hands-on versus when to delegate, with examples that show both capabilities applied appropriately to different situations.

THE TECHNICAL VISION VS. EXECUTION BALANCE

Engineering Managers must balance setting technical vision with ensuring effective execution. This balance requires demonstrating both strategic thinking and operational excellence.

Strategy: Include examples that show both dimensions—how you've established technical direction and strategy, and how you've ensured effective implementation and delivery of that vision through team execution.

THE INDIVIDUAL VS. TEAM SUCCESS BALANCE

Engineering Managers are evaluated on team outcomes rather than personal achievements. This requires a shift in emphasis from individual contribution to team enablement.

Strategy: Frame your impact in terms of team outcomes and organizational results rather than personal technical accomplishments. Use phrases like "I built a team that..." or "Through my leadership, the team achieved..." to emphasize your focus on collective success.

8.4. CONCLUSION: DEMONSTRATING ENGINEERING LEADERSHIP THROUGH BEHAVIOR

Effective behavioral interviewing for Engineering Manager roles requires demonstrating a sophisticated balance of technical credibility and leadership capabilities. The examples in this chapter illustrate this balance across different question types and competency areas.

Remember that Engineering Manager interviews assess not just what you've built or delivered, but how you lead—your approach to team development, technical decision-making, organizational influence, and business partnership. By preparing examples that demonstrate these dimensions, you position yourself as a complete engineering leader who can drive both technical excellence and team success.

In the next chapter, we'll explore behavioral examples specifically tailored for Solution Architect roles, examining how the expectations and emphasis shift when moving from team leadership to broader architectural and customer-focused positions.

CHAPTER 9. SOLUTION ARCHITECT EXAMPLES

> The architect must be a prophet... a prophet in the true sense of the term... if he can't see at least ten years ahead don't call him an architect.
>
> — Frank Lloyd Wright

"We don't need architects—we need builders who can whiteboard."

The AWS principal architect folded his arms as he rejected my candidate. After six years and 500+ solution architect interviews at Amazon (and countless conversations with peers at Google and Microsoft), I've learned this hard truth: The best technical designs fail behavioral interviews when they're explained like academic exercises rather than customer-obsessed journeys.

This chapter is about the stories that separate theoretical architects from hired ones—the kind who:

- Defend a cloud migration decision by showing its impact on a CFO's balance sheet

- Explain technical trade-offs with the clarity of a product manager

- Turn "Why didn't you use Kubernetes?" into a strategic discussion about team skills and long-term maintenance costs

I'll share what I learned from hiring top solution architects across three FAANG companies, including:

1. The one question that eliminates 80% of candidates (and how to ace it)

2. Why the best architects spend more time talking about failed designs than

successful ones

3. How to discuss technical debt without sounding like you're making excuses

(And yes—we'll dissect that rejected "builder" candidate, who later became one of our highest-performing hires after reframing his approach.)

9.1. THE SOLUTION ARCHITECT BEHAVIORAL ASSESSMENT

Before diving into specific examples, let's understand what companies are actually evaluating when they conduct behavioral interviews for Solution Architect roles.

CORE COMPETENCIES FOR SOLUTION ARCHITECTS

While each company has its own framework, most solution architect interviews assess some combination of these core competencies:

TECHNICAL BREADTH AND DEPTH

- Understanding diverse technologies and their appropriate applications
- Making sound architectural decisions across multiple domains
- Balancing technical trade-offs across complex system landscapes
- Maintaining sufficient technical depth to establish credibility

CUSTOMER OBSESSION

- Understanding customer needs beyond stated requirements
- Translating business problems into technical solutions
- Balancing immediate customer requests with long-term success
- Advocating for customer interests in technical decisions

BUSINESS ACUMEN

- Understanding business models and value drivers
- Aligning technical solutions with business objectives
- Quantifying the business impact of architectural decisions
- Making appropriate cost-benefit trade-offs

STRATEGIC VISION

- Developing forward-looking architectural roadmaps
- Anticipating future technical and business needs
- Balancing immediate solutions with long-term direction
- Communicating technical vision to diverse stakeholders

INFLUENCE AND LEADERSHIP

- Driving architectural decisions without direct authority
- Building consensus across diverse stakeholder groups
- Communicating complex technical concepts to various audiences
- Leading through expertise rather than position

PROBLEM-SOLVING APPROACH

- Breaking down complex business and technical challenges
- Developing innovative solutions to multifaceted problems
- Navigating ambiguity and incomplete information
- Balancing theoretical ideals with practical constraints

These competencies are assessed through behavioral questions that probe for specific examples of how you've demonstrated these capabilities in your past architectural roles.

THE TECHNICAL VS. BUSINESS VS. CUSTOMER BALANCE

Solution Architect interviews present a unique challenge: balancing technical depth with business understanding and customer focus. This balance requires careful calibration:

- **Too technical**: Focusing exclusively on technology without connecting to business value or customer needs

- **Too business-focused**: Emphasizing business outcomes without demonstrating the technical substance to achieve them

- **Too customer-focused**: Prioritizing customer requests without the strategic perspective to ensure long-term success

The most effective Solution Architect responses strike a careful balance—demonstrating technical credibility while clearly connecting architectural decisions to business outcomes and customer success.

This balance varies by company:

- **Amazon**: Emphasizes customer obsession and ownership, with technical depth as a foundation

- **Google**: Values technical depth alongside strategic thinking, with user focus as a guiding principle

- **Microsoft**: Balances technical expertise with customer empathy and business alignment

- **AWS/Azure/Cloud Providers**: Focuses heavily on customer success through appropriate technology application

Understanding this balance for your specific target companies helps you calibrate your responses appropriately.

9.2. QUESTION TYPES AND EFFECTIVE RESPONSES

Let's examine common behavioral question types for Solution Architects and analyze what makes an effective response for each.

TECHNICAL DECISION MAKING QUESTIONS

These questions assess how you make architectural choices, evaluate trade-offs, and ensure technical quality.

COMMON QUESTIONS

- "Tell me about a time when you had to make a significant architectural decision with long-term implications."

- "Describe a situation where you had to choose between competing technical approaches."

- "Give me an example of how you've balanced technical ideals against practical constraints."

- "Tell me about an architectural decision you made that you're particularly proud of."

WHAT MAKES AN EFFECTIVE RESPONSE

Effective responses to technical decision questions demonstrate:

- **Structured decision-making process** rather than intuitive judgments
- **Explicit identification of trade-offs** considered in the decision
- **Connection between technical decisions and business/customer**

outcomes

- **Appropriate balance** between immediate needs and long-term considerations
- **Technical depth** without excessive implementation details

EXAMPLE STAR+ RESPONSE

Question: "Tell me about a time when you had to make a significant architectural decision with long-term implications."

Situation: "At Enterprise Financial Services, I was the Solution Architect for a strategic initiative to modernize our core banking platform. This platform processed approximately $50 billion in transactions annually and supported 5 million customer accounts. The existing system was a 20-year-old monolithic application running on mainframe technology, with high maintenance costs and increasingly difficult regulatory compliance. The business had allocated $25 million for this multi-year transformation, with the primary goals of reducing operational costs, improving time-to-market for new features, and enhancing regulatory compliance capabilities."

Task: "As the Solution Architect, I needed to make a fundamental architectural decision that would shape the entire modernization approach: whether to pursue a complete rewrite using modern cloud-native technologies, implement a progressive modernization using a strangler pattern, or adopt a commercial off-the-shelf (COTS) banking platform. This decision would have profound implications for the organization's technology strategy for the next decade, affecting everything from technology investments to hiring strategies to vendor relationships."

Action: "I approached this decision with a comprehensive, multi-dimensional analysis. First, I established clear evaluation criteria that balanced technical, business, and risk considerations, including implementation timeline, total cost of ownership, regulatory compliance capabilities, integration complexity, and talent availability.

For each option, I conducted deep technical assessments. For the rewrite approach, I developed reference architectures using microservices and event-driven patterns, and created proof-of-concepts to validate key technical assumptions. For the progressive modernization, I identified decomposition boundaries and integration patterns that would enable incremental replacement. For the COTS option, I conducted detailed vendor evaluations, including site visits to reference customers.

Beyond the technical analysis, I engaged extensively with stakeholders across the organization. I conducted workshops with business leaders to understand their strategic priorities and growth plans. I worked with the finance team to develop detailed TCO models for each option. I consulted with our risk and compliance teams to assess regulatory implications. I also engaged with our talent acquisition team to evaluate our ability to hire for different technology stacks.

To ensure I wasn't operating in a vacuum, I formed an architectural review board with senior technical leaders from across the organization. We conducted structured evaluations of each option, challenging assumptions and identifying blind spots in the analysis.

After this comprehensive assessment, I recommended a hybrid approach: adopting a COTS platform for standardized banking functions while implementing a custom, cloud-native architecture for differentiating capabilities. This approach would be executed through a progressive migration pattern, allowing incremental business value delivery rather than a 'big bang' transition."

Result: "The executive leadership team approved my recommended approach, which has guided our modernization journey for the past three years. We've successfully migrated 60% of our core banking functions to the new architecture, achieving significant business outcomes: operational costs have decreased by 30%, time-to-market for new features has improved from months to weeks, and our regulatory compliance capabilities have been recognized as industry-leading by our auditors.

The hybrid approach has proven particularly valuable as market conditions evolved. When a major regulatory change was announced with an aggressive timeline, we were able to leverage the COTS platform's compliance capabilities to meet the deadline. Simultaneously, when a competitive threat emerged in our lending business, we rapidly developed differentiating features using our custom architecture that the COTS platform couldn't have supported.

Perhaps most importantly, this architectural decision has positioned the organization for long-term success. We've established modern engineering practices, attracted top technical talent, and created a technology foundation that can evolve incrementally rather than requiring another wholesale replacement in the future."

Plus (Lessons Learned): "This experience taught me several profound lessons about architectural decision-making that have shaped my approach since. First, I learned that the most impactful architectural decisions are rarely purely technical—they sit at the intersection of technology, business strategy, and organizational capabilities. By explicitly considering all three dimensions in my analysis, I developed a more robust and sustainable solution than a technically-focused approach would have produced.

Second, I recognized the power of hybrid approaches that combine the best elements of different options rather than treating architecture decisions as binary choices. This 'third way' thinking has become a cornerstone of my architectural approach, recently helping navigate a similar decision between build vs. buy for our digital customer experience platform.

Third, I discovered the importance of progressive value delivery in large-scale architectural transformations. By structuring our approach to deliver business value incrementally rather than requiring years of investment before benefits materialized, we maintained organizational momentum and support throughout the journey. This incremental value approach has influenced all subsequent large initiatives I've architected.

Most significantly, I learned that architectural decisions of this magnitude require both analytical rigor and collaborative engagement. The structured analysis provided the foundation for a sound decision, but the extensive stakeholder engagement ensured the solution addressed the full spectrum of organizational needs and built the consensus necessary for successful execution. This balanced approach to major architectural decisions has become my standard practice, most recently guiding our organization's AI and machine learning strategy development."

Why This Response Is Effective: * Demonstrates a structured, multi-dimensional decision-making process * Balances technical considerations with business and organizational factors * Shows long-term strategic thinking alongside practical execution * Provides specific, measurable business outcomes resulting from the decision * Reflects thoughtfully on architectural approach with clear subsequent application

CUSTOMER-FOCUSED QUESTIONS

These questions assess how you understand customer needs, translate them into solutions, and ensure customer success.

COMMON QUESTIONS

- "Tell me about a time when you had to design a solution for a customer with complex or ambiguous requirements."

- "Describe a situation where you had to balance a customer's immediate requests with their long-term needs."

- "Give me an example of how you've advocated for a customer's interests in a technical decision."

- "Tell me about a time when you had to say no to a customer request and propose an alternative solution."

WHAT MAKES AN EFFECTIVE RESPONSE

Effective responses to customer-focused questions demonstrate:

- **Deep understanding** of customer needs beyond stated requirements

- **Translation skills** between business problems and technical solutions

- **Appropriate balance** between customer requests and technical best practices

- **Long-term perspective** on customer success, not just immediate satisfaction

- **Effective communication** with both technical and non-technical stakeholders

EXAMPLE STAR+ RESPONSE

Question: "Tell me about a time when you had to design a solution for a customer with complex or ambiguous requirements."

Situation: "While working as a Solution Architect at Cloud Solutions Inc., I was assigned to work with a major healthcare provider who was undertaking their first significant cloud migration. The customer operated 15 hospitals and over 100 clinics, serving approximately 2 million patients annually. They had a complex landscape of legacy systems, including critical clinical applications with strict availability requirements and sensitive patient data subject to HIPAA regulations. Their stated goal was to 'move to the cloud to reduce costs and improve agility,' but beyond this high-level objective, their requirements were ambiguous and sometimes contradictory. Different stakeholders within their organization had varying priorities and concerns, from the CIO's focus on cost reduction to the CISO's security concerns to the clinical directors' emphasis on system reliability."

Task: "As the Solution Architect, I needed to develop a comprehensive cloud migration strategy that would address their business objectives while navigating their complex technical landscape and diverse stakeholder priorities. The challenge was particularly difficult because the customer lacked cloud expertise, had inconsistent documentation of their current systems, and operated in a highly regulated environment where mistakes could impact patient care."

Action: "I approached this challenge by first focusing on understanding the customer's environment and needs before proposing solutions. I conducted a series of structured discovery workshops with different stakeholder groups, using a framework I developed that covered business drivers, technical constraints, regulatory requirements, and operational considerations.

Rather than accepting the initial stated goal of 'moving to the cloud for cost and agility' at face value, I worked with the customer's executive team to define specific, measurable objectives. Through this process, we refined their goals to include 30% infrastructure cost reduction, 50% improvement in deployment frequency for key applications, enhanced disaster recovery capabilities, and strengthened security controls for protected health information.

To address the ambiguity in their technical landscape, I led a systematic application portfolio assessment. We evaluated each major system against multiple dimensions: business criticality, technical complexity, data sensitivity, integration dependencies, and cloud readiness. This assessment revealed that their environment was more heterogeneous than initially understood, requiring different migration approaches for different systems.

Based on this comprehensive understanding, I designed a multi-phase migration strategy that addressed their specific needs rather than following a generic cloud migration playbook. The strategy included:

1. A hybrid architecture that kept certain clinical systems on-premises while moving appropriate workloads to the cloud

2. A security and compliance framework specifically designed for healthcare data in cloud environments

3. A phased migration approach starting with non-critical systems to build cloud capabilities before tackling mission-critical applications

4. A detailed economic model showing cost implications across the migration journey, not just the end state

Throughout this process, I maintained transparent communication about trade-offs and constraints. When stakeholders had conflicting priorities, I facilitated structured decision-making processes that made trade-offs explicit and created shared understanding of the rationale behind architectural choices."

Result: "The customer approved the migration strategy and has successfully implemented the first three phases of the plan over the past 18 months. They've migrated 60% of their application portfolio to the cloud, achieving significant business outcomes: infrastructure costs have decreased by 35% (exceeding the target), deployment frequency has improved by 70% for migrated applications, and they've established a robust disaster recovery capability that reduced their recovery time objective from 24 hours to 2 hours for critical systems.

The security and compliance framework we developed has successfully passed two HIPAA audits with zero findings, giving their security team confidence in their cloud environment. The phased approach allowed their team to develop cloud skills incrementally, reducing their initial concerns about talent gaps.

Perhaps most significantly, the customer has evolved from viewing cloud merely as a cost-saving measure to recognizing it as a strategic enabler. They've since launched three new digital health initiatives leveraging cloud capabilities that wouldn't have been feasible in their previous environment."

Plus (Lessons Learned): "This experience taught me valuable lessons about handling complex and ambiguous customer requirements that I've applied to numerous engagements since. First, I learned the importance of looking beyond stated requirements to understand underlying business objectives. By reframing their generic goal of 'cloud migration for cost and agility' into specific, measurable outcomes, we created a much more effective foundation for architectural decisions.

Second, I recognized that technical discovery and business alignment must happen before solution design, not in parallel. The comprehensive assessment we conducted revealed critical insights that significantly shaped the architecture, avoiding what would have been costly assumptions had we started designing solutions immediately.

Third, I discovered the power of structured frameworks for bringing clarity to ambiguous situations. The application portfolio assessment framework I developed for this engagement has since become a standard tool in my approach, which I've refined and applied to twelve subsequent cloud migration projects across different industries.

Most importantly, I learned that effective solution architecture in complex environments requires balancing technical expertise with stakeholder alignment skills. The technical aspects of the cloud migration were actually less challenging than the process of aligning diverse stakeholders around a common approach. This insight has fundamentally shaped my solution architecture practice, leading me to invest as much in developing stakeholder management and communication skills as in deepening my technical knowledge."

Why This Response Is Effective: * Demonstrates deep customer focus beyond surface requirements * Shows systematic approach to navigating complexity and ambiguity * Balances technical solution with business outcomes and stakeholder needs * Provides specific, measurable customer results * Reflects thoughtfully on customer engagement approach with subsequent application

BUSINESS VALUE QUESTIONS

These questions assess how you connect technical solutions to business outcomes and make value-driven decisions.

COMMON QUESTIONS

- "Tell me about a time when you had to justify a significant technical investment based on business value."

- "Describe a situation where you had to make trade-offs between cost, time, and quality in an architectural decision."

- "Give me an example of how you've aligned a technical solution with business objectives."

- "Tell me about a time when you had to adapt an architectural approach due to business constraints."

WHAT MAKES AN EFFECTIVE RESPONSE

Effective responses to business value questions demonstrate:

- **Clear connection** between technical decisions and business outcomes

- **Quantification** of business impact where possible

- **Value-based prioritization** rather than technical preference

- **Appropriate trade-off decisions** that balance multiple business considerations

- **Business acumen** alongside technical expertise

EXAMPLE STAR+ RESPONSE

Question: "Tell me about a time when you had to justify a significant technical investment based on business value."

Situation: "At Digital Retail Inc., I was the Solution Architect for our e-commerce platform that generated approximately $300 million in annual revenue. The platform had evolved over seven years and was showing signs of significant technical debt: slow page load times (averaging 4.5 seconds), frequent small outages (2-3 per month), and increasingly lengthy deployment cycles (2-3 weeks for major features). These technical issues were beginning to impact business performance, with conversion rates declining 5% year-over-year and customer satisfaction scores dropping from 4.2 to 3.8 out of 5. Despite these challenges, the business was reluctant to invest in technical modernization, preferring to focus resources on new feature development and marketing initiatives."

Task: "As the Solution Architect, I needed to develop and justify a significant platform modernization investment—estimated at $4.5 million and 12 months of engineering effort—based on business value rather than technical merits alone. The challenge was particularly difficult because the investment would temporarily reduce our capacity for new feature development, the benefits would be realized incrementally rather than immediately, and previous technical debt discussions had failed to gain executive support."

Action: "I approached this challenge by reframing the modernization from a technical initiative to a business value proposition. First, I collaborated with our analytics team to quantify the business impact of our technical issues. We conducted A/B tests comparing conversion rates between user segments experiencing different page load times, analyzed customer drop-off patterns during system slowdowns, and calculated the opportunity cost of delayed feature deployments.

Rather than presenting a monolithic modernization plan, I developed a phased approach with clear business value milestones. Each phase targeted specific business metrics: the first focused on reliability improvements to reduce lost sales from outages, the second on performance enhancements to improve conversion rates, and the third on deployment automation to accelerate time-to-market.

For each phase, I created a detailed business case that included: 1. Current business impact of the technical issues (quantified in revenue and customer terms) 2. Expected business outcomes of the proposed improvements 3. Implementation approach and timeline 4. Required investment and resource allocation 5. Risk mitigation strategies 6. Success metrics and measurement approach

To make the investment more palatable, I designed an implementation approach that would deliver incremental business value rather than requiring the full investment before seeing returns. I also identified opportunities to combine modernization work with planned feature enhancements, reducing the perceived opportunity cost.

Perhaps most importantly, I engaged business stakeholders throughout the process, ensuring the modernization plan addressed their specific pain points and priorities. I conducted workshops with product, marketing, and sales teams to understand how technical limitations were affecting their objectives and incorporated their feedback into the plan."

Result: "The executive team approved the full modernization investment, allocated as a separate budget line item rather than competing with feature development resources. We successfully implemented the plan over 14 months, delivering significant business outcomes: page load times improved from 4.5 seconds to 1.2 seconds, platform reliability increased to 99.98% uptime (from approximately 99.8%), and deployment cycles reduced from weeks to days for major features and hours for minor changes.

These technical improvements translated directly to business results: conversion rates increased by 15% compared to pre-modernization baseline, generating approximately $45 million in incremental annual revenue. Customer satisfaction scores improved from 3.8 to 4.5 out of 5, and our Net Promoter

Score increased by 18 points.

The modernization also enabled business capabilities that weren't previously possible, including personalized product recommendations, real-time inventory visibility, and rapid A/B testing of new features. These capabilities have become central to the company's competitive strategy, with the CEO highlighting the platform's 'digital agility' in recent investor presentations."

Plus (Lessons Learned): "This experience taught me valuable lessons about connecting technical decisions to business value that have influenced my approach to solution architecture ever since. First, I learned that technical debt must be translated into business impact terms to gain appropriate attention. By quantifying the revenue and customer experience implications, we transformed the conversation from technical preference to business necessity.

Second, I recognized the power of incremental value delivery in gaining support for large technical investments. By structuring the modernization to deliver business benefits throughout the journey rather than only at the end, we maintained momentum and executive support even when challenges arose. This incremental approach has become my standard practice for large technical initiatives.

Third, I discovered that business stakeholder engagement is as critical as technical excellence in major architectural initiatives. By involving business teams in defining the modernization priorities, we ensured the technical improvements directly addressed their most significant pain points, creating natural advocates for the investment.

Most significantly, I learned that solution architects must be bilingual—fluent in both technical and business languages—to be truly effective. The ability to translate between these domains, connecting architectural decisions to business outcomes, has become the foundation of my approach to solution architecture. This business value orientation has since helped me secure investment for several other major technical initiatives, including our recent API platform modernization and cloud migration."

Why This Response Is Effective: * Demonstrates clear connection between technical decisions and business outcomes * Shows quantification of business impact in revenue and customer terms * Balances technical approach with business considerations * Provides specific, measurable business results * Reflects thoughtfully on business value approach with subsequent application

STRATEGIC VISION QUESTIONS

These questions assess how you develop forward-looking architectural roadmaps and balance immediate solutions with long-term direction.

COMMON QUESTIONS

- "Tell me about a time when you developed a long-term technical vision or roadmap."

- "Describe a situation where you had to balance immediate solutions with long-term architectural direction."

- "Give me an example of how you've anticipated and prepared for future technical needs."

- "Tell me about a time when you had to evolve an architecture to address changing business requirements."

WHAT MAKES AN EFFECTIVE RESPONSE

Effective responses to strategic vision questions demonstrate:

- **Forward-looking perspective** beyond immediate requirements

- **Balanced approach** to immediate needs and future flexibility

- **Systematic roadmap development** rather than vague aspirations

- **Alignment between technical vision and business strategy**
- **Practical implementation path** for strategic direction

EXAMPLE STAR+ RESPONSE

Question: "Tell me about a time when you developed a long-term technical vision or roadmap."

Situation: "At InsureTech Inc., I was the Lead Solution Architect during a period of significant business transformation. The company was transitioning from a traditional insurance provider to a digital-first organization, facing new competitive threats from insurtech startups and changing customer expectations for digital experiences. Our technology landscape consisted of 75+ systems accumulated through decades of operation and multiple acquisitions, creating a complex, fragmented architecture that couldn't support the company's digital ambitions. The executive team recognized the need for technological transformation but lacked a coherent vision for the future state architecture and a practical path to achieve it."

Task: "As the Lead Solution Architect, I needed to develop a comprehensive technical vision and roadmap that would enable the company's digital transformation while addressing the complexity of our existing landscape. The challenge was particularly difficult because the vision needed to balance ambitious transformation with practical reality, span multiple technology domains from core insurance systems to customer-facing applications, and align diverse stakeholders from business and IT with different priorities and perspectives."

Action: "I approached this challenge by developing a multi-horizon architectural vision with a practical implementation roadmap. First, I established a clear understanding of the business strategy and objectives through extensive engagement with executive leadership. I conducted structured interviews and workshops to identify key business drivers, competitive differentiators, and growth priorities for the next 3-5 years.

Based on this business context, I defined an architectural vision organized around four key principles: customer-centricity, data as a strategic asset, operational excellence, and innovation agility. For each principle, I articulated specific architectural patterns and capabilities that would enable the business strategy.

Rather than presenting a monolithic 'target state' that would be outdated before it could be achieved, I developed a horizon-based roadmap: 1. Horizon 1 (0-18 months): Establishing foundational capabilities and addressing critical pain points 2. Horizon 2 (18-36 months): Accelerating digital capabilities and reducing legacy constraints 3. Horizon 3 (36+ months): Enabling innovation and differentiation through advanced technologies

For each horizon, I defined specific architectural initiatives, their business value, implementation approach, dependencies, and success metrics. I paid particular attention to the transition architecture—how we would evolve from the current state to the future vision while maintaining business operations.

To ensure the vision was actionable, I developed detailed architecture blueprints for key domains (customer experience, policy administration, claims, etc.) and identified integration patterns that would enable incremental modernization rather than requiring wholesale replacement.

Throughout this process, I maintained extensive stakeholder engagement, conducting regular reviews with both business and technology leaders to refine the vision and build shared ownership. I also established governance mechanisms to ensure architectural decisions would align with the vision while allowing for adaptation as business needs evolved."

Result: "The executive team unanimously approved the architectural vision and roadmap, allocating $25 million for the initial horizon of implementation. Over the past two years, we've successfully executed the Horizon 1 initiatives, delivering significant business outcomes: customer digital adoption increased from 35% to 65%, new product launch time reduced from 9 months to 3 months, and operational efficiency improved by 22% through automation and process optimization.

The architectural vision has become a cornerstone of the company's transformation strategy, with the CEO regularly referencing it in communications with investors and employees. It has provided a framework for prioritizing technology investments, with all major initiatives now evaluated against their contribution to the target architecture.

Perhaps most importantly, the vision has created alignment between business and technology teams around a common direction. Cross-functional teams now collaborate more effectively with shared understanding of how their work contributes to the broader transformation journey."

Plus (Lessons Learned): "This experience taught me valuable lessons about developing effective architectural visions that I've applied to subsequent strategic initiatives. First, I learned that architectural visions must be explicitly connected to business strategy to be meaningful. By anchoring our technical direction in business drivers and outcomes, we created a vision that resonated beyond the technology organization.

Second, I recognized the importance of horizon-based planning rather than fixed target states. Technology and business environments change too rapidly for static end-state architectures to remain relevant. The multi-horizon approach allowed us to maintain a clear direction while adapting to evolving needs and emerging technologies. This dynamic approach to architectural planning has become central to my practice.

Third, I discovered that transition architecture is often more critical than target architecture. The path from current state to future vision—including the intermediate states—determines the practical viability of a transformation. I now place equal emphasis on transition planning and target state definition in all architectural roadmaps I develop.

Most significantly, I learned that architectural visions succeed through stakeholder alignment more than technical elegance. The extensive engagement process we conducted created shared ownership that sustained momentum through inevitable challenges and competing priorities. This insight has fundamentally shaped my approach to architectural leadership, emphasizing collaborative vision development over top-down technical directives."

Why This Response Is Effective: * Demonstrates strategic thinking and long-term perspective * Shows practical approach to vision development and implementation * Balances technical architecture with business strategy alignment * Provides specific business outcomes resulting from the vision * Reflects thoughtfully on strategic planning approach with subsequent application

INFLUENCE AND LEADERSHIP QUESTIONS

These questions assess how you drive architectural decisions without direct authority and build consensus across diverse stakeholder groups.

COMMON QUESTIONS

- "Tell me about a time when you had to influence a significant architectural decision without having formal authority."

- "Describe a situation where you had to build consensus among stakeholders with different priorities."

- "Give me an example of how you've communicated complex technical concepts to non-technical audiences."

- "Tell me about a time when you had to drive architectural standards or governance across an organization."

WHAT MAKES AN EFFECTIVE RESPONSE

Effective responses to influence and leadership questions demonstrate:

- **Influence strategies** beyond positional authority
- **Stakeholder management** across diverse groups
- **Effective communication** adapted to different audiences
- **Consensus building** rather than forcing decisions
- **Architectural leadership** through expertise and collaboration

EXAMPLE STAR+ RESPONSE

Question: "Tell me about a time when you had to influence a significant architectural decision without having formal authority."

Situation: "At Global Financial Services, I was working as a Solution Architect on a strategic initiative to modernize our customer onboarding experience. This initiative spanned multiple business units and technology teams, each with their own leadership and priorities. A critical architectural decision emerged regarding the customer data management approach: whether to create a new centralized customer data platform or continue with the existing federated model where each business unit maintained its own customer data with point-to-point integrations. The centralized approach would provide significant long-term benefits for customer experience and analytics but required substantial investment and organizational change. As a Solution Architect, I had no formal authority over this decision—it required agreement from five business unit leaders and their respective technology teams, all of whom had historically operated autonomously."

Task: "I needed to influence this significant architectural decision toward the centralized approach, which I believed was technically superior and better aligned with the company's strategic direction. The challenge was particularly difficult because several influential stakeholders initially favored the federated approach due to concerns about implementation complexity, timeline impact, and perceived loss of control over their customer data."

Action: "I developed a multi-faceted influence strategy focused on building consensus through evidence, collaboration, and strategic alignment. First, I conducted a comprehensive analysis comparing the two approaches across multiple dimensions: customer experience impact, implementation complexity, total cost of ownership, regulatory compliance, and future flexibility. This analysis quantified the long-term benefits of the centralized approach while acknowledging the legitimate short-term concerns.

Rather than advocating for my preferred solution in isolation, I formed a cross-functional working group with representatives from each affected business unit and technology team. This group collaboratively defined the evaluation criteria and reviewed the analysis, ensuring all perspectives were considered and building shared ownership of the process.

To address concerns about implementation complexity, I developed a phased migration approach that would deliver incremental benefits while managing risk. This approach included a proof-of-concept phase to validate key assumptions before full commitment, addressing the 'show me, don't tell me' skepticism of several key stakeholders.

I recognized that different stakeholders had different priorities and communication preferences. For business leaders focused on customer experience and revenue, I created business-oriented presentations highlighting how the centralized approach would enable personalized customer journeys and cross-selling opportunities. For technology leaders concerned about implementation risk, I developed detailed technical designs and migration plans. For the CFO and finance team, I prepared a comprehensive TCO analysis showing the long-term cost advantages despite higher initial investment.

To build broader support, I identified and engaged influential advocates within each business unit who understood the strategic benefits. These allies helped socialize the approach within their organizations and provided valuable feedback on how to address specific concerns.

Perhaps most importantly, I explicitly connected the architectural decision to the company's strategic priorities. Our CEO had recently announced a 'customer-first' transformation initiative, and I demonstrated how the centralized customer data platform was essential to delivering on this strategic direction."

Result: "After three months of collaborative evaluation and refinement, all five business units agreed to pursue the centralized customer data platform approach. The executive committee approved the required investment ($12 million over two years), and we established a cross-functional implementation team with representation from each business unit.

We've since completed the first phase of implementation, migrating two business units to the centralized platform. This has already delivered significant business benefits: customer onboarding time reduced from 12 days to 3 days, cross-selling conversion rates improved by 35%, and regulatory reporting efficiency increased by 40%.

Beyond the immediate project outcomes, this process established a new model for cross-organizational architectural decisions. The collaborative approach we developed has since been adopted as a standard practice for enterprise-wide technology decisions, with three subsequent initiatives using similar methods to build consensus around complex architectural choices."

Plus (Lessons Learned): "This experience taught me valuable lessons about architectural influence that have shaped my leadership approach. First, I learned that effective influence requires understanding and addressing the specific concerns of each stakeholder rather than treating them as a homogeneous group. By tailoring my approach to different perspectives and priorities, I built broader support than a one-size-fits-all advocacy would have achieved.

Second, I recognized the power of collaborative processes in building consensus. By involving stakeholders in defining evaluation criteria and reviewing analysis, we created shared ownership that was more effective than presenting a predetermined solution, however well-reasoned. This collaborative approach to architectural decisions has become a cornerstone of my practice.

Third, I discovered the importance of connecting architectural decisions to strategic business priorities. By explicitly linking the technical approach to the CEO's customer-first initiative, we elevated the discussion from a technical preference to a strategic enabler. This strategic alignment approach has proven effective in numerous subsequent situations where I needed to influence without authority.

Most significantly, I learned that architectural influence is about building bridges between different perspectives rather than advocating for a particular position. By acknowledging legitimate concerns and incorporating them into a refined approach, we developed a solution that was ultimately stronger than my initial proposal. This insight fundamentally changed my view of architectural leadership from technical advocacy to collaborative problem-solving."

Why This Response Is Effective: * Focuses on influence and leadership rather than technical details * Demonstrates sophisticated stakeholder management across diverse groups * Shows multiple influence strategies adapted to different audiences * Provides concrete results that validate the approach * Reflects thoughtfully on leadership lessons with subsequent application

PROBLEM-SOLVING QUESTIONS

These questions assess how you approach complex business and technical challenges and develop innovative solutions.

COMMON QUESTIONS

- "Tell me about the most complex problem you've solved as a Solution Architect."

- "Describe a situation where you had to develop an innovative solution to a challenging business problem."

- "Give me an example of how you've approached a problem with significant constraints or limitations."

- "Tell me about a time when you had to solve a problem with incomplete information or ambiguity."

WHAT MAKES AN EFFECTIVE RESPONSE

Effective responses to problem-solving questions demonstrate:

- **Structured approach** to complex problem decomposition
- **Creative thinking** in developing non-obvious solutions
- **Pragmatic innovation** within real-world constraints
- **Balanced consideration** of technical and business dimensions
- **Resilience** in navigating ambiguity and incomplete information

EXAMPLE STAR+ RESPONSE

Question: "Tell me about the most complex problem you've solved as a Solution Architect."

Situation: "At Global Logistics Inc., I was the Solution Architect for a mission-critical initiative to modernize our supply chain visibility platform. This platform tracked approximately 5 million shipments annually across 120 countries, integrating with 200+ partners including carriers, customs authorities, and distribution centers. The existing system had evolved over 15 years and was struggling with increasing data volumes, new real-time tracking requirements, and the need to support emerging IoT devices and sensors. Business stakeholders needed enhanced capabilities to maintain competitive advantage, while simultaneously facing pressure to reduce operational costs by 20%."

Task: "I needed to design a solution that would transform our supply chain visibility capabilities while addressing several seemingly contradictory constraints: significantly enhanced functionality, reduced operational costs, minimal disruption to ongoing operations, compatibility with hundreds of existing integration points, and implementation within 18 months to meet competitive pressures. The challenge was particularly complex because it spanned multiple technology domains (IoT, data platforms, integration, analytics) and required balancing immediate business needs with long-term architectural sustainability."

Action: "I approached this complex problem through a structured, multi-dimensional process. First, I decomposed the challenge into distinct but interconnected domains: data ingestion and processing, storage and persistence, analytics and intelligence, integration and APIs, and user experience. For each domain, I identified specific requirements, constraints, and potential solution approaches.

Rather than attempting to solve all aspects simultaneously, I prioritized the core capabilities that would deliver the most significant business value: real-time shipment tracking, predictive delivery estimates, and exception management. This focused approach allowed us to manage complexity while still addressing critical business needs.

To navigate the tension between enhanced capabilities and cost reduction, I developed an innovative architecture that leveraged cloud-native services for scalability and cost efficiency, combined with a domain-driven design that isolated core business logic from technical implementation details. This approach enabled incremental modernization without requiring a complete replacement of existing systems.

For the critical challenge of maintaining compatibility with existing integration points while enabling new capabilities, I designed an API gateway pattern with adapter services that provided backward compatibility for legacy interfaces while exposing new capabilities through modern APIs. This pattern allowed partners to migrate at their own pace without disrupting ongoing operations.

To address the data volume and real-time processing requirements, I developed a hybrid data architecture combining stream processing for real-time events with batch processing for historical analysis. This approach optimized for both immediacy of information and depth of analysis while managing infrastructure costs.

Throughout this process, I maintained close collaboration with business stakeholders, technical teams, and external partners. I conducted regular design reviews, created prototypes to validate key assumptions, and established feedback loops to refine the solution based on emerging insights."

Result: "We successfully implemented the modernized supply chain visibility platform within the 18-month timeframe and under the allocated budget. The solution delivered transformative business capabilities: real-time tracking reduced average shipment visibility gaps from 4 hours to 5 minutes, predictive delivery estimates improved accuracy from ±24 hours to ±2 hours, and automated exception management reduced manual interventions by 65%.

These capabilities translated directly to business outcomes: customer satisfaction scores increased from 3.7 to 4.5 out of 5, operational efficiency improved by 25% (exceeding the 20% target), and the enhanced visibility enabled the company to offer premium service tiers that generated $15 million in incremental annual revenue.

From a technical perspective, the solution achieved remarkable results: data processing costs decreased by 40% despite a 300% increase in data volume, system reliability improved from 99.9% to 99.99% availability, and the modular architecture has enabled 15 subsequent enhancements to be deployed without service disruption."

Plus (Lessons Learned): "This experience taught me valuable lessons about solving complex architectural problems that have influenced my approach ever since. First, I learned the power of structured decomposition in managing complexity. By breaking the challenge into distinct domains while maintaining a clear understanding of their interdependencies, we made the problem tractable without losing sight of the holistic solution. This domain-based decomposition approach has become a standard part of my architectural toolkit.

Second, I recognized that innovation often emerges from embracing constraints rather than fighting them. The tension between enhanced capabilities and cost reduction actually drove us toward a more elegant solution than we might have developed without these competing pressures. I now actively use constraints as creative catalysts rather than viewing them as obstacles.

Third, I discovered the importance of focusing on core business value when navigating complexity. By prioritizing the capabilities that would deliver the most significant impact, we maintained momentum and demonstrated value early, which built support for the broader transformation. This value-focused approach has guided my solution development in all subsequent complex initiatives.

Most significantly, I learned that complex problems require balanced consideration of both technical and business dimensions throughout the solution development process. The continuous collaboration with business stakeholders ensured we were solving the right problem, while the technical rigor ensured we were solving it right. This integrated approach to business and technical problem-solving has become the foundation of my practice as a Solution Architect."

Why This Response Is Effective: * Demonstrates structured approach to a genuinely complex problem * Balances technical innovation with practical business considerations * Shows creative problem-solving within real-world constraints * Provides specific, measurable outcomes across multiple dimensions * Reflects thoughtfully on problem-solving approach with subsequent application

9.3. THE TECHNICAL BREADTH VS. DEPTH BALANCE

Solution Architect interviews often probe for the balance between technical breadth across multiple domains and sufficient depth in key areas. Let's explore this balance and strategies for demonstrating both dimensions effectively.

THE T-SHAPED KNOWLEDGE MODEL

Effective Solution Architects typically exhibit a "T-shaped" knowledge profile: * The horizontal bar represents breadth across multiple technology domains * The vertical bar represents depth in specific areas of expertise

This balance allows architects to make sound decisions across the technology landscape while maintaining sufficient credibility in core domains.

Strategy: In your responses, demonstrate both dimensions by: 1. Showing how you connect different technology domains in holistic solutions 2. Providing specific technical details in areas most relevant to the role 3. Explaining how you leverage specialist expertise when needed in areas outside your core depth

THE SPECIALIST VS. GENERALIST TENSION

Different organizations have different expectations for the specialist/generalist balance in Solution Architects: * Some value deep expertise in their specific technology stack * Others prioritize broad knowledge across multiple domains *

Most seek a balance with emphasis determined by role specifics

Strategy: Research your target company's expectations and calibrate your responses accordingly. When in doubt, demonstrate your primary areas of depth while showing how you effectively work across domains where you have less specialized knowledge.

THE IMPLEMENTATION KNOWLEDGE BALANCE

Solution Architects must balance high-level design knowledge with sufficient implementation understanding to ensure solutions are practical. This requires: * Enough implementation knowledge to design viable solutions * Sufficient practical experience to anticipate challenges * The wisdom to know when to consult specialists on implementation details

Strategy: Include specific implementation considerations in your examples without becoming overly focused on coding or configuration details. Show how you balance architectural thinking with practical implementation awareness.

9.4. CONCLUSION: DEMONSTRATING ARCHITECTURAL EXCELLENCE THROUGH BEHAVIOR

Effective behavioral interviewing for Solution Architect roles requires demonstrating a sophisticated balance of technical expertise, business acumen, and customer focus. The examples in this chapter illustrate this balance across different question types and competency areas.

Remember that Solution Architect interviews assess not just what you've designed, but how you design—your approach to problems, your collaboration with stakeholders, your technical judgment, and your ability to connect technology decisions to business outcomes. By preparing examples that demonstrate these dimensions, you position yourself as not just a technical expert, but a trusted advisor who can guide organizations through complex technology decisions.

In the next chapter, we'll explore behavioral examples specifically tailored for Program Manager roles, examining how the expectations and emphasis shift when moving from technical architecture to program execution and stakeholder management.

CHAPTER 10. PROGRAM MANAGER EXAMPLES

Plans are only good intentions unless they immediately degenerate into hard work.

— Peter Drucker

"Your Gantt chart is beautiful. Now tell me about the time it blew up."

The Amazon Principal PM leaned back, waiting for my candidate's answer. After years of working closely with hiring managers across FAANG—including hundreds of late-night conversations with my Principal PM mentor at Amazon—I've learned this brutal truth: **Program Managers get hired for their ability to recover from disaster, not prevent it.**

This chapter is about the messy reality behind polished program plans—the stories that separate theoretical PMs from hired ones:

- How you convinced an engineering team to work weekends after your timeline miscalculation

- Why you canceled a $2M initiative three months in (and how you sold it to leadership)

- The spreadsheet hack that saved a launch when your project management tool failed

I'll share what I learned from watching top PMs navigate these make-or-break moments, including:

1. The one interview answer that makes hiring managers sit up straighter (used by 90% of L6+ hires)

2. Why the best PMs talk about failed milestones more than successful ones

3. How to discuss stakeholder conflicts without sounding like you're assigning blame

10.1. THE PROGRAM MANAGER BEHAVIORAL ASSESSMENT

Before diving into specific examples, let's understand what companies are actually evaluating when they conduct behavioral interviews for Program Manager roles.

CORE COMPETENCIES FOR PROGRAM MANAGERS

While each company has its own framework, most program manager interviews assess some combination of these core competencies:

STAKEHOLDER MANAGEMENT

- Building relationships across diverse organizational functions

- Managing competing priorities and expectations

- Communicating effectively with different audiences

- Navigating organizational politics constructively

EXECUTION EXCELLENCE

- Driving complex initiatives from concept to completion

- Managing dependencies and coordinating cross-functional efforts

- Identifying and mitigating risks proactively

- Ensuring quality and timeliness of deliverables

STRATEGIC THINKING

- Connecting program activities to broader business objectives
- Prioritizing efforts based on business impact
- Anticipating future needs and challenges
- Making appropriate trade-off decisions

PROBLEM-SOLVING

- Breaking down complex challenges into manageable components
- Developing creative solutions to obstacles
- Navigating ambiguity and incomplete information
- Balancing competing constraints effectively

LEADERSHIP AND INFLUENCE

- Driving alignment without formal authority
- Building consensus among diverse stakeholders
- Motivating teams through challenging situations
- Demonstrating ownership and accountability

ADAPTABILITY

- Responding effectively to changing requirements or conditions
- Adjusting approaches based on new information
- Managing uncertainty and ambiguity
- Learning and applying insights from experience

These competencies are assessed through behavioral questions that probe for specific examples of how you've demonstrated these capabilities in your past program management roles.

THE EXECUTION VS. STRATEGY BALANCE

Program Manager interviews present a unique challenge: balancing execution focus with strategic thinking. This balance requires careful calibration:

- **Too execution-focused**: Demonstrating tactical capability without connecting to broader business objectives
- **Too strategic**: Emphasizing vision and planning without showing the ability to drive practical implementation

The most effective Program Manager responses strike a careful balance—showing strong execution skills while clearly connecting program activities to strategic business outcomes.

This balance varies by company and level:

- **Microsoft**: Values strategic thinking alongside execution, with increasing emphasis on strategy at higher levels
- **Google**: Emphasizes analytical problem-solving and data-driven decision making in program execution
- **Amazon**: Focuses heavily on ownership, customer obsession, and bias for action in program delivery
- **Meta**: Prioritizes speed, impact, and scale in program execution

Understanding this balance for your specific target companies helps you calibrate your responses appropriately.

10.2. QUESTION TYPES AND EFFECTIVE RESPONSES

Let's examine common behavioral question types for Program Managers and analyze what makes an effective response for each.

STAKEHOLDER MANAGEMENT QUESTIONS

These questions assess how you build relationships, manage expectations, and navigate organizational dynamics.

COMMON QUESTIONS

- "Tell me about a time when you had to manage stakeholders with competing priorities."

- "Describe a situation where you had to influence a decision without having direct authority."

- "Give me an example of how you've built alignment across diverse organizational functions."

- "Tell me about a time when you had to deliver difficult news to a stakeholder."

WHAT MAKES AN EFFECTIVE RESPONSE

Effective responses to stakeholder management questions demonstrate:

- **Proactive relationship building** rather than reactive engagement

- **Nuanced understanding** of different stakeholder perspectives and motivations

- **Transparent communication** adapted to different audiences

- **Constructive navigation** of organizational politics and conflicts

- **Balance between advocacy** and accommodation in stakeholder interactions

EXAMPLE STAR+ RESPONSE

Question: "Tell me about a time when you had to manage stakeholders with competing priorities."

Situation: "At Enterprise Solutions Inc., I was the Program Manager for a major digital transformation initiative that affected multiple business units. The program involved implementing a new customer relationship management (CRM) system that would replace three legacy systems and standardize customer engagement processes across the organization. The key stakeholders included the Sales leadership team, who wanted enhanced opportunity management capabilities; the Customer Service organization, who prioritized case management and customer history features; the Marketing team, who focused on campaign management and analytics; and the IT department, who was concerned about integration complexity and long-term supportability. Each group had different priorities, timelines, and definitions of success for the program."

Task: "As the Program Manager, I needed to build alignment among these stakeholders with competing priorities to ensure the program's success. The challenge was particularly complex because each group had legitimate business needs, limited resources to contribute to the implementation, and different levels of urgency. Additionally, there was a fixed budget and timeline for the overall program, making it impossible to fully satisfy all stakeholder requests simultaneously."

Action: "I approached this stakeholder management challenge systematically. First, I conducted individual meetings with each key stakeholder group to deeply understand their specific requirements, priorities, and concerns. Rather than just collecting feature requests, I focused on understanding their underlying business objectives and success metrics.

Based on these discussions, I created a comprehensive stakeholder map that documented each group's priorities, influence level, support level, and key concerns. This mapping helped me identify potential conflicts and alignment opportunities that weren't immediately obvious.

To address the competing priorities, I facilitated a series of structured workshops bringing together representatives from all stakeholder groups. In these sessions, I first established shared program objectives that transcended individual department goals, focusing on customer experience improvement and operational efficiency that benefited everyone.

I then introduced a prioritization framework that evaluated features based on multiple dimensions: business impact, implementation complexity, dependency relationships, and alignment with strategic objectives. This framework provided an objective basis for decision-making that stakeholders perceived as fair rather than arbitrary.

For particularly contentious issues, I used a phased implementation approach, scheduling certain capabilities for later releases to manage the scope while still addressing critical needs for all groups. I created a visual roadmap showing how each group's priorities would be addressed across the program timeline.

Throughout the program, I maintained transparent communication through multiple channels: a weekly status dashboard showing progress against key milestones, bi-weekly steering committee meetings with senior stakeholders, and department-specific updates tailored to each group's particular interests. When trade-offs were necessary, I clearly communicated the rationale and ensured all stakeholders understood the decision-making process."

Result: "Through this structured stakeholder management approach, we successfully implemented the CRM system on time and within budget, with high adoption across all business units. The program delivered 85% of the initially requested capabilities in the first release, with the remaining 15% implemented in a subsequent phase three months later.

Key business outcomes included a 35% reduction in customer onboarding time, 28% improvement in sales conversion rates, and 40% faster resolution of customer service issues. Each stakeholder group achieved their primary objectives, though some had to accept compromises on timing or specific feature implementations.

Perhaps most significantly, the collaborative approach transformed the organizational dynamics around technology initiatives. The cross-functional governance model we established has since been adopted as a standard practice for major programs, and stakeholder satisfaction with IT-led initiatives increased from 65% to 88% in the annual business survey."

Plus (Lessons Learned): "This experience taught me valuable lessons about stakeholder management that have shaped my program management approach. First, I learned the importance of understanding the 'why' behind stakeholder requests rather than just the 'what.' By focusing on business objectives rather than specific features, we found creative solutions that addressed underlying needs while managing scope.

Second, I recognized that transparency in decision-making processes is often more important than the specific decisions themselves. When stakeholders understood how and why decisions were made, they were more likely to accept outcomes even when they didn't get everything they wanted. This principle of process transparency has become central to my stakeholder management approach.

Third, I discovered the power of creating shared objectives that transcend departmental boundaries. By establishing program goals that all stakeholders could support, we created a foundation for collaborative problem-solving rather than competitive positioning. I've since applied this approach to all cross-functional programs I've managed, most recently in our enterprise data governance initiative.

Most significantly, I learned that effective stakeholder management requires both structure and empathy—systematic processes for alignment combined with genuine understanding of each stakeholder's perspective and constraints. This balanced approach has become a cornerstone of my program management philosophy, enabling me to navigate complex organizational dynamics while maintaining focus on program outcomes."

Why This Response Is Effective: * Demonstrates a structured approach to a common program management challenge * Shows nuanced understanding of different stakeholder perspectives * Balances accommodation of diverse needs with program delivery requirements * Provides specific, measurable outcomes that benefited all stakeholders * Reflects thoughtfully on stakeholder management approach with subsequent application

EXECUTION EXCELLENCE QUESTIONS

These questions assess how you drive complex initiatives, manage dependencies, and ensure quality delivery.

COMMON QUESTIONS

- "Tell me about a complex program you managed from initiation to completion."

- "Describe a situation where you had to overcome significant obstacles to deliver a program successfully."

- "Give me an example of how you've managed dependencies across multiple workstreams or teams."

- "Tell me about a time when a program was at risk of missing critical deadlines and how you handled it."

WHAT MAKES AN EFFECTIVE RESPONSE

Effective responses to execution excellence questions demonstrate:

- **Structured program management** methodology and tools

- **Proactive risk identification** and mitigation

- **Effective dependency management** across workstreams

- **Clear metrics and milestones** for tracking progress

- **Decisive action** when facing delivery challenges

EXAMPLE STAR+ RESPONSE

Question: "Tell me about a complex program you managed from initiation to completion."

Situation: "At TechCorp, I led a strategic program to consolidate and modernize our customer-facing digital platforms. Prior to this initiative, the company operated seven separate digital properties that had been developed independently by different business units, resulting in inconsistent customer experiences, duplicated functionality, and inefficient maintenance. The program scope included consolidating these properties into a unified platform, implementing a consistent design system, migrating approximately 500,000 active customers, and establishing new operational processes—all while ensuring business continuity throughout the transition."

Task: "As the Program Manager, I was responsible for leading this complex initiative from concept through completion. The program involved 12 cross-functional teams totaling about 85 people, including product management, UX design, engineering, data analytics, marketing, customer support, and compliance. We had an 18-month timeline and $12 million budget. The challenge was particularly complex because it required coordinating technical work across multiple technology stacks, managing change for both internal teams and customers, and navigating competing priorities from different business units who were concerned about losing control of their digital presence."

Action: "I approached this complex program with a comprehensive management framework. First, I established a clear program structure with defined workstreams, each with specific deliverables, milestones, and accountabilities. The workstreams included platform architecture, UX/UI standardization, content migration, data integration, customer migration, and operational readiness.

For planning and tracking, I implemented a multi-level approach: a high-level roadmap showing major phases and dependencies, quarterly objectives and key results (OKRs) for each workstream, and two-week sprint plans for execution teams. This structure provided both strategic visibility and tactical clarity.

To manage the extensive dependencies across workstreams, I created a centralized dependency management system that tracked inter-team dependencies with clear owners and due dates. We conducted weekly dependency review meetings where teams coordinated handoffs and addressed potential blockers.

For risk management, I established a structured process for identifying, assessing, and mitigating risks. Each workstream maintained a risk register that fed into a program-level risk dashboard, which we reviewed bi-weekly with senior leadership. For critical risks, we developed detailed mitigation plans with trigger points for contingency actions.

To ensure quality throughout the program, we implemented a phased release approach with comprehensive testing at multiple levels. We created a dedicated testing environment that simulated the full customer journey across all integrated components, and established clear quality gates that had to be passed before functionality could progress to the next stage.

For stakeholder management, I established a governance structure with multiple engagement forums: a monthly steering committee with executive sponsors, bi-weekly business unit reviews, and weekly technical coordination meetings. I tailored communication to each audience, focusing on business outcomes for executives and detailed progress for implementation teams.

Perhaps most importantly, I recognized that this program was as much about organizational change as technical implementation. I worked closely with our change management team to develop comprehensive training, communication, and support plans for both internal teams and customers affected by the transition."

Result: "We successfully completed the program within the 18-month timeline and approximately 5% under the allocated budget. The consolidated platform launched with 99.99% availability and received positive feedback from both customers and internal stakeholders.

The business impact was significant: customer satisfaction scores increased by 18 points, digital conversion rates improved by 25%, and operational costs decreased by approximately $3.5 million annually through reduced maintenance and streamlined operations. The unified data model enabled cross-selling opportunities that generated an additional $7 million in revenue in the first year.

From a technical perspective, we reduced our technology footprint by 60%, improved page load times by 45%, and established a component-based architecture that has accelerated subsequent feature development by approximately 30%.

The program also transformed our organizational approach to digital initiatives, establishing cross-functional collaboration patterns and shared governance models that have been applied to multiple subsequent programs."

Plus (Lessons Learned): "This experience taught me valuable lessons about managing complex programs that I've applied to all subsequent initiatives. First,

I learned that multi-level planning is essential for complex programs—maintaining alignment between strategic objectives and day-to-day execution requires explicit connection points between different planning horizons. The quarterly OKR approach bridging long-term roadmaps and sprint planning has become my standard practice for program management.

Second, I recognized that dependency management is often the critical factor in program success or failure. The centralized dependency system we implemented, while initially seen as overhead by some teams, proved invaluable in preventing cascading delays and has become a core component of my program management toolkit.

Third, I discovered the importance of balancing standardization with flexibility in program execution. While we established consistent processes for planning, risk management, and reporting, we allowed teams to adapt their specific implementation approaches based on their unique challenges. This balanced governance approach has proven effective across various program types and organizational contexts.

Most significantly, I learned that successful program delivery requires equal attention to technical implementation and organizational change. By treating stakeholder alignment, team readiness, and customer transition as integral parts of the program rather than afterthoughts, we achieved adoption levels that technical excellence alone couldn't have delivered. This integrated approach to technical and organizational change has fundamentally shaped my program management philosophy."

Why This Response Is Effective: * Demonstrates structured approach to managing a genuinely complex program * Shows mastery of multiple program management disciplines (planning, risk, dependencies, etc.) * Balances technical execution with organizational change management * Provides specific, measurable outcomes across multiple dimensions * Reflects thoughtfully on program management approach with subsequent application

STRATEGIC THINKING QUESTIONS

These questions assess how you connect program activities to business objectives and make strategic trade-off decisions.

COMMON QUESTIONS

- "Tell me about a time when you had to make strategic trade-offs in a program."
- "Describe a situation where you aligned a program with changing business priorities."
- "Give me an example of how you've translated business strategy into program execution."
- "Tell me about a time when you had to cancel or significantly pivot a program based on strategic considerations."

WHAT MAKES AN EFFECTIVE RESPONSE

Effective responses to strategic thinking questions demonstrate:

- **Clear connection** between program activities and business objectives
- **Value-based prioritization** rather than simply following plans
- **Appropriate trade-off decisions** balancing multiple considerations
- **Adaptability** to changing strategic priorities
- **Business acumen** alongside program management expertise

EXAMPLE STAR+ RESPONSE

Question: "Tell me about a time when you had to make strategic trade-offs in a program."

Situation: "At FinTech Inc., I was the Program Manager for a major initiative to launch a new mobile banking platform. This program was strategically important for the company as mobile was becoming the primary channel for customer engagement, and our existing app was significantly behind competitors in functionality and user experience. The program had three primary objectives: improving customer experience to increase engagement, adding new revenue-generating features, and replacing aging backend systems to reduce operational costs. We had a fixed launch date tied to a major marketing campaign, and the scope had been defined based on competitive analysis and customer research."

Task: "Six months into the 12-month program, we encountered significant challenges that forced strategic trade-offs. We discovered that integrating with several legacy systems was much more complex than initially estimated, consuming more resources than planned. Additionally, user testing of early prototypes revealed that certain features were more important to customers than our initial prioritization had indicated. As Program Manager, I needed to make strategic trade-offs to ensure we delivered a successful product within our fixed timeline and budget constraints, while still achieving the core business objectives."

Action: "I approached these trade-off decisions through a structured, business-value focused process. First, I worked with product management to reassess all planned features against three dimensions: customer impact (measured through user research), revenue potential (quantified by our finance team), and technical foundation (evaluated by architecture and engineering).

Rather than making isolated scope decisions, I developed a comprehensive trade-off framework that explicitly connected potential changes to business outcomes. For each major feature area, we created scenarios showing the impact of full implementation, reduced implementation, or deferral to a future release.

To ensure decisions were strategically sound, I facilitated a workshop with senior leadership where we revisited the program's strategic objectives and established clear priorities among them. This discussion revealed that customer experience impact should be the primary decision driver, as it would ultimately influence both revenue and operational efficiency.

Based on this strategic clarity, I proposed a revised approach that maintained all features with high customer impact, reduced scope for some revenue-generating features, and implemented a phased approach for backend modernization. This proposal included a detailed analysis showing how it would affect our key performance indicators, along with a roadmap for addressing deferred capabilities in subsequent releases.

Throughout this process, I maintained transparent communication with all stakeholders about the challenges, options, and trade-off rationale. Rather than presenting the revised plan as a fait accompli, I engaged key stakeholders in the decision-making process, building shared ownership of the strategic choices."

Result: "The executive team approved the revised approach, and we successfully launched the mobile banking platform on schedule. The strategic trade-offs proved effective: customer adoption exceeded targets by 25%, with mobile engagement increasing from 4.2 to 8.7 sessions per week on average. The Net Promoter Score for mobile banking improved from 12 to 42, significantly outperforming our main competitors.

While we had reduced scope for some revenue-generating features, the ones we prioritized performed better than projected, achieving 85% of the original revenue target despite implementing only 60% of the planned features. The phased approach to backend modernization allowed us to meet our launch date while still reducing operational costs by 15% in the first release.

Perhaps most importantly, the transparent trade-off process strengthened trust with senior leadership. When we proposed the subsequent release plan addressing the deferred capabilities, it received immediate approval with an increased budget allocation based on the success of the initial launch."

Plus (Lessons Learned): "This experience taught me valuable lessons about strategic trade-offs that have influenced my program management approach ever since. First, I learned that effective trade-off decisions must be explicitly connected to business strategy rather than made in isolation. By reframing decisions around strategic priorities rather than simply what could be cut to meet the timeline, we maintained focus on long-term business value rather than short-term expediency.

Second, I recognized the importance of multi-dimensional evaluation in trade-off decisions. By assessing options across customer impact, revenue potential, and technical foundation, we developed more nuanced and effective solutions than a one-dimensional prioritization would have produced. This balanced evaluation approach has become standard practice in all programs I manage.

Third, I discovered that transparency in trade-off processes is essential for stakeholder alignment. By involving key stakeholders in the decision-making rather than simply informing them of outcomes, we built shared ownership that sustained support through implementation challenges. This collaborative approach to strategic decisions has proven valuable in numerous subsequent situations.

Most significantly, I learned that strategic trade-offs should focus on maximizing value delivered rather than minimizing scope reduced. By prioritizing high-impact capabilities rather than simply cutting the most difficult items, we created a product that exceeded expectations despite having less functionality than originally planned. This value-maximization mindset has fundamentally shaped my approach to program management, guiding trade-off decisions across multiple subsequent initiatives."

Why This Response Is Effective: * Demonstrates strategic thinking connected to business outcomes * Shows structured approach to trade-off decisions rather than ad hoc cuts * Balances multiple considerations (customer, revenue, technical) in decision-making * Provides specific business results validating the strategic choices * Reflects thoughtfully on strategic approach with subsequent application

PROBLEM-SOLVING QUESTIONS

These questions assess how you approach complex challenges, develop solutions, and navigate ambiguity.

COMMON QUESTIONS

- "Tell me about a significant problem you encountered in a program and how you solved it."

- "Describe a situation where you had to develop a creative solution to an unexpected challenge."

- "Give me an example of how you've approached a problem with significant constraints or limitations."

- "Tell me about a time when you had to solve a problem with incomplete information or ambiguity."

WHAT MAKES AN EFFECTIVE RESPONSE

Effective responses to problem-solving questions demonstrate:

- **Structured approach** to problem definition and analysis

- **Creative thinking** in developing non-obvious solutions

- **Data-driven decision making** where possible

- **Pragmatic solutions** within real-world constraints

- **Resilience** in navigating ambiguity and uncertainty

EXAMPLE STAR+ RESPONSE

Question: "Tell me about a significant problem you encountered in a program and how you solved it."

Situation: "At TechSolutions Inc., I was managing a program to implement a new enterprise resource planning (ERP) system across our global operations. This was a mission-critical initiative as our legacy systems were approaching end-of-life and limiting our business growth. The program involved 10 workstreams across finance, supply chain, manufacturing, and HR functions, with implementation planned across 12 countries in a phased approach. We were six months into the 18-month program when we encountered a significant problem: the system integration testing revealed that the ERP solution couldn't handle our complex transfer pricing model, which was essential for our international operations and tax compliance. The vendor had assured us during selection that this capability was standard, but it became clear that our specific requirements exceeded their standard functionality."

Task: "As the Program Manager, I needed to find a solution to this critical gap that wouldn't derail the entire implementation. The challenge was particularly difficult because we had already invested $4 million in the implementation, our legacy systems had a firm decommissioning deadline, and the transfer pricing functionality was non-negotiable for regulatory compliance. Initial estimates suggested that custom development would take 6-8 months and cost an additional $1.2 million, which would exceed both our timeline and budget constraints."

Action: "I approached this problem systematically, starting with a comprehensive analysis to ensure we fully understood the gap. I assembled a task force with subject matter experts from finance, tax, IT, and the implementation partner. We conducted detailed workshops to document our exact requirements and identify specifically where the standard functionality fell short.

313

Rather than accepting the initial 'full custom development' approach, I pushed the team to explore multiple solution options. We identified four potential approaches: full custom development within the ERP, a hybrid approach using standard modules with targeted customization, a separate bolt-on solution integrated with the ERP, or process redesign to align with standard functionality.

For each option, we conducted a rigorous assessment covering implementation time, cost, risk, maintenance implications, and business impact. This analysis revealed that the hybrid approach—using standard modules with targeted customization—could potentially meet our needs with significantly less time and cost than full custom development.

To validate this approach, I authorized a two-week proof-of-concept where our technical team and the vendor worked together to prototype the hybrid solution using actual company data. This rapid prototyping confirmed the viability of the approach but identified additional integration points that would need to be addressed.

Based on the proof-of-concept results, I developed a revised implementation plan that incorporated the hybrid solution while adjusting dependent workstreams to minimize overall impact. This included resequencing certain country implementations to align with the new development timeline and implementing temporary workarounds for the earliest deployments.

Throughout this process, I maintained transparent communication with executive sponsors and stakeholders, providing regular updates on the problem, solution options, and revised approach. I secured additional budget allocation for the customization work by demonstrating how the solution would actually enhance our long-term operational capabilities beyond the original requirements."

Result: "We successfully implemented the hybrid transfer pricing solution, which ultimately delayed the overall program by only 6 weeks instead of the 6-8 months initially estimated for full custom development. The additional cost was $450,000, significantly less than the $1.2 million estimated for the full custom approach.

The solution not only met our compliance requirements but actually improved our transfer pricing capabilities, providing better visibility and control than our legacy systems. This enhanced functionality has since enabled more efficient international operations, reducing the time to close financial periods by 40% and improving tax efficiency by approximately $2 million annually.

Beyond the immediate problem resolution, this experience transformed our approach to vendor management across the program. We implemented more rigorous validation processes for vendor capabilities, which identified and addressed three other potential gaps before they became critical issues."

Plus (Lessons Learned): "This experience taught me valuable lessons about problem-solving in complex programs that have shaped my approach ever since. First, I learned the importance of thorough problem definition before jumping to solutions. By investing time to understand exactly where the standard functionality fell short, we identified a more targeted approach than the comprehensive redevelopment initially proposed.

Second, I recognized the value of exploring multiple solution options rather than accepting the first viable approach. By systematically evaluating four different strategies, we discovered a hybrid solution that delivered better results at lower cost and risk than the obvious path. This multi-option approach has become standard practice in my problem-solving toolkit.

Third, I discovered the power of rapid prototyping for validating solutions to complex problems. The two-week proof-of-concept provided insights that no amount of theoretical analysis could have revealed, significantly de-risking our approach. I've since incorporated targeted prototyping into numerous problem-solving situations, most recently when addressing data migration challenges in our customer platform consolidation.

Most significantly, I learned that effective problem-solving in program management requires balancing technical solutions with program constraints and business objectives. By considering implementation timeline, cost, and business impact together rather than focusing solely on the technical gap, we developed a solution that better served the organization's overall needs. This integrated approach to problem-solving has become a cornerstone of my program management philosophy."

Why This Response Is Effective: * Demonstrates structured approach to a significant program challenge * Shows creative problem-solving beyond the obvious solution * Balances technical considerations with program constraints * Provides specific, measurable outcomes from the solution * Reflects thoughtfully on problem-solving approach with subsequent application

LEADERSHIP AND INFLUENCE QUESTIONS

These questions assess how you drive alignment, build consensus, and lead without formal authority.

COMMON QUESTIONS

- "Tell me about a time when you had to influence stakeholders to support a program direction."

- "Describe a situation where you had to build consensus among teams with different perspectives."

- "Give me an example of how you've led through a challenging situation without formal authority."

- "Tell me about a time when you had to drive a significant change as part of a program."

WHAT MAKES AN EFFECTIVE RESPONSE

Effective responses to leadership and influence questions demonstrate:

- **Influence strategies** beyond positional authority
- **Stakeholder alignment** across diverse perspectives
- **Resilience** in the face of resistance or challenges
- **Authentic leadership** that inspires commitment
- **Change management** approaches that drive adoption

EXAMPLE STAR+ RESPONSE

Question: "Tell me about a time when you had to influence stakeholders to support a program direction."

Situation: "At Global Financial Services, I was leading a program to implement a new digital customer onboarding system that would replace manual, paper-based processes across our retail banking division. This initiative was strategically important as it would reduce onboarding time from days to minutes, significantly improving customer experience and competitive position. However, the program faced significant resistance from multiple stakeholders: branch managers were concerned about changing customer interactions, compliance officers worried about regulatory risks with digital processes, and operations leaders feared job impacts from automation. Despite executive sponsorship, the program was stalling due to passive resistance and lack of active support from these key stakeholder groups."

Task: "As the Program Manager, I needed to influence these diverse stakeholders to actively support the new direction rather than simply comply minimally or passively resist. The challenge was particularly difficult because I had no direct authority over any of these groups, each had legitimate concerns that needed to be addressed, and previous technology initiatives had created skepticism about change. Without their genuine support, the program might deliver the technical solution but fail to achieve the business transformation needed for success."

Action: "I developed a comprehensive influence strategy focused on building understanding, addressing concerns, and creating ownership rather than simply pushing for compliance. First, I conducted extensive stakeholder analysis to understand each group's specific concerns, motivations, and communication preferences. This analysis revealed that different groups required different approaches—branch managers were primarily concerned about customer relationships, compliance officers about regulatory risk, and operations leaders about team impacts.

Rather than trying to 'sell' a predetermined solution, I created structured engagement forums where stakeholders could directly contribute to shaping the approach. For branch managers, I established a Branch Advisory Council that provided input on customer experience design. For compliance officers, I formed a Regulatory Working Group with authority to define compliance requirements. For operations leaders, I created a Workforce Transition Committee focused on role evolution rather than headcount reduction.

To build credibility and address skepticism, I arranged site visits to peer institutions that had successfully implemented similar digital transformations. Seeing concrete examples of success and speaking directly with counterparts who had navigated similar changes proved particularly influential for skeptical stakeholders.

I recognized that data would be more persuasive than assertions for many stakeholders. We conducted a controlled pilot in three branches, carefully measuring customer satisfaction, processing time, error rates, and employee experience. The positive results from this pilot provided compelling evidence that addressed many concerns more effectively than conceptual arguments.

For executive stakeholders, I developed a strategic narrative that connected the program to broader business objectives and competitive pressures. This narrative emphasized how digital onboarding would enable growth strategies that all leaders were already committed to, positioning the program as an enabler of shared goals rather than a competing priority.

Throughout this process, I maintained transparent communication about both progress and challenges. When legitimate issues were raised, I acknowledged them openly and incorporated appropriate adjustments rather than defending the original approach, building trust through responsiveness."

Result: "This influence strategy transformed stakeholder engagement from resistance to active support. The Branch Advisory Council evolved from skeptical questioning to proactive advocacy, with members ultimately serving as change champions during implementation. The Regulatory Working Group developed a compliance framework that actually streamlined requirements while maintaining regulatory integrity, and the Workforce Transition Committee created a role evolution plan that was endorsed by both leadership and staff representatives.

The program successfully delivered the digital onboarding system on schedule and within budget. More importantly, the business adoption exceeded expectations: 85% of new accounts were processed through the digital system within three months of launch (versus a target of 60%), customer satisfaction with onboarding increased from 67% to 92%, and processing time decreased from an average of 2.5 days to 12 minutes.

The influence approach created sustainable change beyond the immediate program. The engagement models we established have been adopted as standard practice for major initiatives, and several stakeholders who were initially resistant have become advocates for digital transformation more broadly."

Plus (Lessons Learned): "This experience taught me valuable lessons about influence and leadership that have shaped my approach to program management. First, I learned that effective influence requires understanding and addressing stakeholders' actual concerns rather than the ones we assume they have. The detailed stakeholder analysis revealed nuances that wouldn't have been apparent from general stakeholder categories, enabling much more targeted and effective engagement.

Second, I recognized the power of contribution in building commitment. By creating structured opportunities for stakeholders to shape the solution rather than simply react to it, we not only improved the approach but created psychological ownership that transformed resistance into advocacy. This co-creation approach has become central to my stakeholder engagement strategy.

Third, I discovered that evidence is more persuasive than assertions for overcoming skepticism. The pilot results provided concrete data that addressed concerns more effectively than any amount of conceptual discussion could have. I now incorporate targeted pilots or proof points into all major change initiatives to build confidence through demonstration rather than declaration.

Most significantly, I learned that influence is ultimately about connecting change to value that stakeholders already care about, not convincing them to care about what we value. By linking the program to growth strategies, customer relationships, and professional development—things stakeholders were already committed to—we created alignment that couldn't have been achieved through persuasion alone. This value-connection approach has fundamentally shaped my leadership philosophy and has proven effective across diverse organizational contexts."

Why This Response Is Effective: * Focuses on influence and leadership rather than program mechanics * Shows sophisticated understanding of different stakeholder perspectives * Demonstrates multiple influence strategies adapted to different audiences * Provides concrete results that validate the approach * Reflects thoughtfully on leadership lessons with subsequent application

ADAPTABILITY QUESTIONS

These questions assess how you respond to changing conditions, adjust approaches, and learn from experience.

COMMON QUESTIONS

- "Tell me about a time when you had to significantly adjust a program due to changing requirements or conditions."

- "Describe a situation where you had to manage through high ambiguity or uncertainty."

- "Give me an example of how you've applied lessons from a previous experience to improve a program outcome."

- "Tell me about a time when a program didn't go as planned and how you responded."

WHAT MAKES AN EFFECTIVE RESPONSE

Effective responses to adaptability questions demonstrate:

- **Resilience** in the face of changing conditions

- **Agile decision-making** based on new information

- **Comfort with ambiguity** and uncertainty

- **Learning orientation** that applies insights from experience

- **Balance between persistence** and flexibility in approach

EXAMPLE STAR+ RESPONSE

Question: "Tell me about a time when you had to significantly adjust a program due to changing requirements or conditions."

Situation: "At TechInnovate Inc., I was leading a program to develop and launch a new customer analytics platform that would provide our retail clients with advanced insights into consumer behavior. The program had been planned as an 18-month initiative with a traditional waterfall approach, based on detailed requirements gathered from our top clients and internal stakeholders. We were eight months into execution, with development approximately 40% complete, when two significant changes occurred simultaneously: a major competitor launched a similar platform with features we hadn't anticipated, and our company acquired a startup with complementary AI technology that could potentially enhance our solution. These changes substantially altered the competitive landscape and technical possibilities for our program."

Task: "As the Program Manager, I needed to rapidly assess these changes and determine how to adjust our approach to ensure we still delivered a market-relevant solution. The challenge was particularly complex because we had already invested significantly in the current direction, had commitments to clients based on the original timeline, and needed to balance competitive response with thoughtful integration of the new technology. Simply continuing with the original plan would result in a product that was competitively disadvantaged, while completely restarting would cause unacceptable delays."

Action: "I approached this situation with a structured yet flexible adaptation process. First, I called a temporary pause on non-critical development activities to create space for reassessment without completely halting momentum. During this two-week period, I organized three parallel workstreams: competitive analysis, technology integration assessment, and impact evaluation.

The competitive analysis team conducted detailed research on the competitor's offering, gathering feedback from clients and sales teams to understand which features were most valued in the market. The technology integration team worked with the acquired startup to evaluate how their AI capabilities could be incorporated into our platform and what timeline was realistic. The impact team assessed the implications of potential changes on our schedule, budget, resources, and client commitments.

Based on these assessments, I facilitated a strategic options workshop with key stakeholders, including product management, engineering leadership, sales, and executive sponsors. Rather than presenting a single recommendation, I developed three scenarios with different trade-offs between competitive response, technology integration, and time-to-market.

Through this collaborative process, we decided to pivot to an incremental delivery approach: we would accelerate development of a core platform with features matching the competitor's offering for release within six months, followed by differentiated AI capabilities leveraging the acquired technology in subsequent quarterly releases. This approach required significant changes to our development methodology, moving from waterfall to an agile approach with quarterly releases.

To implement this shift, I restructured the program into cross-functional teams aligned with feature sets rather than technical components, established new governance and planning processes appropriate for agile delivery, and developed a revised roadmap showing the incremental value delivery. I also created a transparent communication plan for both internal stakeholders and clients, explaining the rationale for the changes and the enhanced value of the new approach."

Result: "We successfully executed the adjusted program approach, delivering the core platform five months after the pivot (13 months into the overall program) and the first AI-enhanced capabilities three months later. Despite the significant mid-course adjustment, we launched only one quarter later than the original target date, but with a substantially stronger product.

The market response exceeded expectations: we signed 40% more clients in the first six months than projected in the original business case, and client satisfaction scores averaged 4.6/5 compared to 3.8/5 for the competitor's offering. The incremental delivery approach also generated earlier revenue, with the core platform generating $3.2 million in the first quarter after launch while we continued enhancing the product.

Perhaps most significantly, the program's adaptation became a catalyst for broader organizational change. The agile delivery model we implemented has since been adopted as the standard approach for product development initiatives across the company, and the cross-functional team structure has improved collaboration between previously siloed departments."

Plus (Lessons Learned): "This experience taught me valuable lessons about adaptability in program management that have profoundly influenced my approach. First, I learned that effective adaptation requires creating deliberate space for reassessment. The two-week pause, while initially concerning to some stakeholders, ultimately saved months of potential rework by ensuring our pivot was strategic rather than reactive. I now build explicit reassessment points into all program plans, creating structured opportunities to adapt rather than treating changes as exceptions.

Second, I recognized that options-based decision-making is essential when navigating significant changes. By developing multiple scenarios rather than a single recommendation, we engaged stakeholders in evaluating trade-offs rather than simply accepting or rejecting a change. This collaborative approach led to a more robust solution and stronger commitment to the adjusted direction. I've since applied this options-based approach to all major program adjustments.

Third, I discovered that communication transparency during changes builds rather than undermines confidence. By openly sharing the reasons for the pivot and the process we used to make decisions, we maintained stakeholder trust despite significant adjustments to commitments. This transparent approach to change communication has become a cornerstone of my program management practice.

Most significantly, I learned that adaptability isn't just about responding to change but leveraging it to create new opportunities. By embracing the disruption rather than minimizing it, we ultimately delivered a stronger product and catalyzed positive organizational change that wouldn't have occurred otherwise. This perspective shift from seeing changes as obstacles to viewing them as potential catalysts has fundamentally altered my approach to program management in dynamic environments."

Why This Response Is Effective: * Demonstrates thoughtful adaptation to significant changes rather than rigid plan adherence * Shows structured approach to reassessment and decision-making * Balances responsiveness with strategic thinking * Provides specific outcomes that validate the adaptation approach * Reflects deeply on adaptability lessons with subsequent application

10.3. THE EXECUTION VS. STRATEGY BALANCE

Program Manager interviews often probe for the balance between execution focus and strategic thinking. Let's explore this balance and strategies for demonstrating both dimensions effectively.

THE TACTICAL VS. STRATEGIC SPECTRUM

Different Program Manager roles fall at different points on the tactical-strategic spectrum: * **Tactical Program Managers**: Focus primarily on execution, coordination, and delivery * **Strategic Program Managers**: Balance execution with business alignment, value optimization, and strategic impact * **Transformational Program Managers**: Lead initiatives that fundamentally change business capabilities or direction

Understanding where your target role falls on this spectrum helps you calibrate your responses appropriately.

Strategy: For tactical roles, emphasize execution excellence while showing strategic awareness. For strategic roles, demonstrate both dimensions with emphasis on connecting program activities to business outcomes. For transformational roles, lead with strategic thinking while showing the execution capability to deliver on the vision.

THE BUSINESS IMPACT CONNECTION

Regardless of where a role falls on the tactical-strategic spectrum, effective Program Managers connect execution activities to business outcomes. This connection demonstrates that you understand the "why" behind the "what" and "how" of program management.

Strategy: In your responses, explicitly articulate: * The business context and objectives driving the program * How specific program decisions connected to business priorities * The measurable business outcomes resulting from program execution * How you balanced business value with execution constraints

This business impact connection elevates your responses from showing competent execution to demonstrating strategic program leadership.

THE STAKEHOLDER LEVEL ADAPTATION

Program Managers must communicate effectively with stakeholders at different organizational levels, from technical teams focused on implementation details to executives concerned with strategic outcomes. This requires adapting your communication to different audiences without losing substance.

Strategy: In your interview responses, demonstrate this adaptation by: * Showing how you tailored communication to different stakeholder groups * Articulating both detailed execution considerations and strategic implications * Demonstrating comfort discussing both tactical challenges and business impact * Explaining how you created alignment across different organizational levels

This stakeholder level adaptation demonstrates the versatility needed in effective program management.

10.4. CONCLUSION: DEMONSTRATING PROGRAM MANAGEMENT EXCELLENCE THROUGH BEHAVIOR

Effective behavioral interviewing for Program Manager roles requires demonstrating a sophisticated balance of execution excellence and strategic thinking. The examples in this chapter illustrate this balance across different question types and competency areas.

Remember that Program Manager interviews assess not just what you've delivered, but how you deliver—your approach to stakeholder management, execution, strategic alignment, problem-solving, leadership, and adaptability. By preparing examples that demonstrate these dimensions, you position yourself as not just a coordinator, but a program leader who can drive complex initiatives to successful outcomes that deliver business value.

In the next chapter, we'll explore how to adapt your behavioral interview responses to align with the specific cultural values and assessment frameworks of different companies, examining how to tailor your examples for Amazon, Google, Meta, Microsoft, and other major technology organizations.

CHAPTER 11. ADAPTING TO COMPANY CULTURE

> Culture eats strategy for breakfast.

— Peter Drucker

"Tell us about a time you disagreed with your manager's technical decision."

The Amazon interviewer gets ready to type as they asked this question. They haven't mentioned Leadership Principles once, but their question perfectly mirrors the "Have Backbone; Disagree and Commit" principle. After analyzing hundreds of interview transcripts and anecdotes across tech companies, I've found that 90% of cultural assessment happens through stealth questions like these—never through direct mentions of company values.

This chapter decodes the hidden cultural patterns in tech interviews: * The 3 subtle differences between Amazon's "customer obsession" questions and Microsoft's "customer focus" questions * Why Google asks about "ambiguous situations" while Meta probes for "fast decisions"—and how to answer both with the same story * How to retrofit your experiences using each company's cultural lens (without fabrication)

Based on my work with hiring managers at all major tech firms, I'll show you:

1. The unwritten scoring rubrics behind common behavioral questions at each company

2. How to diagnose cultural priorities from the interviewer's word choices

3. Adaptation frameworks that work when you don't have a perfect cultural match

(Includes the exact formula a candidate used to reframe her Amazon project for a successful Google interview.)

11.1. UNDERSTANDING COMPANY CULTURE FRAMEWORKS

Before diving into specific companies, let's understand what cultural frameworks are and how they impact behavioral interviews.

WHAT ARE CULTURAL FRAMEWORKS?

Cultural frameworks are the formalized articulation of a company's values, principles, and expectations for employee behavior. They serve multiple purposes:

- **Guiding decision-making** across the organization
- **Shaping performance evaluation** and career advancement
- **Influencing hiring decisions** and candidate assessment
- **Defining the company's identity** and approach to business

While all companies have cultures, not all have explicit frameworks. The major technology companies we're focusing on have developed highly structured frameworks that are deeply integrated into their hiring processes.

HOW CULTURAL FRAMEWORKS IMPACT BEHAVIORAL INTERVIEWS

Cultural frameworks influence behavioral interviews in several critical ways:

QUESTION SELECTION AND FRAMING

Interview questions are often directly derived from cultural frameworks, with specific questions designed to assess alignment with particular values or principles. For example, Amazon interviewers explicitly ask about Leadership Principles like "Customer Obsession" or "Dive Deep."

EVALUATION CRITERIA

Responses are evaluated not just for general effectiveness but for specific evidence of behaviors aligned with the company's cultural values. Interviewers often use rubrics that directly reference cultural framework elements.

EXPECTED RESPONSE STRUCTURE

Some companies have specific expectations for how responses should be structured beyond the general STAR format. For example, Amazon places particular emphasis on data-driven results and lessons learned.

LANGUAGE AND TERMINOLOGY

Companies often have specific terminology associated with their cultural frameworks that interviewers listen for in responses. Using this language appropriately signals cultural alignment.

TRADE-OFF PRIORITIZATION

Cultural frameworks often reveal how companies prioritize certain values over others when trade-offs are necessary. Understanding these priorities helps candidates emphasize the aspects of their experiences that will resonate most strongly.

Understanding these impacts allows you to adapt your behavioral responses to each company's specific expectations without changing the fundamental experiences you're sharing.

11.2. AMAZON: LEADERSHIP PRINCIPLES

Amazon's Leadership Principles are perhaps the most explicit and thoroughly integrated cultural framework among major technology companies. These principles are not just aspirational values but practical guidelines that Amazonians use daily to make decisions, evaluate performance, and assess candidates.

THE LEADERSHIP PRINCIPLES FRAMEWORK

Amazon has 16 Leadership Principles that define its culture:

1. **Customer Obsession**: Leaders start with the customer and work backward.

2. **Ownership**: Leaders act on behalf of the entire company, beyond just their team.

3. **Invent and Simplify**: Leaders expect and require innovation and invention.

4. **Are Right, A Lot**: Leaders have strong judgment and good instincts.

5. **Learn and Be Curious**: Leaders are never done learning and always seek to improve.

6. **Hire and Develop the Best**: Leaders raise the performance bar with every hire and promotion.

7. **Insist on the Highest Standards**: Leaders have relentlessly high standards.

8. **Think Big**: Leaders create and communicate a bold direction.

9. **Bias for Action**: Speed matters in business.

10. **Frugality**: Accomplish more with less.

11. **Earn Trust**: Leaders listen attentively, speak candidly, and treat others respectfully.

12. **Dive Deep**: Leaders operate at all levels, stay connected to the details.

13. **Have Backbone; Disagree and Commit**: Leaders are obligated to respectfully challenge decisions.

14. **Deliver Results**: Leaders focus on key inputs and deliver with the right quality and timely fashion.

15. **Strive to be Earth's Best Employer**: Leaders work every day to create a safer, more productive, higher performing, more diverse, and more just work environment.

16. **Success and Scale Bring Broad Responsibility**: Leaders create more than they consume and always leave things better than they found them.

HOW LEADERSHIP PRINCIPLES IMPACT AMAZON INTERVIEWS

Amazon's behavioral interviews are explicitly structured around Leadership Principles, with several distinctive characteristics:

DIRECT PRINCIPLE ASSESSMENT

Each interview question directly targets one or more specific Leadership Principles. Interviewers are trained to probe for evidence of these principles and evaluate responses against them.

DATA-DRIVEN EXPECTATIONS

Amazon places strong emphasis on quantifiable results and metrics in behavioral responses. Vague or qualitative outcomes are generally viewed less favorably than specific, measurable impacts.

OWNERSHIP FOCUS

Amazon interviewers look for evidence that candidates take personal responsibility for outcomes rather than attributing success to teams or circumstances. The use of "I" rather than "we" is often encouraged.

DIVE DEEP EXPECTATION

Interviewers expect candidates to demonstrate detailed knowledge of their examples, often asking probing follow-up questions to test depth of understanding and involvement.

TRADE-OFF AWARENESS

Amazon recognizes that Leadership Principles can sometimes conflict (e.g., Bias for Action vs. High Standards). Interviewers assess how candidates navigate these tensions.

ADAPTING YOUR RESPONSES FOR AMAZON

To effectively adapt your behavioral responses for Amazon interviews, consider these strategies:

MAP YOUR EXAMPLES TO SPECIFIC PRINCIPLES

Before your interview, analyze your key professional experiences and map them to specific Leadership Principles. Identify which examples most strongly demonstrate each principle and prepare them accordingly.

EMPHASIZE METRICS AND RESULTS

Strengthen your responses by including specific, quantifiable outcomes. If your original experience lacks metrics, consider what data points you could reasonably estimate or what qualitative results could be framed more concretely.

HIGHLIGHT PERSONAL AGENCY

While maintaining honesty about team contributions, emphasize your personal actions, decisions, and impacts. Be prepared to clearly articulate your specific role and contributions.

PREPARE FOR DEPTH

For each example, ensure you can discuss details at multiple levels—from high-level strategy to specific implementation challenges. Anticipate and prepare for follow-up questions that probe deeper.

ADDRESS PRINCIPLE TENSIONS

When relevant, acknowledge tensions between different Leadership Principles in your examples and explain how you prioritized and balanced competing considerations.

EXAMPLE ADAPTATION FOR AMAZON

Let's examine how the same professional experience might be adapted for an Amazon interview:

Original Response (Generic): "In my previous role, I worked on improving our customer onboarding process. We redesigned the workflow and made it more user-friendly. The team was happy with the results, and we received positive feedback from customers."

Adapted Response (Amazon - Customer Obsession & Deliver Results): "In my previous role, I noticed our customer onboarding process was causing friction, with 23% of new users abandoning before completion. I took ownership of this problem and worked backward from the customer experience to identify pain points. I analyzed drop-off data at each step and conducted 15 user interviews to understand specific frustrations.

Based on this customer feedback, I proposed and led a redesign of the onboarding workflow, reducing steps from 12 to 5 while maintaining all necessary data collection. I collaborated with engineering and design but personally drove the requirements and success metrics. After implementation, we saw abandonment rates decrease from 23% to 8%, resulting in approximately 1,200 additional completed onboardings per month and $360,000 in annual recurring revenue that would have otherwise been lost.

Beyond the metrics, I learned the importance of continuously collecting customer feedback rather than making assumptions about their needs. I've since implemented a regular customer interview practice that has informed three subsequent feature improvements."

Why This Adaptation Works for Amazon: * Demonstrates Customer Obsession by working backward from customer pain points * Shows Ownership by taking personal responsibility for the problem * Includes specific metrics and quantifiable business results * Demonstrates Dive Deep through detailed understanding of the problem and solution * Includes lessons learned, showing Learn and Be Curious * Uses "I" language to emphasize personal agency while acknowledging collaboration

11.3. GOOGLE: GOOGLEYNESS AND LEADERSHIP

Google's approach to cultural assessment is less explicitly structured than Amazon's but equally important in their hiring process. Google evaluates candidates across multiple dimensions, with particular emphasis on "Googleyness" alongside technical and leadership capabilities.

THE GOOGLE CULTURAL FRAMEWORK

Google's cultural assessment includes several key components:

GOOGLEYNESS

This somewhat ambiguous term encompasses the cultural attributes Google values: * **Comfort with ambiguity**: Thriving in uncertain or rapidly changing situations * **Intellectual humility**: Acknowledging what you don't know and being open to learning * **Collaborative orientation**: Working effectively with others across boundaries * **Conscientiousness**: Being thorough, careful, and reliable * **Bias to action**: Moving forward despite uncertainty when appropriate * **User focus**: Deeply understanding and advocating for user needs

GENERAL COGNITIVE ABILITY

Beyond specific skills, Google values: * **Problem-solving approach**: How candidates break down complex problems * **Learning ability**: How quickly candidates acquire and apply new knowledge * **Analytical thinking**: How candidates evaluate information and draw conclusions

LEADERSHIP

Google assesses leadership through several lenses: * **Emergent leadership**: Stepping up when needed rather than relying on formal authority * **Thought leadership**: Contributing innovative ideas and perspectives * **People leadership**: Developing others and building effective teams * **Navigating ambiguity**: Making progress despite unclear or changing circumstances

HOW GOOGLE'S FRAMEWORK IMPACTS INTERVIEWS

Google's behavioral interviews have several distinctive characteristics:

SITUATION COMPLEXITY

Google interviewers often look for examples involving complex, ambiguous situations rather than straightforward challenges. They assess how candidates navigate uncertainty and incomplete information.

LEARNING EMPHASIS

Interviewers place significant value on candidates' ability to learn, adapt, and grow from experiences. They look for intellectual humility and openness to new perspectives.

COLLABORATIVE ASSESSMENT

Google evaluates how candidates work with others, particularly across organizational boundaries or with diverse perspectives. They look for evidence of effective collaboration rather than individual heroics.

DATA-INFORMED DECISION MAKING

While less metrics-focused than Amazon, Google values data-informed approaches to problem-solving and decision-making. They look for evidence of analytical thinking in behavioral examples.

USER-CENTERED THINKING

Google interviewers assess whether candidates naturally consider user perspectives and needs in their decision-making and problem-solving approaches.

ADAPTING YOUR RESPONSES FOR GOOGLE

To effectively adapt your behavioral responses for Google interviews, consider these strategies:

HIGHLIGHT COMPLEXITY AND AMBIGUITY

Choose examples that demonstrate your ability to navigate uncertain or ambiguous situations effectively. Explain how you made progress despite incomplete information or changing circumstances.

EMPHASIZE LEARNING AND GROWTH

Include specific insights and lessons learned from your experiences. Demonstrate intellectual humility by acknowledging limitations and explaining how you addressed them through learning.

SHOWCASE COLLABORATIVE APPROACHES

Highlight how you've worked effectively across organizational boundaries or with diverse perspectives. Demonstrate respect for others' contributions while still showing your impact.

INCORPORATE DATA-INFORMED THINKING

Explain how you used data and evidence to inform your decisions and approaches. Show analytical rigor without becoming overly focused on metrics alone.

CENTER USER/CUSTOMER PERSPECTIVES

Demonstrate how you considered user or customer needs in your approach. Show empathy and understanding for the people affected by your work.

EXAMPLE ADAPTATION FOR GOOGLE

Let's examine how the same professional experience might be adapted for a Google interview:

Original Response (Generic): "In my previous role, I worked on improving our customer onboarding process. We redesigned the workflow and made it more user-friendly. The team was happy with the results, and we received positive feedback from customers."

Adapted Response (Google - Googleyness & Leadership): "In my previous role, I noticed our customer onboarding process was creating friction, but we lacked clear data on exactly where and why users were struggling. This presented an ambiguous problem that required both user empathy and analytical thinking to solve.

I initiated a collaborative investigation involving product, design, and engineering team members. Rather than assuming I knew the answer, I facilitated a process where we combined quantitative funnel analysis with qualitative user research. The data revealed surprising insights—users weren't dropping off where we expected, and their frustrations stemmed from unclear expectations rather than technical friction.

Based on these insights, I brought together cross-functional perspectives to redesign the experience. When we encountered disagreements about the approach, I encouraged evidence-based discussion rather than deferring to the highest-paid person's opinion. This collaborative approach led to creative solutions we wouldn't have discovered through a top-down process.

After implementation, we established a measurement framework that combined completion metrics with user satisfaction scores. The results showed a significant improvement, with completion rates increasing by 15 percentage points and satisfaction scores improving from 3.2 to 4.5 out of 5.

What I learned from this experience was the importance of balancing data with user empathy. Our initial assumptions were wrong precisely because we hadn't deeply understood the user perspective. I've since applied this balanced approach to other projects, most recently when redesigning our subscription management interface, where it helped us avoid similar assumption-based mistakes."

Why This Adaptation Works for Google: * Demonstrates comfort with ambiguity in approaching an unclear problem * Shows intellectual humility by acknowledging limitations and learning needs * Highlights collaborative approach across functional boundaries * Incorporates data-informed decision making while maintaining user focus * Demonstrates emergent leadership by initiating and facilitating without formal authority * Includes specific learning and growth from the experience

11.4. META: MOVE FAST, BE BOLD, FOCUS ON IMPACT

Meta (formerly Facebook) has a distinctive culture characterized by speed, impact, and scale. While less formally structured than Amazon's Leadership Principles, Meta's cultural values significantly influence their behavioral interviews and candidate assessment.

THE META CULTURAL FRAMEWORK

Meta's culture is defined by several core values:

MOVE FAST

- Emphasis on speed and rapid iteration
- Valuing progress over perfection
- Quick decision-making and execution
- Comfort with changing direction based on new information

BE BOLD

- Taking calculated risks
- Challenging conventional approaches
- Thinking at scale rather than incrementally
- Pursuing ambitious goals

FOCUS ON IMPACT

- Prioritizing work based on potential impact
- Measuring and quantifying results
- Focusing on outcomes rather than process
- Making data-driven decisions

BE OPEN

- Transparent communication
- Sharing information broadly
- Giving and receiving direct feedback
- Collaborating across boundaries

BUILD SOCIAL VALUE

- Connecting work to broader social impact
- Considering long-term implications of decisions
- Building technology that brings people together
- Addressing potential negative consequences

HOW META'S CULTURE IMPACTS INTERVIEWS

Meta's behavioral interviews have several distinctive characteristics:

SCALE ORIENTATION

Interviewers look for examples that demonstrate thinking and operating at scale. They value experiences that show the ability to impact large systems or user populations.

IMPACT QUANTIFICATION

Meta places strong emphasis on measuring and quantifying impact. Interviewers expect candidates to articulate the specific outcomes and value of their work.

SPEED AND ITERATION

Meta values rapid execution and iteration over perfect planning. Interviewers look for evidence of shipping quickly and improving based on feedback.

BOLD DECISION MAKING

Interviewers assess candidates' willingness to take calculated risks and make difficult decisions with incomplete information.

DIRECT COMMUNICATION

Meta values clear, direct communication. Interviewers expect concise, straightforward responses that get to the point quickly.

ADAPTING YOUR RESPONSES FOR META

To effectively adapt your behavioral responses for Meta interviews, consider these strategies:

EMPHASIZE SCALE AND SCOPE

Highlight the scale at which your examples operated—number of users affected, size of systems, or breadth of impact. If your experience wasn't inherently large-scale, explain how your approach could scale to larger contexts.

QUANTIFY IMPACT CLEARLY

Include specific metrics and quantifiable outcomes in your responses. Focus on business or user impact rather than just technical accomplishments.

HIGHLIGHT SPEED AND ITERATION

Demonstrate how you moved quickly, shipped incrementally, and improved based on feedback rather than seeking perfection before release.

SHOWCASE BOLD DECISIONS

Include examples where you took calculated risks or made difficult decisions despite uncertainty. Explain your reasoning and how you managed potential downsides.

BE DIRECT AND CONCISE

Structure your responses efficiently, getting to the key points quickly. Avoid unnecessary details or lengthy context-setting.

EXAMPLE ADAPTATION FOR META

Let's examine how the same professional experience might be adapted for a Meta interview:

Original Response (Generic): "In my previous role, I worked on improving our customer onboarding process. We redesigned the workflow and made it more user-friendly. The team was happy with the results, and we received positive feedback from customers."

Adapted Response (Meta - Move Fast, Focus on Impact): "In my previous role, I identified that our customer onboarding process was a critical growth bottleneck affecting our entire user base of 2 million customers. Rather than conducting extensive research, I pushed for a rapid, data-informed approach to maximize impact quickly.

I analyzed our funnel metrics and identified that we were losing 23% of potential customers during onboarding, representing approximately $4.2 million in annual recurring revenue. Instead of planning a perfect end-to-end solution, I broke the problem down into components and prioritized the three highest-impact friction points based on drop-off data.

I assembled a small, cross-functional team and set an aggressive two-week timeline for our first iteration. We shipped a simplified version that addressed the most critical issues while deferring less impactful improvements. This initial version reduced the abandonment rate from 23% to 15% within the first week.

Based on this data and user feedback, we quickly iterated with two subsequent releases over the following month, ultimately reducing abandonment to 8% and recovering an estimated $2.8 million in annual recurring revenue. The entire initiative went from identification to final implementation in six weeks.

The key decision that drove our success was prioritizing speed and impact over comprehensive redesign. By focusing on the highest-impact friction points first and iterating based on real-world data, we delivered significant business value much faster than a traditional approach would have allowed."

Why This Adaptation Works for Meta: * Demonstrates Move Fast through rapid timelines and iterative approach * Shows Focus on Impact by quantifying business results and prioritizing based on potential value * Illustrates Be Bold by pushing for aggressive timelines and making prioritization trade-offs * Emphasizes scale by referencing the entire user base of 2 million customers * Uses direct, concise communication that gets to the point quickly * Highlights data-driven decision making throughout the process

11.5. MICROSOFT: GROWTH MINDSET AND MODEL, COACH, CARE

Microsoft's culture has evolved significantly under CEO Satya Nadella's leadership, with a shift toward growth mindset, inclusivity, and collaborative leadership. This cultural transformation is reflected in their behavioral interview approach.

THE MICROSOFT CULTURAL FRAMEWORK

Microsoft's culture is built around several key elements:

GROWTH MINDSET

- Embracing challenges and persisting through obstacles
- Learning from criticism and feedback
- Finding inspiration in others' success
- Believing abilities can be developed through dedication and hard work

MODEL, COACH, CARE LEADERSHIP

- **Model**: Leading by example and demonstrating desired behaviors
- **Coach**: Helping others develop their capabilities and perspectives
- **Care**: Showing genuine concern for team members' wellbeing and growth

CUSTOMER OBSESSION

- Deeply understanding customer needs and pain points
- Building products and services that deliver meaningful value
- Measuring success through customer outcomes

DIVERSITY AND INCLUSION

- Seeking and valuing diverse perspectives
- Creating inclusive environments where everyone can contribute
- Recognizing and addressing bias in decision-making

ONE MICROSOFT

- Collaborating across organizational boundaries
- Prioritizing company success over team or individual success
- Building on others' work rather than reinventing

HOW MICROSOFT'S CULTURE IMPACTS INTERVIEWS

Microsoft's behavioral interviews have several distinctive characteristics:

LEARNING AND ADAPTATION

Interviewers look for evidence of growth mindset through how candidates have learned from challenges, adapted to feedback, and developed their capabilities over time.

PEOPLE DEVELOPMENT

Microsoft values candidates who develop others, not just themselves. Interviewers assess how candidates have coached, mentored, and helped team members grow.

INCLUSIVE COLLABORATION

Interviewers evaluate how candidates work with diverse perspectives and create environments where everyone can contribute effectively.

CUSTOMER CONNECTION

Microsoft assesses how candidates understand and address customer needs in their work, particularly in product development roles.

CROSS-ORGANIZATION EFFECTIVENESS

Interviewers look for evidence that candidates can work effectively across organizational boundaries and contribute to broader company objectives.

ADAPTING YOUR RESPONSES FOR MICROSOFT

To effectively adapt your behavioral responses for Microsoft interviews, consider these strategies:

HIGHLIGHT LEARNING AND GROWTH

Demonstrate how you've embraced challenges, learned from setbacks, and developed your capabilities over time. Show a willingness to receive and apply feedback.

EMPHASIZE PEOPLE DEVELOPMENT

Include examples where you've helped others grow and develop, whether through formal mentoring or informal coaching and support.

SHOWCASE INCLUSIVE COLLABORATION

Highlight how you've worked with diverse perspectives and created environments where everyone could contribute effectively.

CONNECT TO CUSTOMER OUTCOMES

Demonstrate how your work connected to customer needs and delivered meaningful value, not just technical accomplishments.

ILLUSTRATE CROSS-BOUNDARY COLLABORATION

Show how you've worked effectively across organizational boundaries and contributed to broader objectives beyond your immediate team.

EXAMPLE ADAPTATION FOR MICROSOFT

Let's examine how the same professional experience might be adapted for a Microsoft interview:

Original Response (Generic): "In my previous role, I worked on improving our customer onboarding process. We redesigned the workflow and made it more user-friendly. The team was happy with the results, and we received positive feedback from customers."

Adapted Response (Microsoft - Growth Mindset, Model-Coach-Care): "In my previous role, I led an initiative to improve our customer onboarding process, approaching it with a growth mindset and focus on both customer and team outcomes.

The challenge began when our customer success team shared feedback that our onboarding process was causing frustration. Rather than becoming defensive about the product my team had built, I embraced this as an opportunity to learn and improve. I partnered with the customer success team to understand the specific pain points, reviewing support tickets and conducting joint customer interviews to develop deeper empathy for the user experience.

As I formed a cross-functional team to address the issue, I recognized that we had team members with varying experience levels. Instead of simply assigning tasks based on current capabilities, I created development opportunities by pairing less experienced developers with more senior team members. I modeled the behavior I wanted to see by taking on challenging aspects myself while also being open about where I needed to learn and improve.

Throughout the project, I coached team members through challenges, providing support while encouraging them to develop their own solutions. When one designer was struggling with a particularly complex workflow, I didn't just provide the answer but helped them develop a framework for approaching similar problems in the future.

We implemented a redesigned workflow that reduced onboarding time from 45 minutes to 12 minutes on average, significantly improving the customer experience. Customer satisfaction scores for the onboarding process increased from 3.2 to 4.7 out of 5.

Beyond the customer impact, I'm particularly proud of how the team grew through this project. Two junior developers gained confidence in customer-facing feature development, and our designer has since led three subsequent user experience initiatives based on the skills developed during this project. The collaborative approach also strengthened our partnership with the customer success team, creating an ongoing feedback channel that has informed several other product improvements."

Why This Adaptation Works for Microsoft: * Demonstrates Growth Mindset by embracing feedback and viewing it as an opportunity to improve * Shows Model-Coach-Care leadership through developing team members and supporting their growth * Highlights Customer Obsession by deeply understanding user needs and measuring success through customer outcomes * Illustrates cross-organizational collaboration with the customer success team * Balances business results with people development outcomes * Demonstrates inclusive approach that values diverse perspectives

11.6. AUTHENTIC ADAPTATION VS. FABRICATION

While adapting your responses to align with company cultures is important, there's a critical distinction between authentic adaptation and fabrication.

Authentic adaptation presents your genuine experiences through the lens most relevant to the company, while fabrication involves creating fictional examples or exaggerating your role and impact.

THE RISKS OF FABRICATION

Fabricating or significantly exaggerating examples carries substantial risks:

- **Credibility Loss**: Experienced interviewers can often detect inconsistencies or unrealistic claims
- **Follow-up Vulnerability**: Detailed follow-up questions can quickly expose fabricated examples
- **Ethical Concerns**: Misrepresentation raises serious ethical questions about integrity
- **Cultural Misalignment**: Ironically, fabrication demonstrates poor alignment with the values of trust and integrity that all companies seek

PRINCIPLES FOR AUTHENTIC ADAPTATION

To adapt your responses authentically while maintaining integrity:

START WITH TRUTH

Always begin with your actual experiences and accomplishments. Adaptation should involve framing and emphasis, not invention.

EMPHASIZE RELEVANT ASPECTS

Different experiences have multiple dimensions. Authentic adaptation highlights the aspects most relevant to the company's values without distorting the fundamental facts.

TRANSLATE TERMINOLOGY

Using company-specific language to describe your experiences is appropriate as long as the underlying concepts align. This is translation, not fabrication.

ACKNOWLEDGE LIMITATIONS

If your experience doesn't perfectly align with a company's values, acknowledge this honestly while explaining how you would apply their principles going forward.

PREPARE SUFFICIENT EXAMPLES

Having a diverse portfolio of genuine examples allows you to select the most appropriate ones for each company rather than stretching a limited set to fit all situations.

WHEN YOU LACK PERFECT EXAMPLES

If you don't have experiences that perfectly align with a company's cultural values:

- **Use Adjacent Experiences**: Identify examples that demonstrate related qualities or principles

- **Discuss Partial Alignment**: Acknowledge where your experience aligns and where it differs

- **Express Value Alignment**: Explain why you resonate with their values even if your past roles haven't fully expressed them

- **Demonstrate Learning Orientation**: Show how you would apply their principles based on your understanding

11.7. PREPARATION STRATEGIES FOR COMPANY-SPECIFIC ADAPTATION

Effectively adapting your responses to different company cultures requires thoughtful preparation. Here are strategies to develop this capability:

RESEARCH BEYOND THE OBVIOUS

While company values are typically published on websites, deeper research provides more nuanced understanding:

- **Employee Blogs and Interviews**: These often contain practical examples of how values are applied
- **Conference Presentations**: Technical talks by company employees frequently reference cultural elements
- **Leadership Communications**: Earnings calls, all-hands meetings, and executive interviews often emphasize cultural priorities
- **Books and Articles**: Many companies have books written about their culture (e.g., "Working Backwards" for Amazon)

CREATE A CULTURAL ALIGNMENT MATRIX

Develop a systematic way to map your experiences to different company cultures:

1. List your key professional experiences in rows
2. Create columns for each company's core cultural elements
3. Identify where each experience demonstrates each cultural element
4. Note specific aspects of each experience that align with each element
5. Highlight your strongest examples for each company

This matrix helps you quickly identify which examples to use for which companies and how to adapt them appropriately.

DEVELOP COMPANY-SPECIFIC STAR+ TEMPLATES

Create response templates tailored to each company's expectations:

- **Amazon**: Emphasize metrics, personal ownership, and lessons learned

- **Google**: Highlight complexity, learning orientation, and collaborative approaches

- **Meta**: Focus on scale, impact quantification, and speed of execution

- **Microsoft**: Emphasize growth mindset, people development, and customer connection

These templates help you structure your responses appropriately while ensuring you include the elements each company values most.

PRACTICE ADAPTIVE STORYTELLING

Develop the ability to tell the same core story with different emphasis:

1. Select a rich professional experience with multiple dimensions

2. Practice telling it four different ways, each adapted to a specific company

3. Record yourself and review for authentic alignment

4. Refine your approach based on what sounds natural versus forced

This practice builds the mental flexibility to adapt in real time during interviews.

PREPARE FOR COMPANY-SPECIFIC FOLLOW-UPS

Different companies tend to ask different types of follow-up questions:

- **Amazon**: Expects detailed knowledge of metrics and specific actions you took
- **Google**: Often probes for alternative approaches you considered
- **Meta**: Frequently asks about how solutions could scale to larger contexts
- **Microsoft**: May explore how you developed others or handled inclusion challenges

Anticipating these follow-ups helps you prepare more comprehensive examples.

11.8. CONCLUSION: CULTURAL ALIGNMENT AS A COMPETITIVE ADVANTAGE

Effectively adapting your behavioral responses to align with company cultures provides a significant competitive advantage in technical interviews. By understanding each company's unique cultural framework and tailoring your examples accordingly, you demonstrate not just technical capability but cultural fit—a critical factor in hiring decisions.

Remember that authentic adaptation is about presenting your genuine experiences through the most relevant lens for each company, not fabricating or exaggerating your accomplishments. This approach maintains your integrity while maximizing your chances of success.

As you prepare for interviews with different companies, invest time in understanding their specific cultural frameworks and how they impact behavioral assessment. This investment pays dividends not just in interview success but in identifying organizations where you'll genuinely thrive based on cultural alignment.

In the next section of this book, we'll explore advanced behavioral interviewing strategies, including how to navigate ambiguous questions and master follow-up questions that frequently arise in technical interviews.

PART 4: ADVANCED STRATEGIES

CHAPTER 12. NAVIGATING AMBIGUOUS AND UNEXPECTED QUESTIONS

> In preparing for battle I have always found that plans are useless, but planning is indispensable.

— Dwight D. Eisenhower

The virtual interview room at Google falls silent as the interviewer leans forward with an enigmatic smile. You've navigated the technical portions successfully and prepared meticulously for standard behavioral questions. But now comes a question that wasn't in any of your preparation materials:

"Tell me about a time when you had to make a decision with no clear right answer."

Your heart rate quickens. This question doesn't fit neatly into your prepared examples. It's ambiguous, open-ended, and potentially a minefield of wrong approaches. In this critical moment, your ability to navigate ambiguity could make the difference between success and failure.

While previous chapters have focused on preparing for expected behavioral questions with structured responses, this chapter addresses a different challenge: how to handle ambiguous, unexpected, or seemingly impossible questions that inevitably arise in behavioral interviews. These questions often reveal more about your thinking process, adaptability, and authentic self than standard questions ever could.

In this chapter, we'll explore the psychology behind ambiguous questions, develop frameworks for categorizing and approaching different types of ambiguity, and provide strategies for maintaining composure and structure when facing the unexpected. We'll also examine how to turn these challenging moments into opportunities to demonstrate your unique value as a candidate.

12.1. UNDERSTANDING AMBIGUOUS QUESTIONS

Before diving into specific strategies, let's understand what makes a question ambiguous and why interviewers deliberately use ambiguity in behavioral interviews.

TYPES OF AMBIGUOUS QUESTIONS

Behavioral interview questions can be ambiguous in several distinct ways:

CONCEPTUALLY AMBIGUOUS

These questions contain terms or concepts that could be interpreted in multiple ways:

- "Tell me about a time when you demonstrated innovation."
- "Describe a situation where you showed good judgment."
- "Give me an example of when you displayed leadership."

The ambiguity lies in how terms like "innovation," "good judgment," or "leadership" can be defined and interpreted differently.

CONTEXTUALLY AMBIGUOUS

These questions lack sufficient context to determine what kind of example would be most appropriate:

- "Tell me about a difficult decision you made."
- "Describe a time when you failed."

- "Give me an example of how you handle pressure."

Without additional context, it's unclear whether the interviewer is looking for personal or professional examples, technical or interpersonal situations, or recent or formative experiences.

STRUCTURALLY AMBIGUOUS

These questions don't follow the typical pattern that prompts a STAR response:

- "What would you do if your team disagreed with your approach?"
- "How do you determine when to stop improving a solution?"
- "What's your philosophy on balancing quality and speed?"

These questions blend behavioral and hypothetical elements or ask for general approaches rather than specific examples.

DELIBERATELY CHALLENGING

Some questions are intentionally designed to be difficult or uncomfortable:

- "Tell me about your biggest professional regret."
- "Describe a time when your integrity was tested."
- "Give me an example of when you had to admit you were wrong."

These questions probe sensitive areas and often reveal how candidates handle vulnerability and self-reflection.

WHY INTERVIEWERS USE AMBIGUOUS QUESTIONS

Understanding the interviewer's intent helps you respond more effectively to ambiguous questions. Interviewers typically use ambiguity for several specific purposes:

ASSESSING CLARIFICATION SKILLS

In real work environments, requirements and expectations are rarely perfectly clear. Ambiguous questions test your ability to seek clarification appropriately—a critical skill in technical roles where understanding requirements is essential for success.

EVALUATING THINKING PROCESS

How you approach an ambiguous question reveals your thinking process more clearly than prepared responses to standard questions. Interviewers observe how you structure your thinking, make assumptions, and navigate uncertainty.

TESTING ADAPTABILITY

Technical environments constantly present unexpected challenges. Ambiguous questions assess how you adapt to unexpected situations and maintain effectiveness when thrown off your prepared path.

REVEALING AUTHENTIC PRIORITIES

When faced with ambiguity, candidates often default to what they genuinely value or prioritize. This gives interviewers insight into your authentic professional values and instincts.

CREATING DIFFERENTIATION

Standard questions often elicit similar responses from well-prepared candidates. Ambiguous questions create space for candidates to differentiate themselves through unique perspectives and approaches.

Understanding these motivations helps you recognize that ambiguous questions are opportunities, not traps. They allow you to demonstrate valuable skills that might not emerge in response to more straightforward questions.

12.2. THE CLARIFICATION FRAMEWORK

When faced with an ambiguous question, your first and most powerful tool is appropriate clarification. However, there's an art to clarification that demonstrates thoughtfulness rather than confusion or stalling.

THE CLEAR CLARIFICATION MODEL

The CLEAR model provides a structured approach to clarifying ambiguous questions effectively:

CONSIDER THE CORE QUESTION

Before asking for clarification, take a moment to identify what you believe is the core intent behind the question. This demonstrates that you're thinking critically rather than reflexively asking for help.

Example: "I understand you're asking about a time when I had to make a decision with no clear right answer. This seems to be about how I navigate ambiguity and make decisions with incomplete information."

LEVERAGE WHAT YOU KNOW

Reference any context from earlier in the interview or from your research about the company that might inform your understanding of the question.

Example: "Based on our earlier discussion about cross-functional collaboration, I'm assuming this relates to decisions in collaborative contexts rather than purely technical decisions."

EXPLORE SPECIFIC DIMENSIONS

Rather than asking "What do you mean?" (which puts the burden entirely on the interviewer), suggest specific interpretations and ask which is most relevant.

Example: "I have examples ranging from technical architecture decisions with multiple valid approaches to stakeholder prioritization decisions with competing valid perspectives. Would you prefer I focus on technical decision-making or cross-functional prioritization?"

ACKNOWLEDGE THE AMBIGUITY

Briefly acknowledge that you recognize the question's open-ended nature, showing comfort with ambiguity rather than anxiety about it.

Example: "I appreciate that this question intentionally leaves room for interpretation, as many important workplace decisions involve similar ambiguity."

REFRAME WITH PRECISION

Based on any clarification received, reframe the question with greater precision before answering.

Example: "So to confirm, you'd like me to discuss a technical decision where multiple approaches had merit, focusing on how I evaluated options and made a final choice despite the lack of a clearly superior solution."

CLARIFICATION PITFALLS TO AVOID

While clarification is valuable, certain approaches can create negative impressions:

EXCESSIVE CLARIFICATION

Asking multiple clarifying questions in succession can appear as stalling or lack of confidence. Limit yourself to one or two focused clarifications.

PASSING RESPONSIBILITY

Phrases like "What exactly are you looking for?" put the entire burden on the interviewer and can appear evasive. Instead, offer your interpretation and ask for confirmation.

REVEALING ANXIETY

Statements like "I'm not sure I understand what you're asking" can signal discomfort with ambiguity. Instead, demonstrate comfort by offering multiple possible interpretations.

PREMATURE NARROWING

Immediately narrowing to a very specific interpretation without exploring the question's breadth can miss the interviewer's intent. Start with the broader purpose before narrowing.

WHEN CLARIFICATION ISN'T FORTHCOMING

Sometimes interviewers intentionally maintain ambiguity even after clarification attempts. In these cases:

- Explicitly acknowledge that you'll proceed with your best interpretation
- Briefly explain the assumptions you're making
- Proceed with a well-structured response based on those assumptions
- If time permits, briefly mention how your response might differ under alternative interpretations

This approach demonstrates comfort with ambiguity while still providing a structured, thoughtful response.

12.3. THE ADAPT FRAMEWORK FOR AMBIGUOUS QUESTIONS

Once you've attempted appropriate clarification, you need a framework for structuring your response to ambiguous questions. The ADAPT framework provides this structure:

ACKNOWLEDGE THE AMBIGUITY

Begin by briefly acknowledging the question's open-ended or multifaceted nature. This demonstrates awareness rather than confusion.

Example: "This question about innovation could be approached from multiple angles, from technical creativity to process improvement to business model innovation."

DEFINE YOUR INTERPRETATION

Clearly state how you're interpreting the question, including any assumptions you're making. This demonstrates decisive thinking while maintaining transparency.

Example: "I'll focus on innovation in the context of technical problem-solving, specifically finding non-obvious solutions to complex challenges that created unexpected value."

ARTICULATE A SPECIFIC EXAMPLE

Provide a concrete example that fits your interpretation, using the STAR+ format to ensure structure and completeness.

Example: "At TechCorp, we faced a persistent performance issue with our data processing pipeline that standard optimization approaches hadn't resolved..."

PRINCIPLES AND PATTERNS

Extract broader principles or patterns from your example that demonstrate your general approach to similar situations. This shows that your capabilities extend beyond the specific example.

Example: "This experience reinforced several principles I apply when innovating: questioning fundamental assumptions, looking for inspiration in adjacent domains, and creating rapid prototypes to test non-obvious approaches."

TRANSITION TO ALTERNATIVES

If time permits, briefly acknowledge how your response might differ under alternative interpretations of the question. This demonstrates flexibility and breadth of thinking.

Example: "If we were to consider innovation in terms of process improvement rather than technical problem-solving, I could share how I redesigned our deployment workflow to reduce release friction, which had different challenges but similar principles of questioning assumptions and rapid experimentation."

This framework allows you to provide a structured, thoughtful response to even the most ambiguous questions while demonstrating awareness of multiple perspectives.

12.4. STRATEGIES FOR SPECIFIC TYPES OF AMBIGUOUS QUESTIONS

Different types of ambiguous questions require slightly different approaches.

Let's explore strategies for the most common categories.

NAVIGATING CONCEPTUALLY AMBIGUOUS QUESTIONS

These questions contain terms that could be interpreted in multiple ways, such as "innovation," "leadership," or "impact."

STRATEGY: DEFINE, THEN DEMONSTRATE

1. Briefly define how you interpret the key concept
2. Explain why this interpretation is relevant to the role or company
3. Provide a specific example that clearly demonstrates this interpretation
4. Connect your example back to the definition to reinforce alignment

Example Response to "Tell me about a time when you demonstrated innovation":

"I view innovation as developing non-obvious solutions that create significant new value, rather than just incremental improvements. In software engineering, this often means questioning fundamental assumptions about how problems should be approached.

At DataSystems Inc., we faced a challenge with our recommendation engine that was becoming increasingly compute-intensive as our user base grew. The conventional approach would have been to optimize the existing algorithms or add more computing resources. Instead, I questioned whether we needed to generate recommendations in real-time for all scenarios.

I proposed and implemented a hybrid approach that pre-computed recommendations for common user patterns while maintaining real-time processing only for edge cases and new users. This required developing a classification system to identify which users needed real-time processing and which could use pre-computed recommendations.

The result was a 78% reduction in computing costs while actually improving recommendation relevance by 12% according to our A/B tests. This approach has since been applied to three other systems within the company.

This experience reinforced my belief that innovation often comes from questioning whether the problem itself is framed correctly, rather than just seeking better solutions to the problem as initially presented."

HANDLING CONTEXTUALLY AMBIGUOUS QUESTIONS

These questions lack sufficient context to determine what kind of example would be most appropriate, such as "Tell me about a difficult decision" or "Describe a time when you failed."

STRATEGY: CONTEXT, CRITERIA, CASE

1. Briefly acknowledge the breadth of possible contexts

2. Establish criteria for selecting a particularly relevant example

3. Present your example using the STAR+ format

4. Explain why this example is especially illustrative of your approach

Example Response to "Tell me about a difficult decision you made":

"Difficult decisions can arise in many contexts—technical architecture, resource allocation, career choices, or ethical dilemmas. Given that this role involves leading engineering teams through technical transformations, I'll share a difficult decision that involved balancing technical debt against delivery timelines.

At TechSolutions, I was leading the development of a new customer-facing API that would replace three legacy systems. Six weeks before our committed launch date, we discovered a fundamental design flaw in our authentication system that worked for our test cases but would fail for approximately 15% of edge cases in production.

We had three options: delay the launch to properly redesign the authentication system, implement a quick but suboptimal fix that would accumulate technical debt, or launch with known limitations and communicate them to customers.

This decision was particularly difficult because it involved trade-offs between multiple valid priorities: our commitment to customers, technical excellence, and business revenue targets. After consulting with security, engineering, and business stakeholders, I decided to delay the launch by three weeks to implement a proper solution.

I made this decision based on three criteria: first, authentication issues would affect trust in the entire platform; second, the technical debt from a quick fix would compound over time and eventually require more time to address than the initial delay; and third, we could mitigate most of the business impact by providing early access to key customers during the extended development period.

The result validated this approach—we launched three weeks late but with a robust solution that has scaled without issues as we've grown from 50 to 500 enterprise customers. The early access program actually increased engagement with key customers and led to valuable refinements before the general launch.

This experience reinforced my decision-making framework for these situations: clearly identify the trade-offs, consult diverse perspectives, establish clear criteria for the decision, and create mitigation strategies for the downsides of whatever option is selected."

ADDRESSING STRUCTURALLY AMBIGUOUS QUESTIONS

These questions don't follow typical patterns that prompt a STAR response, such as "What would you do if..." or "How do you approach..."

STRATEGY: BRIDGE TO EXPERIENCE

1. Acknowledge the forward-looking or general nature of the question

2. Bridge to relevant past experiences that inform your approach

3. Extract principles from these experiences

4. Apply these principles to the scenario in the question

Example Response to "What would you do if your team disagreed with your technical approach?":

"While this question asks about a hypothetical future scenario, my approach would be informed by my past experiences navigating technical disagreements within teams.

At CloudTech, I led a project to redesign our data processing architecture. I proposed a microservices approach, but several experienced team members strongly advocated for a monolithic architecture with clear service boundaries instead. They had valid concerns about operational complexity and debugging challenges in distributed systems.

Rather than simply pushing my preferred approach, I facilitated a structured evaluation process. First, I asked each team member to articulate their concerns and priorities in writing to ensure all perspectives were fully understood. Then, I organized a workshop where we collectively defined evaluation criteria, including development velocity, operational complexity, scalability, and team expertise.

We then evaluated both approaches against these criteria, which revealed that while microservices offered theoretical advantages for our long-term scalability needs, the team's current expertise and our operational tooling were better aligned with a monolithic approach in the near term.

Based on this process, we aligned on a compromise: a modular monolith with clear service boundaries designed for eventual decomposition into microservices as our needs and capabilities evolved. This approach addressed immediate concerns while preserving our long-term architectural direction.

Drawing from this and similar experiences, if my team disagreed with my technical approach in this role, I would:

1. Ensure all perspectives are fully articulated and understood
2. Collaboratively establish evaluation criteria that reflect both technical and organizational considerations
3. Objectively evaluate alternatives against these criteria
4. Seek synthesis rather than binary choices where possible
5. Document the decision-making process and rationale for future reference

This approach respects team members' expertise while ensuring decisions are made systematically rather than based on opinion or authority."

RESPONDING TO DELIBERATELY CHALLENGING QUESTIONS

These questions are intentionally designed to be difficult or uncomfortable, such as "Tell me about your biggest professional regret" or "Describe a time when your integrity was tested."

STRATEGY: AUTHENTIC REFLECTION

1. Briefly acknowledge the challenging nature of the question
2. Respond with genuine self-reflection rather than a polished narrative
3. Focus on learning and growth rather than justification
4. Demonstrate how the experience shaped your current approach

Example Response to "Tell me about your biggest professional regret":

"That's a thought-provoking question that requires honest reflection. My biggest professional regret comes from my time as a technical lead at StartupTech, where I prioritized technical elegance over user needs in a way that ultimately hurt the product.

We were developing a data visualization platform for financial analysts, and I pushed the team to implement a highly sophisticated, technically impressive architecture that would support extreme flexibility and extensibility. I was convinced that our users would eventually need these capabilities, even though our user research didn't explicitly identify them as requirements.

The situation came to a head when we missed a critical market window because the implementation complexity delayed our launch by nearly three months. When we finally launched, we discovered that users found the interface overly complex and struggled to access the core functionality they actually needed.

What I regret most isn't the technical approach itself, but my failure to validate my assumptions with users before committing significant resources. I had substituted my own technical judgment for actual user feedback, despite having access to customers who could have provided guidance.

This experience fundamentally changed how I approach technical leadership. I now insist on continuous user validation throughout the development process, even for seemingly obvious technical decisions. I've learned to treat technical elegance as a means to deliver user value, not an end in itself.

In my subsequent role at DataCorp, I implemented this lesson by establishing bi-weekly user feedback sessions for our development team and creating a framework for evaluating technical decisions based on user impact rather than just architectural purity. This approach led to significantly higher user adoption and satisfaction while still maintaining technical quality where it truly mattered."

12.5. HANDLING SEEMINGLY IMPOSSIBLE QUESTIONS

Occasionally, you may encounter questions that seem impossible to answer effectively, such as:

- Questions about experiences you genuinely don't have

- Questions that appear to have no good answer

- Questions that seem designed to trap you regardless of how you respond

These situations require special strategies to navigate effectively.

THE EXPERIENCE GAP STRATEGY

When asked about an experience you don't have, use this approach:

1. Acknowledge the gap honestly without apologizing or becoming defensive

2. Bridge to the most relevant experience you do have

3. Demonstrate transferable skills or approaches

4. Express enthusiasm for developing in this area

Example Response to "Tell me about a time when you led a large distributed team" (when you haven't):

"I haven't yet had the opportunity to lead a large distributed team in my career, though it's an area I'm eager to develop in. My most relevant experience comes from coordinating across three teams in different locations while leading the authentication system redesign at SecureTech.

While this wasn't formally leading a distributed team, it required many of the same skills: establishing clear communication protocols, creating visibility into work progress across locations, accommodating time zone differences for synchronous collaboration, and building relationships despite limited face-to-face interaction.

For example, I implemented a documentation-first approach where all major decisions and their rationales were recorded in a shared knowledge base, reducing dependency on synchronous communication. I also established a rotating schedule for our coordination meetings to fairly distribute the time zone burden across teams.

These approaches resulted in successful cross-team collaboration despite the distribution challenges, with the project completing on schedule and meeting all technical requirements. I'm excited about the opportunity to build on these experiences and develop formal distributed team leadership skills in this role, particularly by learning established best practices from others in the organization who have this expertise."

THE REFRAME STRATEGY

When faced with a question that seems to have no good answer, consider reframing:

1. Identify the underlying skill or quality the question is likely assessing

2. Acknowledge the complexity or tension inherent in the question

3. Reframe toward the underlying quality rather than the specific scenario

4. Provide an example that demonstrates this quality

Example Response to "Would you rather deliver a project on time with known bugs or delay to fix all issues?":

"This question highlights the fundamental tension between delivery timelines and quality that engineering teams regularly navigate. Rather than seeing this as a binary choice with a single correct answer, I approach these situations by focusing on risk assessment and stakeholder alignment.

At ProductCorp, we faced this exact dilemma with our payment processing system update. Two weeks before launch, we identified several non-critical bugs that would affect approximately 5% of edge cases but wouldn't compromise core functionality or security.

Rather than unilaterally deciding to delay or proceed, I led a structured risk assessment process. We categorized each issue by impact severity, likelihood of occurrence, and remediation difficulty. We then engaged key stakeholders—including product management, customer support, and executive leadership—to evaluate these risks against business priorities and customer expectations.

Through this process, we aligned on launching with documented workarounds for the edge cases while committing to a rapid follow-up release two weeks later with comprehensive fixes. We also implemented enhanced monitoring specifically for the affected scenarios to provide early detection and mitigation.

This approach balanced multiple considerations rather than treating it as a simple time-versus-quality trade-off. The key was making the decision collaboratively with full transparency about the implications, rather than optimizing for a single dimension.

I've found that these situations rarely have universally correct answers—the right approach depends on specific context including the type of product, customer expectations, competitive landscape, and organizational values. The constant is the need for structured risk assessment and transparent stakeholder alignment."

THE META-RESPONSE STRATEGY

For questions that seem designed to trap you, consider a meta-response:

1. Acknowledge the challenging nature of the question

2. Demonstrate awareness of the tensions or trade-offs involved

3. Discuss how you approach such dilemmas generally

4. Provide a specific example of navigating similar tensions

Example Response to "Tell me about a time when you had to choose between what was right for the company and what was right for the customer":

"This question highlights an interesting tension that I believe is often based on a false dichotomy. In my experience, what's truly right for the company in the long term is almost always aligned with what's right for customers, even if short-term metrics might suggest otherwise.

Rather than accepting this framing, I approach these situations by seeking to understand the apparent conflict and looking for solutions that serve both interests. At FinTech Inc., we faced a situation where a major customer requested custom features that would have diverted significant engineering resources from our product roadmap, potentially delaying improvements that would benefit our broader customer base.

The easy framing would have been 'company roadmap versus customer request,' but I approached it differently. I worked with the customer to deeply understand their underlying needs rather than their specific feature requests. This revealed that their core requirements could be addressed through configuration changes and workflow adjustments rather than custom development.

We then collaborated on a solution that met their needs while requiring minimal deviation from our roadmap. This approach not only satisfied the customer but also identified configuration limitations that, once addressed, created value for multiple other customers.

The key insight was refusing to accept the premise that company and customer interests were fundamentally opposed. By digging deeper into the actual needs and constraints, we found alignment that wasn't visible at the surface level.

I've applied this same approach to numerous situations where interests initially appear to conflict—whether between security and usability, performance and maintainability, or immediate delivery and technical debt. The consistent pattern is that apparent dichotomies often dissolve when you examine the underlying needs and take a longer-term perspective."

12.6. MAINTAINING COMPOSURE UNDER PRESSURE

Ambiguous and unexpected questions often create pressure that can undermine your performance if not managed effectively. Here are strategies for maintaining composure when facing challenging questions:

THE PAUSE AND PROCESS TECHNIQUE

When faced with an unexpected question:

1. Take a deliberate pause (3-5 seconds) to process the question

2. Acknowledge the thoughtfulness of the question

3. If needed, take a sip of water to create a natural moment for thinking

4. Structure your thoughts before beginning your response

This brief pause appears thoughtful rather than hesitant and gives you valuable processing time.

THE STRUCTURED THINKING APPROACH

If you need more substantial thinking time:

1. Verbalize your thinking process: "I'd like to consider this from a few angles..."

2. Enumerate the dimensions you're considering: "First, the technical implications; second, the team dynamics; third, the customer impact..."

3. Think aloud in a structured way as you formulate your response

This approach turns thinking time into a demonstration of your analytical process.

THE BRIDGE TECHNIQUE

When completely unsure how to respond:

1. Find any aspect of the question you can confidently address

2. Start by addressing that element thoughtfully

3. Use that foundation to bridge to the more challenging aspects

4. Build your response progressively from the known to the unknown

This technique prevents freezing by giving you a starting point, however small.

THE RESET APPROACH

If you start a response and realize it's not effective:

1. Briefly acknowledge the shift: "Actually, let me approach this differently..."

2. Reframe your response more effectively

3. Proceed with the improved approach without over-apologizing

This demonstrates adaptability rather than confusion and often leads to stronger responses.

12.7. TURNING AMBIGUITY INTO OPPORTUNITY

While ambiguous questions present challenges, they also create unique opportunities to differentiate yourself as a candidate. Here's how to leverage these moments effectively:

DEMONSTRATING INTELLECTUAL FLEXIBILITY

Ambiguous questions allow you to showcase your ability to: * Consider multiple interpretations of a situation * Adapt your thinking based on new information * Navigate complexity without oversimplifying * Balance competing considerations thoughtfully

These qualities are highly valued in technical roles that require navigating trade-offs and uncertainty.

REVEALING AUTHENTIC PRIORITIES

Your response to ambiguous questions often reveals what you naturally prioritize when not guided by explicit structure. Use this to: * Emphasize values that align with the company culture * Demonstrate authentic commitment to principles like user focus, quality, or collaboration * Show how your natural instincts align with the role requirements

This authentic alignment is more convincing than rehearsed responses to standard questions.

SHOWCASING COMMUNICATION SKILLS

Ambiguous questions create opportunities to demonstrate: * Clarity in explaining complex thinking * Skill in making abstract concepts concrete * Ability to structure communication effectively without external scaffolding * Comfort discussing nuance and trade-offs

These communication skills are particularly valuable in senior technical roles that require influencing without authority.

CREATING MEMORABLE MOMENTS

Unexpected questions often lead to more memorable interactions than standard questions. Use these moments to: * Share unique insights from your experience * Demonstrate distinctive thinking approaches * Create authentic connection through genuine reflection * Leave a lasting impression that differentiates you from other candidates

These memorable moments often have disproportionate impact on hiring decisions.

12.8. CONCLUSION: EMBRACING AMBIGUITY AS A COMPETITIVE ADVANTAGE

Ambiguous and unexpected questions are inevitable in behavioral interviews, particularly for senior technical roles where navigating uncertainty is a core requirement. By developing the skills to handle these questions effectively, you transform potential stumbling blocks into opportunities to demonstrate your unique value as a candidate.

Remember that interviewers use ambiguous questions not to trick you but to see beyond your preparation to your authentic capabilities and approach. The frameworks and strategies in this chapter—from the CLEAR clarification model to the ADAPT response framework—provide structure for navigating this ambiguity while still allowing your genuine strengths to shine through.

As you prepare for behavioral interviews, resist the temptation to focus exclusively on rehearsing answers to expected questions. Instead, practice applying these frameworks to unexpected questions, developing the mental flexibility to respond effectively to whatever comes your way. This preparation for ambiguity becomes a competitive advantage that distinguishes you from candidates who can only excel when questions match their preparation.

In the next chapter, we'll explore another advanced behavioral interviewing challenge: mastering follow-up questions and probing. These deeper explorations often follow your initial responses and can be even more consequential than the original questions in determining interview outcomes.

CHAPTER 13. MASTERING FOLLOW-UPS AND PROBING QUESTIONS

The first principle is that you must not fool yourself—and you are the easiest person to fool.

— Richard Feynman

"That's interesting. Now tell me, what would you have done differently if you could do it again?"

This seemingly simple follow-up question suddenly requires you to critically evaluate your own performance, acknowledge imperfections, and demonstrate growth mindset—all while maintaining the positive impression you've worked to establish. Your ability to handle this probing question effectively could reveal more about your candidacy than your initial response ever did.

While previous chapters have focused on preparing initial responses to behavioral questions, this chapter addresses the critical second phase of behavioral interviews: the follow-up questions and deeper probing that often reveal the most significant insights about candidates. These moments frequently separate truly exceptional candidates from those who are merely well-prepared.

In this chapter, we'll explore the psychology behind follow-up questions, develop frameworks for anticipating and preparing for different types of probes, and provide strategies for maintaining authenticity and depth when interviewers dig deeper. We'll also examine how to turn these challenging moments into opportunities to demonstrate your unique value as a candidate.

13.1. UNDERSTANDING FOLLOW-UP QUESTIONS

Before diving into specific strategies, let's understand what makes follow-up questions particularly challenging and why interviewers use them as a critical assessment tool.

TYPES OF FOLLOW-UP QUESTIONS

Follow-up questions in behavioral interviews typically fall into several distinct categories:

DEPTH PROBES

These questions ask you to provide more specific details about your example:

- "Can you walk me through your exact thought process in that moment?"
- "What specific metrics did you use to evaluate success?"
- "How exactly did you implement that solution?"

The intent is to verify your involvement and understanding by testing your ability to provide granular details that someone who wasn't deeply involved wouldn't know.

ALTERNATIVE SCENARIO EXPLORATIONS

These questions ask you to consider how your approach might change under different circumstances:

- "What would you have done if you had half the time/budget?"
- "How would your approach change if you were doing this today?"
- "What would you do differently if you could do it again?"

These questions assess your adaptability, self-awareness, and ability to learn from experience.

MOTIVATION INQUIRIES

These questions probe your underlying motivations and decision-making rationale:

- "Why did you choose that approach over alternatives?"
- "What was most important to you in making that decision?"
- "How did you determine that was the right priority?"

These questions reveal your values, priorities, and decision-making frameworks.

CHALLENGING ASSUMPTIONS

These questions directly challenge aspects of your response:

- "Couldn't that have been solved more simply by...?"
- "Why didn't you just...?"
- "Wasn't that approach risky because...?"

These questions test your ability to defend your decisions without becoming defensive and to acknowledge valid criticisms constructively.

HYPOTHETICAL EXTENSIONS

These questions extend your example into hypothetical territory:

- "How would you apply that learning to [current company's] environment?"
- "What if you faced that situation with a team that disagreed with your approach?"
- "How would you scale that solution to handle 100x the volume?"

These questions assess your ability to transfer experiences to new contexts and think beyond the specific example you provided.

WHY INTERVIEWERS USE FOLLOW-UP QUESTIONS

Understanding the interviewer's intent helps you respond more effectively to follow-up questions. Interviewers typically use follow-ups for several specific purposes:

VERIFYING AUTHENTICITY

Prepared candidates can deliver polished initial responses, but follow-up questions quickly reveal whether the experience is genuine. The depth and specificity of your answers to unexpected probes signal authenticity more reliably than any initial response.

TESTING DEPTH OF INVOLVEMENT

Candidates sometimes claim credit for team accomplishments where their personal contribution was limited. Detailed follow-up questions help interviewers distinguish between peripheral involvement and genuine leadership or significant contribution.

ASSESSING SELF-AWARENESS

How candidates respond to questions about what they would do differently or what they learned reveals their capacity for self-reflection and continuous improvement—critical qualities in high-performing technical professionals.

EVALUATING ADAPTABILITY

Follow-up questions about alternative scenarios assess how candidates might adapt their approaches to different contexts, constraints, or requirements—an essential capability in dynamic technical environments.

CREATING DIFFERENTIATION

Standard questions often elicit similar initial responses from well-prepared candidates. Follow-up questions create space for candidates to differentiate themselves through unique insights, thoughtful reflection, and authentic perspectives.

Understanding these motivations helps you recognize that follow-up questions are opportunities, not traps. They allow you to demonstrate valuable qualities that might not emerge in your initial responses.

13.2. THE DEPTH FRAMEWORK FOR FOLLOW-UP QUESTIONS

When faced with follow-up questions, you need a framework for structuring thoughtful, authentic responses that build on your initial answer while providing new insights. The DEPTH framework provides this structure:

DETAILS ON DEMAND

Provide specific, granular details that demonstrate your deep involvement and understanding. These details should be concrete and precise rather than general or vague.

Example: "The specific metrics we tracked were weekly active users, which increased from 15,300 to 22,700 over the three-month period; average session duration, which improved from 3.2 minutes to 4.8 minutes; and conversion rate, which grew from 2.3% to 3.7%. I personally designed the measurement framework and built the dashboard that tracked these metrics daily, allowing us to identify which specific feature changes were driving improvements."

EVALUATE ALTERNATIVES

Demonstrate thoughtful consideration of alternative approaches, including those you didn't ultimately select. This shows strategic thinking beyond the specific path you took.

Example: "We considered three alternative approaches before selecting our implementation strategy. The first was a complete rewrite using React, which would have provided better long-term maintainability but introduced too much near-term risk given our timeline constraints. The second was a hybrid approach that would have updated the most critical components while leaving others unchanged, which would have been faster but created technical inconsistency. The third, which we ultimately selected, was a phased migration that balanced immediate user experience improvements with sustainable technical architecture."

PERSONAL REFLECTION

Share honest reflections on your learning, growth, or what you might do differently. This demonstrates self-awareness and continuous improvement orientation.

Example: "In retrospect, I would have invested more time in automated testing earlier in the process. We eventually achieved 85% test coverage, but we could have prevented several late-stage issues if we had established that discipline from the beginning. This experience fundamentally changed my approach to new projects—I now insist on test infrastructure as part of initial setup rather than treating it as a later optimization."

TRANSFER TO NEW CONTEXTS

Explain how the principles or learnings from your example could apply to different situations, particularly those relevant to the role you're interviewing for.

Example: "The core principle I took from this experience—that early user feedback is more valuable than perfect execution in isolation—would be directly applicable to how I would approach product development at your company. For instance, I understand you're currently rebuilding your analytics dashboard. I would apply this learning by establishing a small group of power users for weekly feedback sessions throughout the development process rather than waiting for a complete solution."

HONEST LIMITATIONS

Acknowledge the boundaries or constraints of your example without undermining its core value. This demonstrates intellectual honesty and nuanced thinking.

Example: "It's important to note that this approach was particularly effective in our context of a mature product with established users. The same methodology might need adjustment in an early-stage product where usage patterns are still emerging. The principle of data-driven iteration remains valid, but the specific metrics and feedback mechanisms would likely need to be different."

This framework allows you to provide thoughtful, layered responses to follow-up questions while maintaining authenticity and demonstrating sophisticated thinking.

13.3. STRATEGIES FOR SPECIFIC TYPES OF FOLLOW-UP QUESTIONS

Different types of follow-up questions require slightly different approaches. Let's explore strategies for the most common categories.

MASTERING DEPTH PROBES

These questions ask for more specific details about your example. The key challenge is providing sufficient specificity without becoming excessively technical or losing the strategic thread.

STRATEGY: CONCRETE-STRATEGIC BALANCE

1. Provide specific, concrete details that demonstrate deep involvement

2. Connect these details to strategic considerations or broader impact

3. Use precise numbers, names, and technical specifics where relevant

4. Maintain focus on aspects most relevant to the role you're interviewing for

Example Response to "Can you walk me through exactly how you implemented that solution?":

"I implemented the authentication system redesign through a carefully sequenced four-phase approach. In the first phase, I created a parallel authentication service using OAuth 2.0 with JWT tokens, specifically selecting this protocol for its stateless nature and scalability benefits. I personally wrote the core token validation and refresh logic, approximately 2,300 lines of code, while collaborating with our security specialist, Elena, on the encryption implementation.

The second phase involved creating an abstraction layer in our existing services that could route authentication requests to either the legacy system or the new service. This required modifying 17 different microservices to implement the new interface. Rather than attempting all modifications simultaneously, I prioritized services based on user impact and technical risk, starting with the account management service that handled 65% of authentication requests.

For the third phase, I developed a gradual migration strategy using feature flags that allowed us to route specific user segments to the new system while maintaining the legacy system as a fallback. This approach was critical because it allowed us to validate the new system with 5% of users initially, then 20%, and finally 100% over a six-week period, rather than risking a high-impact cutover.

The final phase involved decommissioning the legacy system once we had validated the new system's performance and reliability with our full user base of approximately 3 million active accounts.

Throughout implementation, I maintained a balance between technical correctness and practical delivery. For example, while I initially planned to rewrite all authentication-dependent services to use the new protocol natively, I realized this would extend the project timeline by approximately three months. Instead, I designed the abstraction layer to handle protocol translation, allowing us to modernize the core authentication system immediately while creating a path for incremental service updates over time."

HANDLING ALTERNATIVE SCENARIO EXPLORATIONS

These questions ask you to consider how your approach might change under different circumstances. The key challenge is demonstrating adaptability without undermining the validity of your original approach.

STRATEGY: PRINCIPLED ADAPTATION

1. Acknowledge the value of considering alternative scenarios
2. Identify the core principles that would remain constant
3. Explain specific adaptations you would make to your approach
4. Demonstrate thoughtful prioritization under new constraints

Example Response to "What would you have done if you had half the budget?":

"That's an excellent question about adapting to tighter resource constraints. If I had half the budget for the data platform migration, I would have maintained the same core principles—minimizing business disruption, ensuring data integrity, and creating a sustainable architecture—while making several specific adaptations to the implementation approach.

First, I would have narrowed the initial scope to focus exclusively on the highest-business-value data domains rather than attempting a comprehensive migration. Specifically, I would have prioritized customer and transaction data, which drive 80% of our analytical value, while deferring marketing and operational datasets to a subsequent phase.

Second, I would have leveraged more open-source components rather than the commercial solutions we selected. For example, instead of Snowflake, I would have implemented a PostgreSQL-based solution with appropriate partitioning and optimization. While this would have required more engineering effort to achieve comparable performance, the licensing cost difference would have justified this trade-off under tighter budget constraints.

Third, I would have adopted a more gradual migration timeline, extending from 8 months to approximately 12-14 months. This would have allowed a smaller team to accomplish the work by reducing parallel workstreams, though it would have delayed some business benefits.

Fourth, I would have invested more heavily in automated testing and validation frameworks early in the project. While this might seem counterintuitive when reducing budget, my experience has shown that automation becomes even more critical with smaller teams, as it multiplies the effectiveness of limited resources.

The key would have been maintaining focus on the fundamental business objectives while accepting some compromises on timeline and technical sophistication. In resource-constrained environments, I've found that clearly communicating these trade-offs to stakeholders and establishing explicit prioritization frameworks becomes even more essential than in well-resourced projects."

ADDRESSING MOTIVATION INQUIRIES

These questions probe your underlying motivations and decision-making rationale. The key challenge is articulating your thinking process authentically while demonstrating alignment with values important to the role and company.

STRATEGY: VALUES-BASED REASONING

1. Clearly articulate the key factors that influenced your decision

2. Connect these factors to underlying values and principles

3. Explain how you prioritized competing considerations

4. Demonstrate alignment with values relevant to the target role and company

Example Response to "Why did you choose that approach over alternatives?":

"I chose the incremental refactoring approach over a complete rewrite for three primary reasons, each reflecting values that guide my technical leadership.

First, user impact was my highest priority. The incremental approach allowed us to deliver improvements to users every two weeks rather than asking them to wait 6-8 months for a complete solution. This reflects my belief that technical decisions should ultimately serve user needs rather than technical elegance alone. Each incremental release solved specific pain points that users had identified as high-priority, creating immediate business value while the larger transformation progressed.

Second, I valued risk management over theoretical perfection. Our system processed approximately $3 million in daily transactions, making stability and reliability non-negotiable. The incremental approach allowed us to isolate and mitigate risks in smaller components rather than attempting a high-stakes cutover. We could validate each change with real-world usage before proceeding to the next component, creating multiple feedback loops that improved our overall approach.

Third, I prioritized team learning and ownership throughout the process. The incremental approach enabled engineers to develop deep understanding of both the legacy system and modern alternatives, creating knowledge that remained with the team rather than being concentrated in a separate rewrite team. This reflected my commitment to sustainable engineering practices that build long-term team capability rather than just short-term deliverables.

The decision ultimately reflected my belief that technical leadership requires balancing multiple dimensions—user needs, business continuity, technical excellence, and team development—rather than optimizing for any single factor. While a complete rewrite might have produced a more technically elegant solution in isolation, the incremental approach delivered more holistic value across all these dimensions."

NAVIGATING CHALLENGING ASSUMPTIONS

These questions directly challenge aspects of your response. The key challenge is defending your decisions without becoming defensive and acknowledging valid criticisms constructively.

STRATEGY: BALANCED CONSIDERATION

1. Acknowledge the validity of the challenge without becoming defensive

2. Explain the specific context that influenced your decision

3. Articulate the trade-offs you considered and why you made your choice

4. Demonstrate openness to alternative perspectives

Example Response to "Couldn't you have solved that more simply by using a third-party solution?":

"That's a fair challenge and one we actively considered during our decision process. Third-party authentication solutions like Auth0 or Okta would indeed have simplified certain aspects of the implementation and potentially accelerated our timeline.

We evaluated three leading third-party options against our specific requirements and context. The primary factors that led us to build rather than buy were:

First, our specific compliance requirements in the healthcare domain included maintaining complete data sovereignty within our private cloud infrastructure. At that time, the third-party solutions that met our feature requirements couldn't guarantee data residency in a way that would satisfy our compliance team's interpretation of HIPAA requirements. This constraint was particularly important given our customer base of healthcare providers.

Second, we had complex integration requirements with legacy systems that would have required significant customization of any third-party solution. Our cost-benefit analysis indicated that the licensing costs combined with the necessary customization would actually exceed the cost of an internal implementation tailored to our specific needs.

Third, authentication represented a core security component that our security leadership considered strategically important to maintain internal expertise and control over, particularly given our industry context.

That said, I recognize that third-party solutions have evolved significantly since that decision. If I were approaching the same problem today, I would reevaluate this build-versus-buy decision based on current offerings, particularly as vendors have improved their compliance capabilities for regulated industries. The principle of focusing engineering resources on unique business value rather than reinventing solved problems remains valid, even though our specific context at that time led us to an internal implementation."

MANAGING HYPOTHETICAL EXTENSIONS

These questions extend your example into hypothetical territory. The key challenge is transferring principles from your experience to new contexts while acknowledging the limitations of hypothetical comparisons.

STRATEGY: PRINCIPLED TRANSFER

1. Identify the core principles from your experience that would transfer

2. Acknowledge key differences in the new context

3. Explain how you would adapt your approach to these differences

4. Demonstrate thoughtful consideration of the new context's unique challenges

Example Response to "How would you apply that approach to our environment?":

"Based on my understanding of your environment—a rapidly scaling B2B SaaS platform with a microservices architecture—I would apply several key principles from my experience while adapting to your specific context.

The first transferable principle is the phased migration approach, which would be even more relevant in your microservices environment. Rather than attempting to modernize all services simultaneously, I would identify service boundaries that allow for incremental migration with clearly defined interfaces between new and legacy components. This would be particularly important given your continuous delivery environment, where maintaining system stability throughout the transformation would be critical.

The second principle I would transfer is the data-driven prioritization framework we used. However, I would adapt it to your B2B context by incorporating customer contract requirements and SLAs as additional prioritization factors. Understanding which services support your highest-value enterprise customers would inform sequencing decisions to minimize business risk during the transformation.

The third principle—establishing a robust feature flagging infrastructure—would be directly applicable but would need adaptation for your multi-tenant architecture. I would implement tenant-aware feature flags that allow for customer-by-customer migration rather than the user-segment approach we used in our B2C context.

A key difference in your environment is the enterprise customer relationship model, which would require more extensive communication and coordination than our consumer-focused approach. I would establish a structured customer communication program, potentially including preview access for select customers and longer parallel operation periods to accommodate enterprise testing requirements.

Another significant adaptation would involve your CI/CD pipeline. Based on what you've shared about your deployment frequency, I would implement more sophisticated automated testing and canary deployment capabilities than we needed in our weekly release environment, ensuring that the migration wouldn't disrupt your ability to deploy multiple times daily.

The fundamental approach of incremental, reversible changes with continuous validation would remain constant, but these specific adaptations would address the unique characteristics of your environment."

13.4. MAINTAINING AUTHENTICITY UNDER PRESSURE

Follow-up questions often create pressure that can lead candidates to abandon authenticity in favor of saying what they think interviewers want to hear. This undermines the very purpose of behavioral interviews—to assess your actual capabilities and approach. Here are strategies for maintaining authenticity while still presenting yourself effectively:

THE THOUGHTFUL PAUSE TECHNIQUE

When faced with a challenging follow-up:

1. Take a deliberate pause (3-5 seconds) to consider your authentic response

2. Acknowledge the thoughtfulness of the question

3. Respond based on your actual experience rather than what seems "correct"

4. Be willing to acknowledge limitations or areas of growth

This approach signals confidence in your authentic self rather than rushing to provide an idealized answer.

THE SPECIFIC DETAIL ANCHOR

To maintain authenticity in your responses:

1. Anchor your answers in specific, concrete details from your actual experience

2. Include distinctive elements that wouldn't be present in generic responses

3. Reference particular challenges or constraints unique to your situation

4. Mention specific individuals, technologies, or metrics from your example

These specific details naturally guide you toward authenticity by grounding your response in reality.

THE BALANCED SELF-ASSESSMENT

When discussing your performance or decisions:

1. Acknowledge both strengths and limitations in your approach

2. Discuss what worked well and what you would improve

3. Take appropriate ownership without excessive self-criticism

4. Demonstrate growth mindset without undermining your capabilities

This balanced perspective demonstrates both confidence and self-awareness.

THE CONTEXT CLARIFICATION

When your decisions might seem questionable without proper context:

1. Briefly explain the specific constraints or requirements that influenced your approach

2. Clarify factors that might not be obvious to the interviewer

3. Acknowledge how different contexts might lead to different approaches

4. Demonstrate adaptability while standing by contextually appropriate decisions

This approach helps interviewers understand your reasoning within your specific situation.

13.5. PREPARING FOR FOLLOW-UP QUESTIONS

While you can't predict every follow-up question, you can prepare systematically to handle them effectively. Here are strategies for developing this capability:

THE FIVE WHYS PREPARATION

For each of your prepared examples:

1. Ask yourself "why?" about your key decisions at least five times

2. Explore your underlying motivations and rationales in depth

3. Identify the principles and values that guided your choices

4. Prepare to articulate these deeper layers when probed

This preparation helps you access deeper insights quickly when asked follow-up questions.

THE ALTERNATIVE SCENARIO EXPLORATION

For your key examples:

1. Consider how your approach would change with different constraints (less time, fewer resources, different team composition)

2. Identify which elements would remain constant and which would adapt

3. Prepare to discuss these adaptations thoughtfully

4. Consider how your approach might evolve based on current knowledge and technology

This exploration prepares you for "what if" and "what would you do differently" questions.

THE CRITICISM ANTICIPATION

For each example:

1. Identify potential criticisms or challenges to your approach

2. Consider the validity of these criticisms from different perspectives

3. Prepare thoughtful responses that acknowledge valid points without becoming defensive

4. Identify what you've learned or how you've evolved since the experience

This preparation helps you respond constructively to challenging questions.

THE DETAIL INVENTORY

For your most important examples:

1. Create a detailed inventory of specific metrics, technologies, methodologies, and key decisions

2. Document the specific role you played in each aspect of the example

3. Refresh your memory on technical details you might have forgotten

4. Prepare to discuss implementation specifics at multiple levels of granularity

This inventory ensures you can provide depth when probed for details.

THE TRANSFER PRACTICE

For your key examples:

1. Practice explaining how the principles from your experience would apply to different contexts

2. Consider how your approach would translate to the specific company you're interviewing with

3. Identify which elements are context-specific and which are universally applicable

4. Prepare to discuss these translations thoughtfully

This practice prepares you for questions about applying your experience to new environments.

13.6. THE SEQUENCE DIAGRAM OF EFFECTIVE FOLLOW-UP RESPONSES

Behavioral interviews often follow a predictable pattern of initial question, response, follow-up, and deeper probing. Understanding this sequence helps you navigate the entire conversation effectively rather than focusing solely on individual questions.

INITIAL RESPONSE: SETTING THE FOUNDATION

Your initial STAR+ response should: * Provide a clear, structured overview of your example * Include sufficient detail to demonstrate competence * Highlight key decisions and outcomes * Leave openings for interviewers to probe areas of interest

Think of this as setting the foundation for deeper exploration rather than telling the complete story.

FIRST FOLLOW-UP: EXPANDING DIMENSION

The first follow-up typically explores a specific dimension of your example: * Respond with greater depth in the requested dimension * Maintain connection to your overall narrative * Introduce new insights not covered in your initial response * Demonstrate comfort with deeper exploration

This response should expand the interviewer's understanding rather than simply repeating elements of your initial answer.

SECOND FOLLOW-UP: TESTING BOUNDARIES

Subsequent follow-ups often test the boundaries of your experience or thinking: * Demonstrate flexibility and adaptability in your thinking * Show comfort with hypotheticals and alternative scenarios * Maintain authenticity while exploring new territory * Connect to principles rather than clinging to specifics

These responses demonstrate your ability to think beyond your specific experience.

FINAL PROBES: REVEALING CHARACTER

The deepest follow-ups often reveal character and values: * Respond with genuine reflection rather than calculation * Demonstrate self-awareness and growth orientation * Show comfort with vulnerability where appropriate * Maintain alignment with your authentic professional identity

These moments often have the greatest impact on interviewer impressions.

13.7. TURNING FOLLOW-UPS INTO OPPORTUNITIES

While follow-up questions present challenges, they also create unique opportunities to differentiate yourself as a candidate. Here's how to leverage these moments effectively:

DEMONSTRATING DEPTH BEYOND PREPARATION

Follow-up questions allow you to showcase: * Genuine expertise beyond rehearsed responses * Nuanced understanding of complex situations * Thoughtful consideration of trade-offs and alternatives * Authentic professional judgment developed through experience

These qualities are difficult to demonstrate in initial responses alone.

REVEALING GROWTH MINDSET

Questions about what you would do differently provide opportunities to show: * Comfort with self-evaluation and improvement * Ability to learn from experience * Openness to feedback and alternative perspectives * Continuous evolution of your approach

This growth orientation is particularly valued in technical roles where continuous learning is essential.

SHOWCASING ADAPTABILITY

Alternative scenario questions allow you to demonstrate: * Flexibility in applying principles to different contexts * Comfort with changing constraints and requirements * Pragmatic adjustment without abandoning core values * Resilience in the face of challenging circumstances

These adaptability signals are increasingly important in rapidly changing technical environments.

CREATING AUTHENTIC CONNECTION

The spontaneous nature of follow-up exchanges often creates: * More genuine interaction beyond scripted responses * Opportunities for authentic professional passion to emerge * Moments of shared insight or understanding with interviewers * Memorable exchanges that differentiate you from other candidates

These authentic connections often influence hiring decisions more than technical qualifications alone.

13.8. CONCLUSION: MASTERING THE COMPLETE BEHAVIORAL INTERVIEW

Behavioral interviews are conversations, not presentations. While initial responses are important, your ability to engage thoughtfully with follow-up questions often determines the ultimate outcome. By developing the skills to handle these deeper explorations effectively, you transform potential stress points into opportunities to demonstrate your unique value as a candidate.

Remember that interviewers use follow-up questions not to trip you up but to see beyond your preparation to your authentic capabilities and approach. The frameworks and strategies in this chapter—from the DEPTH response framework to specific techniques for different types of follow-ups—provide structure for navigating these moments while still allowing your genuine strengths to shine through.

As you prepare for behavioral interviews, allocate significant time to practicing follow-up responses, not just initial answers. Engage with colleagues in mock interviews where they deliberately probe beyond your first response, helping you develop the mental flexibility and depth needed for effective follow-up exchanges. This preparation for the complete behavioral interview becomes a competitive advantage that distinguishes you from candidates who focus solely on initial responses.

In combination with the strategies from previous chapters—from STAR+ formatting to role-specific examples to company culture alignment—these follow-up mastery techniques complete your behavioral interview toolkit. With these capabilities, you're prepared not just to survive behavioral interviews but to excel in them, demonstrating the full range of qualities that make you an exceptional candidate for technical roles at the world's leading technology companies.

ABOUT THE AUTHOR

Sanjeet Sahay

Sanjeet is the founder and CEO of LeaderHub, and former Amazon engineering and architecture leader with 20+ years in tech. He is a best-selling author, AI-apps developer, interview and career coach, and a prolific course- and content creator. Sanjeet lives in Redmond.

Sanjeet's other best selling books

The No-Nonsense Guide to Beating Burnout (https://a.co/d/i4L1Ww9)

Solutions Architect Interview (https://a.co/d/6UUG0D6)

Generative AI for Software Developers (https://a.co/d/fRa74lM)

Contact Sanjeet at:

- Email (sanjeet@leaderhub.io)
- LinkedIn (https://www.linkedin.com/in/sanjeetsahay/)
- Twitter (https://x.com/sanj33ts)
- Website (https://leaderhub.io/contact-us)

Saurabh Shrivastava

Saurabh is a renowned inventor, author, and technology leader with over 20 years of IT experience. Currently serving as a Solutions Architect Leader at Amazon Web Services (AWS), he empowers global consulting partners and enterprise customers in their cloud transformation journey. Saurabh has played a pivotal role in establishing global technical partnerships, defining visionary strategies for his team, and fostering the growth of new strategic initiatives. His expertise has earned him a patent in cloud platform automation.

Saurabh's portfolio of books including Generative AI for Software Developers and Solutions Architect Interview here: (https://tinyurl.com/3drpnbed)

As a thought leader and public speaker, Saurabh has shared his insights through various blogs and white papers, covering a wide range of technology domains such as big data, IoT, machine learning, and cloud computing. His passion lies in exploring the latest innovations and understanding their impact on society and everyday life. Among his notable works is the acclaimed book "Solution Architect's Handbook" and "AWS for Solutions Architect," both available on Packt and Amazon.com. This comprehensive book addresses a significant industry gap, drawing from Saurabh's personal experiences and learnings to deliver a relatable and informative read for individuals from diverse backgrounds. It equips readers with invaluable knowledge to succeed as Solutions Architects and unlocks a world of boundless possibilities.

Prior to joining AWS, Saurabh held diverse roles in the IT services industry and R&D space, specializing in enterprise application design, cloud service management, and orchestration. His multifaceted expertise and rich industry experience have shaped him into a prominent figure in the technology landscape.

- LinkedIn (https://www.linkedin.com/in/saurabhtechleader/)

Abhishek Soni

Abhishek is a seasoned technology leader with over two decades of experience spanning cloud architecture, enterprise strategy, and customer success. With a career rooted in deep technical expertise and a passion for enabling organizational transformation, Abhishek has helped numerous global enterprises modernize their IT landscapes, adopt cloud-native architectures, and build scalable, cost-efficient systems.

Currently serving as a Customer Engineer at Google Cloud, Abhishek works with a wide spectrum of clients to design impactful technology strategies using GCP services. Prior to his role at Google, he spent several years at Amazon Web Services (AWS), where he held pivotal roles including Senior Solutions Architect and Senior Technical Consultant. At AWS, he contributed extensively to customer success through architectural reviews, migration strategies, and enablement initiatives, earning accolades such as the Customer Obsession Award.

Abhishek's technical background includes deep expertise in databases, analytics, and cloud platforms, with certifications across both GCP and AWS, including specialties in databases, analytics, and cloud architecture. He has architected critical workloads across industries like finance, logistics, insurance, and telecommunications. His work has been featured in AWS Prescriptive Guidance and blog posts on topics ranging from SQL performance optimization to integrating AI services with legacy infrastructure.

Beyond his technical accomplishments, Abhishek is recognized for his ability to engage with C-level stakeholders, lead cross-functional teams, and serve as a trusted advisor. His career has given him a front-row seat to how organizations hire and scale technical teams — including how behavioral interviewing techniques play a critical role in finding not just the most qualified candidates, but the right ones.

This unique blend of hands-on technical leadership, people-centric consulting, and hiring insight positions Abhishek as a credible and thoughtful voice on behavioral interviewing. In this book, he draws on years of real-world experience mentoring engineers, supporting hiring panels, and working across complex organizational dynamics to offer a structured, practical approach to mastering behavioral interview questions — for both interviewers and candidates

- LinkedIn (https://www.linkedin.com/in/abhishek-soni-877a76117/)

EPILOGUE: THE JOURNEY BEYOND THE INTERVIEW

> The passion for stretching yourself and sticking to it, even (or especially) when it's not going well, is the hallmark of the growth mindset.

— Carol S. Dweck

As our exploration of behavioral interviewing comes to a close, it's worth reflecting on a fundamental truth: mastering behavioral interviews is not merely about securing your next role—it's about developing a deeper understanding of yourself as a professional and cultivating skills that will serve you throughout your career.

The journey we've undertaken together through this book has equipped you with frameworks, strategies, and examples to excel in behavioral interviews at top technology companies. You've learned the STAR+ format, explored role-specific approaches, and developed advanced techniques for handling ambiguous questions and follow-up probes. But the most valuable outcome of this process extends far beyond interview success.

The Lasting Impact of Behavioral Interview Mastery

The skills you've developed through this preparation process create lasting value in several dimensions:

Professional Self-Awareness

The process of identifying and articulating your professional stories forces a level of self-reflection that many of us rarely undertake. By examining your experiences through the lens of behavioral competencies, you've gained deeper insight into your strengths, growth areas, and professional values. This self-awareness becomes a foundation for intentional career development long after any specific interview.

The questions you've learned to answer for interviewers are, in many ways, the same questions you should periodically ask yourself: How do you approach challenges? How do you collaborate with others? How do you learn and grow? How do you drive results? Regular reflection on these questions helps you maintain alignment between your daily work and your long-term professional aspirations.

Structured Communication

The structured communication approaches you've developed for behavioral interviews—particularly the STAR+ format—have applications far beyond the interview context. Whether you're presenting project updates, documenting accomplishments for performance reviews, or simply explaining your work to colleagues, the ability to communicate with clarity, specificity, and impact is invaluable.

Many professionals struggle to articulate their contributions effectively, either understating their impact through excessive modesty or failing to connect their work to broader business outcomes. The frameworks you've learned help you communicate your value authentically and effectively throughout your career.

Strategic Storytelling

The art of strategic storytelling—selecting and shaping experiences to highlight specific competencies—is a powerful professional skill. In leadership roles, storytelling becomes a primary tool for inspiring teams, driving change, and establishing culture. The techniques you've developed for behavioral interviews translate directly to these leadership communication contexts.

Moreover, the ability to recognize and articulate the narrative arc of your experiences—the challenges faced, approaches taken, outcomes achieved, and lessons learned—helps you derive greater meaning from your professional journey. This meaning-making process contributes significantly to career satisfaction and resilience.

Continuous Learning Orientation

The "Plus" in the STAR+ format—the lessons learned component—reinforces perhaps the most valuable professional orientation: a commitment to continuous learning and growth. By habitually reflecting on what you've learned from each significant experience, you accelerate your professional development and build adaptability for an ever-changing technical landscape.

This learning orientation becomes particularly valuable as you advance in your career. Senior technical roles increasingly require the ability to navigate ambiguity, adapt to new contexts, and learn continuously. The reflection habits you've developed through behavioral interview preparation serve as a foundation for this ongoing growth.

From Interview Preparation to Career Development

As you move forward, consider how the work you've done to prepare for behavioral interviews can evolve into a sustainable practice of career development:

The Professional Experience Journal

Consider maintaining a "professional experience journal" where you document significant projects, challenges, and accomplishments using the STAR+ format. This practice serves multiple purposes:

- It creates a repository of examples for future interviews or performance reviews
- It reinforces the habit of reflection and learning from experience

- It provides perspective on your growth over time

- It helps you identify patterns in your strengths and interests

This journal becomes particularly valuable during periods of career transition or when preparing for advancement opportunities. Rather than scrambling to recall examples under pressure, you'll have a rich collection of well-articulated experiences to draw from.

The Feedback Integration Practice

The self-awareness you've developed through behavioral interview preparation provides an excellent foundation for integrating feedback effectively. Consider establishing a regular practice of seeking and processing feedback:

- Actively solicit specific feedback from colleagues, managers, and reports

- Document this feedback alongside your own self-assessments

- Identify patterns and themes across different sources

- Develop focused growth plans based on these insights

This practice helps you maintain an accurate self-image and continuously refine your professional approach based on how others experience your work.

The Intentional Experience Building Approach

As you've prepared for behavioral interviews, you may have identified gaps in your experience—competency areas where you lack compelling examples. Rather than viewing these gaps solely as interview weaknesses, see them as opportunities for intentional career development:

- Seek projects or responsibilities that will help you develop in these areas

- Volunteer for stretch assignments that build new competencies

- Create learning goals that align with your experience gaps

- Document your growth in these areas using the STAR+ format

This approach transforms interview preparation from a reactive exercise into a proactive career development strategy.

The Professional Narrative Review

The work you've done to align your examples with company cultures and role requirements can evolve into a regular practice of reviewing your professional narrative:

- Periodically assess whether your current role aligns with your professional story
- Consider how recent experiences have shaped your professional identity
- Reflect on whether your work reflects your core professional values
- Adjust your career direction to maintain alignment with your evolving narrative

This practice helps ensure that your career develops coherently rather than through disconnected opportunistic moves, creating a professional journey with meaning and purpose.

The Continuous Evolution of Behavioral Interviewing

As you continue your career journey, it's worth noting that behavioral interviewing itself continues to evolve. The approaches that are effective today will likely shift as companies refine their assessment methods and as workplace expectations change. Several trends are worth monitoring:

The Integration of Technical and Behavioral Assessment

The traditional separation between technical and behavioral interviews is increasingly blurring, particularly for senior roles. Companies are developing integrated assessment approaches that evaluate technical decisions through a behavioral lens: How do you make technical choices? How do you navigate trade-offs? How do you lead technical transformation?

This integration requires technical professionals to develop nuanced perspectives on the human and organizational dimensions of technical work—precisely the kind of reflection you've engaged in through behavioral interview preparation.

The Emphasis on Adaptability and Learning

As technical environments become increasingly dynamic, companies are placing greater emphasis on adaptability and learning orientation in their behavioral assessments. The ability to navigate ambiguity, learn continuously, and adapt to changing contexts is becoming as important as specific technical expertise.

The reflection habits and growth mindset you've developed through this preparation process position you well for this evolution in behavioral assessment.

The Focus on Inclusive Leadership

Companies are increasingly incorporating diversity, equity, and inclusion dimensions into their behavioral assessments, particularly for leadership roles. The ability to build inclusive teams, value diverse perspectives, and create environments where everyone can contribute effectively is becoming a core competency rather than a specialized skill.

As you continue to develop your behavioral examples, consider how you demonstrate these inclusive leadership capabilities in your work.

A Final Reflection

As we conclude this journey together, I encourage you to view behavioral interview mastery not as a destination but as an ongoing process of professional development. The frameworks and strategies in this book provide a foundation, but your continued growth will come from applying these approaches to new experiences, reflecting on your evolving professional identity, and adapting to changing expectations.

Remember that the ultimate purpose of behavioral interviewing is not to test your ability to perform in interviews but to assess your potential for real-world impact. By focusing on developing genuine capabilities rather than just interview skills, you create sustainable value that serves you throughout your career.

The most successful technical professionals are those who combine technical excellence with the human dimensions of leadership, collaboration, communication, and continuous growth. The work you've done to prepare for behavioral interviews has strengthened these dimensions of your professional identity, creating value that extends far beyond any specific interview or role.

As you move forward in your career journey, carry with you not just the specific techniques for behavioral interview success but the deeper habits of reflection, structured communication, and continuous learning that will serve you in every professional context. These habits, more than any specific role or company, define a truly successful career in technology.

I wish you not just success in your interviews but fulfillment in the professional journey that follows—a journey of continuous growth, meaningful impact, and authentic contribution to the technical challenges that shape our world.

www.ingramcontent.com/pod-product-compliance
Lightning Source LLC
LaVergne TN
LVHW022332060326
832902LV00022B/4006